Perfect

Perfect your Spanish
Juan Kattán-Ibarra

For UK order enquiries: please contact Bookpoint Ltd,
130 Milton Park, Abingdon, Oxon OX14 4SB.
Telephone: +44 (0) 1235 827720. *Fax:* +44 (0) 1235 400454.
Lines are open 09.00–17.00, Monday to Saturday, with a 24-hour
message answering service. Details about our titles and how to
order are available at www.teachyourself.com

For USA order enquiries: please contact McGraw-Hill Customer
Services, PO Box 545, Blacklick, OH 43004-0545, USA.
Telephone: 1-800-722-4726. *Fax:* 1-614-755-5645.

For Canada order enquiries: please contact McGraw-Hill Ryerson
Ltd, 300 Water St, Whitby, Ontario L1N 9B6, Canada.
Telephone: 905 430 5000. *Fax:* 905 430 5020.

Long renowned as the authoritative source for self-guided learning –
with more than 50 million copies sold worldwide – the *teach yourself*
series includes over 500 titles in the fields of languages, crafts,
hobbies, business, computing and education.

British Library Cataloguing in Publication Data: a catalogue record
for this title is available from the British Library.

Library of Congress Catalog Card Number: on file.

First published in UK 1999 as Improve your Spanish by
Hodder Education, part of Hachette UK, 338 Euston Road,
London NW1 3BH.

First published in US 1999 by The McGraw-Hill Companies, Inc.

This edition published 2011.

The *Teach Yourself* name is a registered trade mark of
Hodder Headline.

Copyright © 1999, 2010, 2011 Juan Kattán-Ibarra

Typeset by MPS Limited, a Macmillan Company.

Printed and bound by CPI Group (UK) Ltd, Croydon, CR0 4YY
for Hodder Education, an Hachette UK Company, 338 Euston Road,
London NW1 3BH.

The publisher has used its best endeavours to ensure that the URLs
for external websites referred to in this book are correct and active
at the time of going to press. However, the publisher and the
author have no responsibility for the websites and can make no
guarantee that a site will remain live or that the content will remain
relevant, decent or appropriate.

Hachette UK's policy is to use papers that are natural, renewable
and recyclable products and made from wood grown in sustainable
forests. The logging and manufacturing processes are expected to
conform to the environmental regulations of the country of origin.

Impression number   10 9 8 7 6 5 4 3 2 1

Year   2014 2013 2012 2011

Acknowledgements

The author and publishers would like to acknowledge the
following for use of their material in this volume: revistas
Cambio 16, *Tiempo*, *Buena Salud*, *Quo* (de divulgación científica),
Guía del Ocio; diarios *Ya*, *El Mundo*, *Diario 16*, *El Mercurio*
(Chile), *Excelsior* (México); radios San Cristóbal, El Conquistador,
Clásica (Chile), La Romántica (México); Universidad de Málaga,
RENFE, OMIC.

Contents

Practise what you have learned with dozens of interactive exercises
online at www.teachyourselfextra.com.

Meet the author

I am an experienced teacher of Spanish and the author of a number of best-selling Spanish courses. I began my career teaching Spanish in the United Kingdom in 1975, at Ealing College in London, and also acted as an external examiner in Spanish for various London examinations boards.

My first Spanish course was published in London in 1978, in a writing career which has lasted until today, and I have written or co-written courses in the **Teach Yourself** series including **Complete Spanish, Perfect your Spanish, Complete Latin American Spanish, Essential Spanish Grammar, Speak Spanish with Confidence** and **Phone Spanish,** and courses for other publishers including the BBC and McGraw-Hill. I am now a full-time author, and very much look forward to being your guide for your continuing journey into the Spanish language. **¡Vamos!**

Juan Kattán-Ibarra

Only got a minute?

There are many ways in which we can enhance our ability to communicate in another language. Living for a time in a country where the language is spoken is certainly the ideal one, but most of us cannot do this and we have to rely on other means. And while a stay in a Spanish-speaking country can help us become more fluent, which is probably what you are aiming at, it does not necessarily lead to greater accuracy, unless you have good linguistic ability, join a regular class or do some serious study on your own.

Of the two, communication and accuracy, the first is more important if you really want to interact with Spanish-speaking people at home or abroad. But most of us would like to achieve both, especially if our objective is to use the language for more serious purposes, at work for example. **Perfect your Spanish** focuses on both. Each of the twelve units which make up the course is centred around a small number of communicative objectives, which are made clear on the opening page of each unit; making enquiries, expressing intentions and giving instructions are just a few of them. Look at these before you start, as they will tell you what you are going to be able to do with the language by the end of that unit or when you have completed the course.

Accuracy, on the other hand, will be achieved through careful study and revision of a number of key grammatical constructions, each one of them linked to the communicative content of the course. Learning how to give directions, for example, involves being able to handle imperative forms as in **Siga todo recto** *Go straight ahead*; expressing uncertainty requires you to learn the forms of the subjunctive, as in **No creo que vuelvan** *I don't think they'll come back*. These and a number of other constructions constitute the core of the grammatical component of the course.

5 Only got five minutes?

The Spanish language

Have you decided to continue with your Spanish to a more advanced level? Then you have made the right choice. With 350 million native speakers in twenty-one countries, from Spain to Africa and the Americas, Spanish, together with English and Chinese, ranks among the top three most widely spoken languages in the world. The majority of Spanish speakers are in the Americas, stretching from Mexico through Central America and the Caribbean to Tierra del Fuego in the south. Mexico, with more than 100 million people, is the largest Spanish-speaking country in the world, followed by Spain with 46 million. In the United States, 34 out of 45 million people of Hispanic origin use Spanish in their homes, making this the second most important language after English in that country. Its presence is evident in many areas, especially in the media, advertising, the retail trade, education and health centres. Millions of other people in places as far apart as China, Japan, Europe and Brazil are learning Spanish as a second or third foreign language and their numbers are growing every day. Among the factors which have contributed to this increase are the expansion in international trade and tourism, and a growing interest in Spanish and Spanish American life and culture, including literature, music, dance, cinema, social and environmental issues and politics. Internet usage, with thousands of websites dealing with Spanish topics or giving access to news from the Spanish-speaking world, has also contributed to this increased interest in the Spanish language.

The enormous areas covered by Spanish and the great distance between different territories has given rise, in the course of history, to many local varieties of the language, just as happened with

English in different parts of the world. This has also been the case in Spain where Castilian Spanish, **el castellano** (the language of the old Kingdom of Castile), of central and northern Spain, sounds quite different from the local varieties of Spanish spoken in areas such as Andalusia in southern Spain, Extremadura in the southwest, or in the Canary Islands, off the northwest coast of Africa. Although Castilian Spanish is considered by many to be the standard, most people in Spain now use other varieties of Spanish and these differences are accepted in all social contexts.

A similar situation to that described above occurs in Latin America, where there are noticeable differences in speech and usage, not only between the various countries but also within the same country. In an area as large as that which extends from Mexico in the north to Chile and Argentina in the south, such differences are not just restricted to pronunciation but also affect vocabulary, determined by a number of geographical, historical and linguistic factors, among them the influence of indigenous languages or even that of non-Spanish European immigrants, such as Italians in Argentina.

In spite of the large numbers of people who use Spanish as their native language in different countries, and the great distance between the Iberian Peninsula and the Americas, the grammar of Spanish has remained largely the same, except for a few differences which are easily identifiable. Written Spanish is the same in all parts of the Spanish-speaking world. A number of factors have contributed to this unity, among these the constant flow of literary texts across the Spanish-speaking world at all times, the role of the press and communications technology, especially in more recent times, and that of the Spanish Royal Academy (*Real Academia Española*), an official academic body with analogous academies in all Spanish-speaking countries, whose main function is to establish norms for Spanish usage, especially in relation to grammar, vocabulary and spelling.

El español or **castellano** is the official language of Spain, though it is not the only language spoken in that country. Three other languages have co-official status in the regions where they are spoken: **gallego**, in Galicia, in the northwestern part of the Peninsula; **catalán**, in Catalonia, in the northeast, with variants of this spoken in Valencia (where it is known officially as **valenciano**, Valencian), and the Balearic Islands (known officially as **mallorquín, menorquín,** and **ibiceño**), and also spoken in Andorra and in southwestern France; **vasco** or **euskera** in the Basque Country, in the French-Spanish border along the western Pyrenees (and also spoken in the French Basque Country). Of these, only Galician and Catalan are, like Spanish, derived from Latin. The exact origins of Basque are subject to much speculation.

The predominance of Castilian over other languages spoken in the Peninsula dates back to the end of the fifteenth century when the old kingdoms of Castile and Aragon, united under *Isabel de Castilla* and *Fernando de Aragón*, brought a large part of the Peninsula under their dominion, and with it the gradual penetration of Castilian into the domains of the Crown, until it became established as the language of Spain. From the Iberian Peninsula, Castilian travelled to the newly discovered territories of the New World. The language of the *conquistadores* was imposed upon millions of indigenous people, many of whom still use their own languages alongside Spanish. By the time of their independence from Spain, at the beginning of the nineteenth century, Spanish had become well established in all the former colonies. Spanish is now an official language in most of these countries, some of which have also granted co-official status to indigenous languages: **quechua** in Ecuador, Peru and Bolivia, **aymara** in Peru and Bolivia, **guaraní** in Paraguay. Mexico has no official language, in spite of the fact that the majority of its people speak Spanish. Indigenous languages, over sixty in all, account for about six million speakers in that country. In Puerto Rico, a self-governing commonwealth in association with the United States, the official languages are Spanish and English.

The word **castellano** instead of **español,** to designate the language, is used by many people in Spain, especially in those regions that have their own language, as it is felt that the word **español** excludes those other languages. Such controversy is not relevant in Latin America, where the word **castellano** is more common.

The roots of **el castellano** can be found in Latin, the language of the Romans, but Arabic rule in large parts of the Peninsula between 710 and 1492 also left an important imprint on the Spanish language, mainly in vocabulary. Many words of everyday use such as **aceite** *oil*, **aceituna** *olive*, **hasta** *until*, **taza** *cup*, and many place names, are derived from Arabic. Starting in the sixteenth century, a number of words from the conquered territories in the Americas began to find their way into Spanish: **chocolate, tomate, cacao** and **patata** are just some of them. Old and then Modern French, especially from the seventeenth century onwards, also had an influence on Spanish, and in more recent times English has been a major contributor. Dozens of English words in as many areas are in current use in Spanish, some in adapted form, others not: examples are **fútbol, tenis, béisbol, jersey, suéter, ticket, film, suspense, sandwich, marketing, email** and **chatear**.

10 Only got ten minutes?

Are you looking for ways to advance your Spanish beyond your present level? Deciding what to do about it is not a simple task, as it depends on a number of factors, among them your own competence in the language, the time you can spare to study on your own or attend a class, and your own needs. Your motivation for furthering your Spanish beyond your current level may be personal or may be to do with your work or travel interests, so you may be wondering whether a self-study course such as *Perfect your Spanish* will be suitable for your circumstances and meet your needs. Whatever these are, it is important to establish that beyond a beginners and intermediate level a self-study course such as this can be an excellent tool to advance and guide your learning, but you will gain much more from it if you supplement the activities in the course with others centred on your own special needs. The following lines will tell you a little about the nature and content of the course and about what you can do to improve your competence in Spanish.

Perfect your Spanish is a general course built around twelve different themes, with a main focus on usage, from which derives the language content of the course. Language functions in the course, about 50 in all, are centred on the user, on the kind of things you might want to say in Spanish. In some, the focus is on you as a person: talking about your daily activities, describing your job and your working conditions, talking about places and people you know, describing minor ailments, etc. Others address your needs when dealing with Spanish speakers either abroad or at home: asking for information about accommodation, asking for and giving directions, making complaints, etc. There are also those language functions of a more general kind that you might need in a wide range of situations: expressing intentions, expressing regret, giving advice, expressing obligation and need, expressing probability and so on.

In terms of the grammar you are going to learn, **Perfect your Spanish** will help you revise verbs and tenses and other key grammatical constructions and will introduce you to new ones. Revision focuses especially on those language forms that English native speakers tend to confuse or find more difficult to produce without making some mistakes, such as the contrast between **ser** and **estar**, **para** and **por**, the present indicative and the present subjunctive, the preterite and the imperfect. New grammatical points include, among others, a look at some of the main uses of the subjunctive and coverage of the present, imperfect and pluperfect subjunctive tenses, and direct and indirect speech. You will also learn the Spanish for conditional sentences such as *If she comes I'll tell her, If she came I'd tell her, If she had come I'd have told her*. All the grammatical forms in the course are presented within a context, a context which is clearly defined at the start of each unit, first with the unit heading, which establishes the main theme, for example Unit 6, **Un lugar donde vivir** *A place to live*; Unit 11, **El mundo que nos rodea** *The world around us*. Then follows a list of the language uses or functions, four to six to each unit, that are the main focus of the unit. In Unit 11, for example, you will learn to ask and give opinions, to express agreement and disagreement, to express relationships of cause and effect, to offer solutions, and to express unfulfilled conditions. The grammatical content, then, stems from these uses, but it also goes beyond them, drawing from some other elements within the unit, for example dialogues and reading passages of different kinds.

The main components of each unit, apart from those mentioned above, are two to four dialogues of various lengths which focus on the main theme, on one or more language uses or functions, and on the grammatical forms or constructions needed to express them. These are followed by different types of questions, key vocabulary and, in some cases, brief **Insights** dealing with language or cultural points or offering you quick tips on how to approach the new material. After the dialogues there is a list of **Key sentences** with English translations. These are followed by a **Grammar** section with explanations of the main language constructions, all with examples in Spanish and English and author guidance on some of the more difficult points. The **Practice** section which follows the **Grammar** contains exercises of various kinds, which draw from the material in the previous sections. Once again, help and further information on language or culture is given where necessary. Each unit ends with a **Test yourself** section, assessing what you have learnt. The answers to the tests and to the exercises in the **Practice** section are in the **Key to the exercises** at the end of the book.

Try planning your own strategy to make the most of what this course has to offer you, to expand your competence in Spanish even further and to satisfy your own needs. There are a number of steps that you can take to do this, some more general, others more dependent on available resources, your ability to handle new technology, and of course your own interests. Here are a few suggestions:

▶ Try to get newspapers and magazines in Spanish and read short news items or select longer articles according to your own interests. This will help you to increase your vocabulary and understanding of written texts. There are two ways to approach this depending on the length of the text or its complexity. Use short articles or news items for *intensive* reading, looking up words you don't know in a dictionary and taking note of phrases that attract your attention. You could keep a notebook specially for this so that you can come back to your notes whenever you like. Use longer or more complex articles for *extensive* reading, *not* looking up every new word, but trying to get the general sense of the passage and deducing meaning from the context, just as we do in our own language sometimes. This will not only further your capacity to understand a longer piece of writing and increase your passive vocabulary, but it will also make you less dependent on your dictionary. Follow the same strategy with short and longer texts in your book, and you can do exactly the same with texts you find on the internet, if you have access to this. The options are wide as there are hundreds of websites, blogs and forums in Spanish to suit your own interests. In one of them, particularly, **La página del idioma español** (elcastellano.org), you will find ample information on the Spanish language and available resources, including direct access to major newspapers in all the main Spanish-speaking countries. The **Taking it further** section at the back of the book contains useful information on resources and websites for those interested in having access to authentic Spanish. If you intend to travel in Spain or Latin America or would like to study Spanish in a Spanish-speaking country this section also includes a few useful websites.

▶ Watch Spanish television if you have access to it and listen to news or other programmes. Don't be discouraged if you find that you cannot understand at first, as this may well be due to the fact that you are not familiar with the context, especially when it comes to news. Spanish newsreaders tend to speak fast, but you will soon get used to it.

▶ Try to find DVDs of Spanish films or of English films with Spanish subtitles. With the first, listen to the Spanish, preferably without looking at the English subtitles if they have them, and focus on the way things are said, and on the accents, even if you do not understand everything at first. With the second, focus on the correspondence between the English and the Spanish.

▶ If you have an MP3 or iPod, use it to listen to Spanish songs. Try to learn the words when you can. You could also download podcasts (digital audio files) in Spanish from the internet to use in your MP3 and listen to their content when you like.

▶ Find **BBC Mundo**, the Spanish web page of the BBC, and either read or listen to news in Spanish. You will find more information on this in the **Taking it further** section.

▶ Try to find Spanish-speaking people with whom you can speak in Spanish in your home town or through the internet. You may even find someone who is learning English and is willing to exchange conversation classes with you.

▶ To increase your vocabulary, place cards around your house with the words or phrases you would like to learn and look at them from time to time. You will be surprised how many words you will be able to remember later on. You can also do this to learn verbs and tenses.

As you progress through **Perfect your Spanish**, try to supplement the material in the units with these extra activities, and when you have finished the course use the suggestions above to carry on learning.

Taking your Spanish further

Before coming across this course you may have wondered what you could do to take your Spanish beyond a basic or intermediate level. A book such as this will help you in a number of ways to increase your capacity to understand and communicate with native speakers. The audio component of the course is there to help you understand people from both Spain and Latin America, while many of the dialogues and exercises are aimed at furthering your ability to speak. Other elements in the course will help you along with reading and to a lesser extent with writing. By reading authentic passages centred around specific themes you will be able to increase your understanding of the written language and expand your vocabulary. Writing focuses mainly on model letters and emails of a utilitarian kind such as those giving references, asking for information, booking a hotel room and giving directions, with follow-up exercises leading you to do your own writing.

The book is organized around twelve themes, covering, among others, subjects such as daily life, leisure, work, education and holidays, while each unit focuses on four to six specific areas of language, and on the grammatical constructions needed to express them. The language covered is the kind you are most likely to need in your dealings with native speakers at home or abroad, either as a tourist, a businessperson, or simply in your social interaction with Spanish-speaking people: making invitations, expressing likes and dislikes, describing your job, describing people and places, booking into a hotel and giving directions. The grammar content serves a dual purpose: firstly, to revise many language constructions which at this stage you should be familiar with, such as most simple and compound tenses, the contrast between the preterite and the imperfect, uses of **ser** and **estar**, **por** and **para**, pronouns, etc.; secondly, to introduce more advanced forms of language, such as the different uses of the subjunctive and its simple and compound tenses, the conditional perfect, conditional sentences, and direct and indirect speech.

What can you do to make better use of the material in this course and further your Spanish beyond what it has to offer? There are in fact a number of steps that you can take. First and foremost, don't be satisfied with just understanding what is in the book or on the audio and answering the questions which precede or follow the introductory **Dialogues**. Go one step further and try to analyse the language content, a particular way of saying something, a turn of phrase or a certain word. Make a list of the things that attract your attention and try to use them in sentences of your own. Make an attempt to memorize some of the phrases that you might want to use in a conversation and make up brief dialogues with them, focusing on a specific point first, then expanding into a longer exchange. Go back to your notes from time to time and practise once again so that you can fix the new forms in your mind. Following the dialogues you will find a **Key sentences** section which brings together some of the main sentences, grouped together according to usage. Use these as a model to produce other similar examples.

The **Grammar** section which follows the **Key sentences** focuses on two or three main points. The limitations of a book such as this make it impossible to treat some of these in great detail, so use the notes as a guideline to find more information on each point. Get yourself a good grammar book, preferably one with exercises, and check those constructions that you find particularly difficult. Go back to them again and again until you feel confident that you have learnt them. One way of learning constructions which are different from English when you are working without a teacher is to place English and Spanish side by side. Take the use of the subjunctive, for example. Write a short list of English sentences that require the subjunctive in Spanish, making sure you understand why: *I hope she calls me* **Espero que me llame**, *I don't think he'll come* **No creo que venga**, *I'll do it when I finish* **Lo haré cuando termine**. Then replace the English verbs that translate as subjunctive in Spanish with others suitable for the context (*I hope he/she writes to me/invites me* etc.) and do likewise with the Spanish. Continue with the rest of the sentences until the construction and the verb forms become automatic.

The exercises in the **Practice** section of the book, which follow the Grammar section, are just one way of reinforcing the new language, but you should try to go beyond these. Whenever possible, use them as a model to produce your own version, drawing from your own experience when appropriate. If you consider a certain exercise to be too easy for you, don't just discard it, but try to adapt it and make it fit your own level. At the start of a course such as this each user will probably be at a different stage with regard to their Spanish, so a more personalized approach to the material is highly recommended. Try also learning from your own mistakes. Don't be satisfied with just checking the correct answers to the exercises in the **Key to the exercises** but try to understand why you made the mistakes that you did and what you can do to improve your performance. Perhaps you need to read the grammar notes again or maybe you require some more practice. Do likewise with the answers to the **Test yourself** section which is at the end of each unit.

There are a number of reading passages in the book and with these the approach should be different depending on their length. Deal with brief texts such as personal letters or letters to the editor, emails or advertisements in detail, just as you did with the dialogues, but use longer pieces for general comprehension, trying to get the gist of what the text says rather than understanding every single word. This is in fact what we usually do when reading something in our own language. We don't look up every single word we don't know, as its meaning is often made clear as we read on. As in English, you will soon get a sense of what is important and what is not. Try to find and read other texts on the same subject, if this interests you, or on a related theme. The internet, if you have access to it, is a useful tool to do this.

Expanding your vocabulary is an essential part of learning a foreign language. One way of doing this is to draw up lists of words and phrases around a certain theme. Choose subjects that interest you, for example sports, cinema, theatre, music, dance, literature, business, etc. and use a dictionary to look up the words and phrases you want. A good dictionary will contain some examples of their use. Some knowledge of word formation in Spanish will also help you expand your passive and active vocabulary. Consider for example English and Spanish prefixes in *undo* – **des**hacer, *untie* – **des**atar, *incapable* – **in**capaz, *invalid* – **in**válido; and compare suffixes in *loyalty* – leal**tad**, *university* – universi**dad**, *manageable* – mane**jable** and *comfortable* – confor**table**. There are some notes on word formation in the book, but if you would like to go beyond these, look up the subject in a grammar book.

The above are only a few hints on what you can do to advance your Spanish. There are many other possible ways. Search on the internet, if you have access to this, and find out what other people have done to improve their competence in the language. You will be surprised at the number of ideas you will find that can help you improve your Spanish and become much more fluent in it.
¡Buena suerte!

Introduction

Welcome to **Perfect your Spanish**. If you have completed a beginners or an intermediate course in Spanish either in a class or studying on your own, or you have learnt the language through contact with Spanish speakers at home or abroad, and are looking to build on what you have learnt and advance your communication skills, then **Perfect your Spanish** is the right course for you. Perhaps you also wish to revise some of the forms and constructions you learnt in a previous course, or certain areas of the language that you are less familiar with. This course offers you ample opportunity to do this in a systematic way, covering a number of key points, with language and usage always going hand in hand.

Although the course has been designed especially for people studying on their own, the material and exercises will also lend themselves to classroom use. Students taking evening classes in Spanish or who are preparing for examinations where the emphasis is on acquiring communicative skills will find plenty of useful material in this book to help them achieve their objectives. By the end of this course you will have increased your capacity to understand the spoken and written language, and advanced your ability to communicate with Spanish speakers, orally or in writing.

The structure of the course

The course book contains

▶ *12 course units with a self-assessment test at the end of each unit*
▶ *a reference section at the back of the book*

In addition there are two CDs which you really need to have if you are going to get maximum benefit from the course.

The course units

The course units can be divided roughly into the following categories, although of course there is a certain amount of overlap from one category to another:

Statement of aims

You will be told what you can expect to learn, in terms of what you will be able to do in Spanish by the end of the unit.

Presentation of new language

You will find two or more dialogues which are recorded on the CDs and also printed in the book. Some assistance with vocabulary is also given. The language in the dialogues covers all the main language structures and tenses, including more advanced forms such as the subjunctive, building on what you have learnt in your beginner's course and taking you further. Each conversation is followed by one or two Language and comprehension check exercises focusing on the content of the dialogue.

Key sentences

All new phrases and expressions with their English translation are listed in this section.

Description and revision of language forms

In the **Grammar** section you learn about the forms of the language, thus enabling you to review structures you may be familiar with and to learn how to use new language forms.

Practice of the new language

In the **Practice** section you will have ample opportunity to use the language that you have learnt and to improve your speaking, reading and writing skills. This section also includes listening comprehension exercises (**¡A escuchar!**) which will help you to increase your capacity to understand spoken Spanish. Transcripts of these exercises are at the back of the book. A **Key to the exercises** in this section will also be found at the back of the book.

Test yourself

A **Test yourself** section at the end of each unit will help you to assess what you have learnt, and allow you to judge whether you have successfully improved your language and communication skills. The keys to these self-assessment tests will be found in the **Key to the exercises** section at the back of the book.

Insights

At different stages throughout the unit you will find Insights with further information related to the content and useful tips for dealing with some of the new language. The information touches not just on grammatical points but also on aspects related to culture.

Reference

At the end of the book there are sections which you can use for reference:

▶ *a key to the activities in the units, including a key to the 'Test yourself' exercises*
▶ *transcripts of the listening comprehension exercises*
▶ *a 'taking it further' section*
▶ *a list of common irregular verbs*
▶ *a Spanish–English vocabulary*
▶ *an English–Spanish vocabulary*
▶ *an index to the grammar*

Online

Once you have completed the course you can practise what you have learned with dozens of interactive exercises online at www.teachyourselfextra.com.

How to use this course

Make sure at the beginning of each unit that you are clear about what you can expect to learn.

First listen to the dialogues on the recording. Try to get the gist of what is being said before you look at the printed text in the book.

Then refer to the printed text and the key vocabulary in order to study the dialogues in more detail. If you want an explanation of new language points at this stage, study the relevant paragraphs in the Grammar section, and the **Insights** which follow some of the dialogues.

You must try to make the most of the audio material by listening to the recordings of the dialogues at every opportunity – sitting on the train or bus, waiting at the dentist's or stuck in a traffic jam, using what would otherwise be 'dead' time. But listening is not enough. You should try to internalize and make sense of what you hear, focusing especially on language forms and expressions which may be new to you. Repeat them to yourself and then use them in sentences of your own. After you have gone through the dialogues, go through the Language and comprehension check questions which follow them to check that you understood what was said. The answers to these are in the **Key to the exercises**.

Move on next to the **Key sentences** section. Try covering up the English translations and producing the English equivalents of the Spanish. If you find that relatively easy, go on to cover the Spanish sentences and produce the Spanish equivalents of the English. You will probably find this more difficult. Trying to recall the context in which words and phrases were used may help you learn them better.

You can then study the explanations in the Grammar section in a systematic way. We have tried to make these as user-friendly as possible, since we recognize that many people find grammar daunting. But in the end, it is up to you just how much time you spend on studying and sorting out the grammar points. Some people find that they can do better by getting an ear for what sounds right, others need to know in detail how the language is put together. You may even want to go beyond the explanations which are offered in this section, in which case there is a number of grammar books, some in the same series, which may help you to expand your knowledge of Spanish grammar. The **Insights** which you will find throughout this section offer useful hints for handling the new language and expand on some of the points covered.

You will then be ready to move on to the Practice section and work through the activities following the instructions that precede them. Most of these are clearly communicative in nature, focusing on the aims outlined at the start of the unit. You are going to be the main actor in this section, carrying out the instructions given for each exercise, which may involve understanding and acting on what a Spanish speaker has said, playing a role, writing a letter, helping a travelling companion who doesn't know any Spanish, and so on.

Some of the activities in this section are listen-only activities. The temptation may be to go straight to the transcriptions at the back of the book, but try not to do this. The whole point of listening exercises is to improve your listening skills. You will not do this by reading first. The transcriptions are there to help you if you get stuck.

Each unit contains, within this section, longer, authentic reading passages designed to help you increase your passive vocabulary and to build on comprehension. Most of these deal with important cultural points related to either Spain or Latin America. Read them through and answer the questions which either precede or follow them. You don't need to understand every single word here, but don't hesitate to use your dictionary if you want to study the passage in more depth.

As you work your way through the activities, check your answers carefully in the **Key to the exercises** at the back of the book. It is easy to overlook your own mistakes. If you have a study buddy it's a good idea to check each other's work. Most of the exercises have fixed answers, but some are a bit more open-ended. For most of these you will find a model answer which you can adapt for your own purposes. The **Insights** in this section offer useful help and information related to some of the activities.

Before you move on to a new unit, go through the **Test yourself** section, which will allow you to assess what you have learnt in the unit. You can check your answers in the **Key to Test yourself**, which is in the **Key to the exercises** section. If you did well in the test move on to the next unit, but if your performance was not satisfactory, study the relevant information in the **Grammar summary** again until you feel confident that you have learnt it.

Symbols and abbreviations

m = masculine gender of noun   V = Verdadero, true

f = feminine gender of noun   F = Falso, false

pl = plural form   sing = singular

◄» Material on the recording.

1

Cosas del diario vivir
Things to do with daily life

In this unit you will learn how to:
- **Talk about daily activities and habits**
- **Say how often you do something**
- **Relate a sequence of events**

1 ¿Qué sueles hacer? *What do you usually do?*

Carlos Salinas, escritor, es entrevistado por una periodista de una revista española. En una parte de la entrevista, Carlos comenta acerca de su vida diaria.

Periodista	Carlos, a veces la gente se pregunta cómo es la vida diaria de un escritor, que no tiene que salir de su casa ni cumplir un horario o vérselas con un jefe autoritario y gruñón.
Carlos	Pues mira, es verdad que trabajar en casa tiene sus grandes ventajas, no tienes que perder el tiempo yendo de un lado a otro de la ciudad en el coche, el metro o lo que sea. Ahora, en cuanto a lo del horario, es cierto que a mí nadie me impone un horario de trabajo determinado como suele ocurrirle a casi todo el mundo. Pero el horario me lo impongo yo mismo. Soy una persona bastante disciplinada.

(Contd)

paro

	Suelo levantarme sobre las siete de la mañana, me doy una ducha y luego bebo un café. No acostumbro comer mucho por la mañana. A veces unas tostadas o algunas pastas. A las ocho me siento frente al ordenador y no paro hasta el mediodía… _until_
Periodista	¿Te molesta que interrumpan tu trabajo?
Carlos	Sí, pero, vamos, no suele ocurrir. Mi familia y mis amistades conocen muy bien mis hábitos y nunca me llaman por la mañana, a no ser que sea para algo importante. Por la tarde, trabajo menos intensamente.
Periodista	¿Qué sueles hacer por la noche?
Carlos	Bueno, yo soy un gran aficionado a la música, principalmente al jazz. A menudo vienen amigos a casa por la noche, escuchamos música, tomamos unas copas, charlamos … A veces vamos al cine o a cenar fuera …
Periodista	¿Cambiarías tu vida por la de una persona normal?
Carlos	No, definitivamente no, prefiero seguir haciendo lo que hago.

unless it is

Insight

Note the use of the present subjunctive in the following phrases: **o lo que sea** or whatever (it may be), **¿Te molesta que interrumpan …?** Does it bother you to be interrupted …?, **a no ser que sea …** unless it is … In all three cases the subjunctive verb refers to something which is not a reality nor a fact.

QUICK VOCAB

diario vivir (m) daily living
¿qué sueles hacer? what do you usually do?
cumplir un horario to keep to a timetable
vérselas con (uno) to deal with (someone)
gruñón grumbling
de un lado a otro from one end to the other
en cuanto a as regards
imponer to impose
darse una ducha to take a shower
ser aficionado a to be fond of, to like

Insight

Sí, pero vamos, no suele ocurrir. The word **vamos** in this context is a filler, used to fill in a gap in the conversation, just as *well* or *you know* do in English. Another common filler in Spanish is **pues** (**Pues mira ...**).

Language and comprehension check 1
Answer the following questions in Spanish.

llegas

a ¿Qué ventajas ve Carlos en trabajar en casa?
b ¿Cómo se describe Carlos?
c ¿Qué hace a las ocho de la mañana?
d ¿Por qué nadie suele interrumpir su trabajo?
e ¿Qué hace normalmente por la noche?

2 Un día normal *An ordinary day*

Alicia Álvarez, ejecutiva de una empresa textil, habla sobre su vida diaria.

Periodista	Alicia, ¿cómo es un día normal para una ejecutiva de una gran empresa?	◆ CD1, TR 2
Alicia	Bueno, difícilmente puedo hablar sobre lo que es un día normal para mí, ya que mis actividades son muchas y muy variadas. Pero, naturalmente, como casi toda la gente que trabaja, estoy sujeta a una cierta rutina que, quiéralo o no, tengo que cumplir. Vivo bastante lejos de la fábrica y por lo general salgo de casa a eso de las ocho, pues si lo hago más tarde el tráfico es fatal. Normalmente, llego a la fábrica sobre las nueve de la mañana, primero consulto mi agenda para ver qué actividades tendré que cubrir y seguidamente planeo el día con mi secretaria. Hay días de mayor actividad que otros, pero casi siempre estoy muy ocupada.	
Periodista	¿Vuelves a casa a comer?	
	(Contd)	

Alicia	No, ¡qué va! Sería imposible, ya que tardaría mucho tiempo. Suelo comer en el restaurante de la empresa que no está nada mal.
Periodista	¿A qué hora vuelves a casa normalmente?
Alicia	Pues, nunca antes de las nueve o las diez de la noche. Lo que pasa es que después de dejar la fábrica hago mis compras o voy a tomar una copa con algún amigo y de vez en cuando visito a mis padres.
Periodista	¿Tienes alguna otra actividad, aparte de tu trabajo y tu vida social?
Alicia	Bueno sí, dos veces por semana voy a un gimnasio para mantenerme en forma y relajarme. En verano suelo ir a la piscina los fines de semana.

(handwritten annotations: "Certainly not" pointing to ¡qué va!, "since" pointing to ya que, "usually" pointing to suelo)

Insight

Quiéralo o no *Whether I like it or not.* This type of phrase with a present subjunctive verb, like **o lo que sea** in Dialogue 1, is common in Spanish. The verb is often repeated in phrases of this kind: **quieran o no quieran** *whether they like it or not*, **sea cuando sea** *whenever it may be*, **diga lo que diga** *whatever he/she may say*, etc.

estar sujeto a *to be tied down*
cubrir *to cover*
planear *to programme*
mantenerse en forma *to keep fit*
relajarse *to relax*

Insight

¡Qué va! Notice this expression which in this context translates into English as *certainly not!* Other translations of this expression, depending on the context, are *nonsense!*, *rubbish!*, *nothing of the sort!*

Language and comprehension check 2

What phrases have been used in the dialogue to express the following:

handwritten at top: difícilmente puedo hablar

a I can hardly speak ...
b Since (or given that) ... *Ya que*
c About or around (eight/ nine o'clock) *a eso de*
d It would take me a long time. *(Ya que) tardaría mucho tiempo*
e It's not bad at all. *no está nada mal*
f What happens is that ... *lo que pasa es que*
g To have a drink. *tomar una copa*
h From time to time. *de vez en cuando*

3 ¿Qué hace usted? *What do you do?*

Teresa González es ama de casa. Teresa habla acerca de su vida diaria. *housewife*

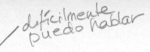

Periodista	Teresa, ¿qué hace Vd. en un día normal?
Teresa	Pues, me levanto a eso de las siete y media para preparar el desayuno para mi marido y mis hijos. Mi marido se va al trabajo a las ocho y media y los chicos salen para el colegio sobre las nueve menos cuarto. Después me arreglo y salgo a hacer la compra del día. Voy al mercado que está a diez minutos de aquí, a la panadería, dos o tres veces por semana voy al supermercado, vamos, depende de lo que haga falta. Nunca es igual. Luego vuelvo a casa para preparar la comida.
Periodista	¿Sus hijos y su marido vienen a casa a comer?
Teresa	Mis hijos sí, pero mi marido no.
Periodista	¿Y por la tarde, qué hace?
Teresa	Pues, veo un rato la tele, a veces echo una siesta, pero vamos, normalmente no. Siempre hay algo que hacer en casa, lavar la ropa, planchar, coser.

handwritten notes: arreglarse – get ready; subj; sew

🎧 CD1, TR 3

Insight

Depende de lo que haga falta *It depends on what(ever) we may need*: another present subjunctive form here, **haga**, referring to something 'unreal'. Compare this with **Hace falta más arroz** *We need more rice*, which is a fact.

arreglarse *to get dressed*
rato *(m) while, moment*
lavar la ropa *to do the washing*
planchar *to iron*
coser *to sew*

Note the use of **para** in: **para** preparar el desayuno **para** mi marido ..., los chicos salen **para** el colegio ...

Language and comprehension check 3

Study the dialogue once more if necessary and then complete these phrases with the missing information.

  a Me levanto a eso de la siete y media para ...
  b Los chicos salen para ...
  c Después me arreglo y salgo a ...
  d Luego, vuelvo a casa para ...
  e Miro un rato la tele, a veces ..., pero vamos, normalmente no.
  f Siempre hay algo que hacer en casa ...

Key sentences

Talking about daily activities and habits

Suelo levantarme sobre las siete.	*I usually get up at about seven.*
Me doy una ducha.	*I take a shower.*
Bebo un café.	*I have a coffee.*
No acostumbro (a) comer mucho.	*I don't usually eat much.*

Saying how often you do something

A veces **(como) unas tostadas.**	*Sometimes I eat some toast.*
Nunca **me llaman por la mañana.**	*They never call me in the morning.*
A menudo **vienen amigos a casa.**	*Friends often come home.*

Other ways of indicating frequency	
por lo general	*generally*
de vez en cuando	*from time to time*
generalmente	*generally*
siempre	*always*
normalmente	*normally*
una vez, dos veces por semana	*once, twice a week*
usualmente	*usually*

Relating a sequence of events

Me doy una ducha y *luego* **bebo un café.**	*I take a shower and then I drink coffee.*
Primero **consulto mi agenda** … *seguidamente* **planeo el día con mi secretaria.**	*First I look up in my diary … then I plan the day with my secretary.*
Después **me arreglo.**	*Then I get dressed.*

Other ways of relating a sequence of events	
en primer lugar	*in the first place*
primeramente	*firstly, first*
antes que nada	*first of all*
a continuación	*next, immediately after*
finalmente	*finally*
por último	*finally*

Grammar

1 Talking about actions you do regularly

a Using the present tense indicative

There are many examples of the use of the present tense in this unit which will help you to revise it. The examples below include different types of verbs: **ir**, irregular; **salir**, irregular in the first person singular (**salgo**); **venir**, irregular in the first person singular (**vengo**), and also a stem-changing verb, like **soler** (o > ue); and **sentarse**, reflexive and stem-changing (e > ie). Refer to your grammar book if you feel you need to revise non-regular and stem-changing forms.

Vamos **al cine.**	*We go to the cinema.*
Salgo **de casa a eso de las 8:00.**	*I leave the house at about 8.00.*
A menudo *vienen* **amigos a casa.**	*Friends often come to our house.*
Me siento **frente al ordenador.**	*I sit in front of the computer.*

b Using **soler** (o > ue) + infinitive

¿Qué sueles hacer **por la noche?**	*What do you usually do in the evening?*
Suelo ir **al cine o a cenar fuera.**	*I usually go to the cinema or to eat out.*

c **Acostumbrar (a)** + infinitive

Acostumbra (a) trabajar **mucho.**	*He/she usually works a lot.*
No *acostumbro (a) salir* **en verano.**	*I don't usually go away in the summer.*

Acostumbrar is used with the preposition **a** by some speakers, especially in Latin America.

2 The subjunctive

There are a few examples of the subjunctive in dialogues 1–3, so a general look at its uses and at the forms of the present subjunctive in particular seems appropriate at this stage.

The subjunctive is not a tense but one of three forms or moods of the verb with tenses of its own (present, imperfect, perfect, pluperfect). The other two are the indicative mood (present, preterite, imperfect indicative, etc.), and the imperative mood (used in commands and instructions). The subjunctive is generally used to refer to actions or states which are unreal or which have not yet taken place. If there is certainty, as in the examples in paragraph 1 above, then you must use the indicative mood. Compare the following sentences:

| **Se alegran cuando** *viene* **su abuela.** | *They are glad when their grandmother comes.* |

This is a fact, therefore the verb is in the *indicative*.

| **Se alegrarán cuando** *venga* **su abuela.** | *They'll be glad when their grandmother comes.* |

This is not yet a fact, therefore the verb is in the *subjunctive*.

The subjunctive often occurs in a construction with a main verb, for example **quiero** *I want*, followed by another clause (the subordinate clause) introduced by **que** and a verb in the subjunctive.

| **No** *quiero que* **me** *interrumpas.* | *I don't want you to interrupt me.* |

In this type of construction the subjunctive is dependent on the main verb, which may express a wish (as in the previous example) or uncertainty, hope, need, possibility, permission, prohibition, some kind of emotion, etc. More examples are given below with the present subjunctive.

3 The present subjunctive

To form the present subjunctive, remove the -**o** of the first person singular of the present indicative and add the appropriate endings: -**e** for -**ar** verbs and -**a** for verbs in -**er** and -**ir** (hablo > hable, como > coma, vivo > viva, vuelvo > vuelva, tengo > tenga, digo > diga, etc.)

	hablar	comer	vivir
yo	hable	coma	viva
tú	hables	comas	vivas
él/ella/usted	hable	coma	viva
nosotros	hablemos	comamos	vivamos
vosotros	habléis	comáis	viváis
ellos/ellas/ustedes	hablen	coman	vivan

No quiero que *hables* **con ella.**	*I don't want you to speak to her. (wish)*
Espero que te lo *comas* **todo.**	*I hope you eat it all. (hope)*
No creo que *viva* **mucho tiempo.**	*I don't think he/she'll live long. (uncertainty)*

In positive statements **creer** is followed by an indicative verb:

Creo que *vivirá* **muchos años.**	*I think he/she'll live for many years.*

A few verbs form the present subjunctive in a different way:

dar *to give*	**dé, des, dé, demos, deis, den**
estar *to be*	**esté, estés, esté, estemos, estéis, estén**
haber *to have*	**haya, hayas, haya, hayamos, hayáis, hayan**
ir *to go*	**vaya, vayas, vaya, vayamos, vayáis, vayan**
saber *to know*	**sepa, sepas, sepa, sepamos, sepáis, sepan**
ser *to be*	**sea, seas, sea, seamos, seáis, sean**

Puede que *estén* **en casa.**	*They may be at home. (possibility)*
Es posible que ya lo *sepan.*	*It's possible that they may already know. (possibility)*
No me permitirán que *vaya.*	*They won't allow me to go. (permission)*
Me alegra que *seas* **sincero.**	*I'm glad you're sincere. (emotion)*

4 Further uses of the subjunctive

The subjunctive is also used after phrases indicating hope, purpose, concession, condition and time:

Ojalá (que) me *den* **un aumento.**	*Let's hope they give me an increase. (hope)*
Lo traeré para que lo *veas.*	*I'll bring it so that you can see it. (purpose)*
Iremos aunque *llueva.*	*We'll go even if it rains. (concession)*
Te lo presto siempre que lo *cuides.*	*I'll lend it to you as long as you take care of it. (condition)*

| **Cuando** *lleguen* **serviré café.** | *When they arrive I'll serve coffee. (time)* |

The subjunctive is used with expressions of time only when these refer to the future, otherwise you need the indicative. Compare the last example with the following one:

| **Cuando** *llegan* **siempre les sirvo café.** | *When they arrive I always serve them coffee.* |

The above are some of the basic rules governing the use of the subjunctive. The subjunctive is important in Spanish and you may wish to expand on what you have learnt, in which case you would do well to refer to a grammar book, especially one with exercises for you to practise on your own.

Practice

1 Complete this passage with the correct form of the verb in the present tense.

Me llamo Ricardo Aguirre, soy ingeniero y vivo en Bilbao. Trabajo en una fábrica de artículos electrodomésticos. Mis actividades habituales son las siguientes: normalmente (**despertarse**) a las 6.30 de la mañana, luego (**levantarse**) y (**ducharse**) y sobre las 7.30 (**desayunar**) con mi mujer y mis tres hijos. A las 8.30 (**salir**) de casa para ir a la fábrica. Por lo general (**ir**) en el coche, pero a veces (**coger**) el autobús. Al mediodía no (**volver**) a casa a comer, ya que normalmente yo (**almorzar**) con unos colegas en un restaurante cerca de la empresa. A las 7.00 (**marcharse**) a casa, pero de vez en cuando (**ir**) a un club deportivo donde (**jugar**) al tenis con algún amigo. Por la noche, después de cenar, a veces (**dar**) un paseo con mi mujer. Nunca (**acostarse**) antes de las 12.00.

2 Now relate Ricardo's daily routine referring to the previous passage. **Ricardo Aguirre es ingeniero y vive en Bilbao. Trabaja …**

3 Match each word on the left with one of similar meaning on the right.

a normalmente — 6   **1** finalmente
b de vez en cuando 3   **2** frecuentemente
c antes que nada 5   **3** a veces
d por último 1   **4** a continuación
e después 4   **5** primero
f a menudo 2   **6** por lo general

4 Imagine a dialogue similar to the ones you have just studied between the same journalist and Carmen Olmo, a secretary. First, you'll need to prepare the questions. Use the familiar form.

a Ask her what time she leaves the house.
b Ask how she goes to work.
c Ask what time she arrives in the office.
d Ask what she does in the morning.
e Ask what time and where she normally has lunch.
f Ask what time she leaves the office.
g Ask what she normally does in the evening.

Now, the following information will help you with the answers.

Nombre: Carmen Olmo García
Profesión: Secretaria
Actividades diarias:
  i 8.30, salida de casa en dirección a la estación de metro más cercana para ir a la oficina.
 ii 8.50–9.00, llegada a la oficina.
iii Lo que suele hacer en el trabajo: abrir la correspondencia, leerla y clasificarla; escribir las cartas que le dicta su jefe; revisar el correo electrónico; recibir a los clientes de la empresa y fijar citas con el gerente; contestar el teléfono; asistir a reuniones …
 iv 1.30, almuerzo con algunos compañeros de trabajo en el bar de la esquina.
  v 7.00, salida de la oficina.
 vi Lo que acostumbra (a) hacer por la noche: cenar, ver la televisión, escuchar música, dar un paseo con su novio.

Check the notes in the Key sentences and Grammar sections and try using some of the words and constructions you've learnt. In the Key to the exercises you will find a basic model dialogue which you may want to look up once you have prepared your own version.

5 ¡A escuchar!

◀) **CD1, TR 4**

Pilar ha encontrado trabajo: Here is a conversation between Pilar Araya, a teacher from Peru, and her friend Antonio. Listen to the conversation if you have the recording or, alternatively, read the transcript in the **¡A escuchar! transcripts** section and use the text for reading comprehension. Look at the vocabulary and the questions first before you read or listen to the conversation.

reunión (f) meeting
acompañar to accompany
regalo (m) present
cumpleaños (m) birthday
¡chao! (esp. Latin America) Bye-bye! (familiar)

QUICK VOCAB

¿Verdadero o falso?
a Pilar trabaja como profesora.
b Trabaja seis horas diarias.
c Empieza a trabajar a las 7.15.
d Por la tarde no hace nada.
e Los sábados no trabaja.

6 Read this passage about the daily activities of a Spanish swimmer, then answer the questions which follow.

> Cristóbal es un gran aficionado a la natación. Cristóbal acostumbra levantarse todos los días a las seis y media de la mañana, se ducha, toma un café y deja su casa para ir a la piscina de un polideportivo donde entrena hasta las ocho y media de la mañana. Normalmente vuelve a casa sobre las
>
> *(Contd)*

regresar = to return

nueve, toma una ducha nuevamente y desayuna algo frugal, tal vez fruta y yogur.

Hacia las diez de la mañana se va a la universidad donde estudia empresariales. A la una acostumbra consumir un almuerzo ligero y sobre las tres suele volver otra vez a casa para descansar. Casi siempre duerme la siesta durante media hora, luego se pone de nuevo el bañador y regresa a la piscina para seguir entrenando. A las seis y media está una vez más de vuelta en casa. Dedica un par de horas a sus estudios, cena algo frugal y luego lee o quizá ve un rato la televisión. Suele acostarse sobre las once. Los fines de semana a lo mejor (maybe) queda con algún amigo, pero su rutina y disciplina nunca cambian mayormente. Sus padres le han dado todo su apoyo y esperan que algún día Cristóbal consiga (subj.) su sueño y sea (subj.) un gran nadador.

QUICK VOCAB

polideportivo *(m) sports centre*
entrenar *to train*
empresariales *(f/pl) business studies*
ligero *light*

a Find two words meaning 'about', with reference to time. Sobre,
b Find four expressions meaning 'again'. otravez,
c Find three expressions meaning 'perhaps'. Talvez,
d Find two expressions meaning 'to shower'.
e Find two opposites of *abundante* in relation to food. ligero, frugal
f Find the phrases meaning 'he puts on his swimming trunks', 'to continue training', 'back at home'.
g Find three expressions indicating how often something is done.
h There are two verbs in the subjunctive in the text. Can you spot them? What are their infinitives?

(a) sobre, hacia
(b) otravez, una vez más, neuevamente, de nuevo
(c) Talvez, quizá, a lo mejor
(d) toma una ducha, se ducha
e) ligero, frugal

7 Put the infinitives in brackets in the appropriate form: the present indicative or the present subjunctive.

a Me quedaré aquí hasta que ellos (*llegar*).

b Cuando Luisa (*salir*) de la oficina se va directamente a casa.

c Cuando Antonio (*regresar*) tomaremos una copa.

d A mi abuela le molesta que la gente la (*llamar*) por teléfono.

e Nos encanta que Ana nos (*invitar*) a su casa. ¡Es preciosa!

f Julia y su marido (*levantarse*) muy temprano cada mañana.

g Traeré a mi novio para que tú le (*conocer*).

h Creo que mi padre (*estar*) cenando.

i No quiero que tú se lo (*decir*) a nadie.

j Carlos siempre (*trabajar*) hasta muy tarde por la noche.

F) se pone del bañador, para seguir entrando, de vuelta en casa

g) Normalmente, casi siempre, suele, nunca

(h) sea (ser)

TEST YOURSELF

1 How would you express the following in English?

   a No acostumbro comer mucho por la noche a menos que *[unless]* tenga que salir.

   b A Julia le molesta que la interrumpan, pero eso no suele ocurrir muy a menudo.

   c Estamos sujetos a una cierta rutina que, querámoslo o no, tenemos que cumplir.

   d Vamos al supermercado una o dos veces por semana, dependiendo de lo que haga falta.

   e No quiero que me llames a no ser que sea absolutamente necesario.

   f Sería imposible volver a casa a comer, ya que perdería mucho tiempo yendo en el coche, el autobús o lo que sea.

2 Choose the correct form of the verb in the following sentences.

   a Espero que (*estás/estés*) bien.

   b Hace mucho tiempo que no (*sé/sepa*) nada de ti.

   c (*Yo*) todavía (*recuerdo/recuerda*) nuestras vacaciones en Estambul y quiero que me (*envías/envíes*) algunas de las fotos de nuestro viaje.

   d No creo que (*yo*) (*puedo/pueda*) ir a España este verano. *[Hopefully]* Ojalá (*es/sea*) posible hacerlo para las Navidades.

   e ¿Cuándo (*vienes/vengas*) tú por aquí? Sabes que puedes venir a mi casa cuando (*quieres/quieras*).

   f Te envío mi nuevo email para que me (*escribes/escribas*) y me (*das/des*) noticias tuyas.

Test 1 has a number of present subjunctive forms used alongside the present indicative. Did you spot the two different forms in Spanish? If you did, perhaps you were also able to choose between both forms of the present in Test 2. Check the 'Test yourself' key in the 'Key to the exercises', and if you did well go on to Unit 2, otherwise go back to the unit and revise all the relevant points.

2

Tiempo de ocio
Leisure time

In this unit you will learn how to:
- *Make invitations*
- *Make suggestions*
- *State preferences*
- *Express likes and dislikes*

1 ¿Qué te parece? *What do you think?*

Pablo Dávila y Ana Ramírez se han conocido durante las vacaciones. En el bar del hotel hablan de cine.

Pablo	¿Has visto la última película de Almodóvar?	
Ana	No, aún no la he visto. Me han dicho que es muy buena. Me gustaría verla. ¿Tú la has visto?	
Pablo	No, tampoco. La ponen en el cine Real en Málaga. ¿Qué te parece si vamos a verla esta noche? Podemos regresar aquí en el último tren.	
Ana	Mira, la verdad es que hoy estoy muy cansada. Prefiero ir mañana. ¿Qué te parece?	
Pablo	De acuerdo. Debe de haber una sesión a las seis y media o siete. Lo veré en el periódico.	
Ana	¿Te gusta mucho el cine?	

CD1, TR 5

(Contd)

Pablo	Bueno, sí, bastante. Suelo ir casi todas las semanas
Ana	A mí también me gusta, pero no voy muy a menudo. Los fines de semana prefiero salir fuera de Madrid.
Pablo	¿Adónde vas?
Ana	Normalmente a la sierra. Mis padres tienen una casa en San Rafael, pero no van mucho por allí. Yo sí. Suelo irme en el coche el viernes por la tarde y no regreso hasta el domingo por la noche. Es un lugar muy bonito y muy tranquilo y la casa tiene una vista espectacular. Tendrás que venir a verme algún día.
Pablo	Gracias. Me gustaría mucho.
Ana	¡Qué calor hace!
Pablo	Sí, mucho. Yo voy a bajar a la playa. ¿Quieres venir conmigo?
Ana	Vale, vamos. _going down_

QUICK VOCAB

poner _to show (a film)_
¿qué te parece si ...? _what about ...?_
debe de haber una session _there must be a show_
sierra _(f) mountain_

Insight

¿Has visto la última película? _Have you seen the latest film?_

Me han dicho que es muy buena. _I've been told it's very good._

Notice the use of the perfect tense in both sentences. **Visto** (_seen_) and **dicho** (_told, said_) are the irregular past participles of **ver** (_to see_) and **decir** (_to tell, say_) respectively. For more information on the perfect tense see Unit 8.

Language and comprehension check 1

Each of the following sentences contains wrong information. Read or listen to the conversation again and try to correct them.

a Ana _no_ ha visto la última película de Almodóvar y le gustaría verla otra vez.

b Ella y Pablo deciden ir al cine esa misma noche.

tardar = take time

ocio = leisure
rato de ocio: leisure time

c Ana acostumbra ir al cine todos los fines de semana.

d Ana se va a la sierra el domingo por la noche y no regresa
hasta el viernes por la tarde.

Insight

Pedro Almodóvar is a well-known Spanish film director.
Among his films are *Matador*, *Mujeres al borde de un ataque
de nervios*, *Todo sobre mi madre*, *Hable con ella*, and *Volver*.

---

2 Tiempo de ocio *Leisure time*

produced by

En unas entrevistas realizadas por una radio española, tres
personas hablan sobre su tiempo libre. El primer entrevistado,
José, es un sudamericano que vive en España.

Presentador	Buenas tardes. En nuestro programa de hoy nos referiremos al tema del ocio. ¿Qué hacen y cómo pasan su tiempo libre algunos de los habitantes de nuestra ciudad? En un mundo dominado por la televisión y por la imagen, en general, hay quienes dedican sus ratos de ocio a otras actividades. Nuestro primer entrevistado es José Ibáñez, de 23 años. José, ¿qué haces en <u>tus ratos de ocio</u>?
José *although*	Pues, normalmente practico deportes, principalmente fútbol, <u>aunque</u> también me gusta la natación. Tengo la suerte de vivir en un barrio donde hay un excelente polideportivo y eso ha incentivado mucho la práctica de los deportes. Antes de que se construyera el polideportivo sólo teníamos el campo de fútbol y si quería ir a la piscina tenía que ir a otro barrio. <u>Tardaba</u> por lo menos media hora en ir allí, por lo que no lo hacía muy a menudo. Ahora sí, practico con regularidad.
It took / used to take	
Presentador	Gracias, José. Y ahora tenemos con nosotros a Antonia Rodríguez, de 35 años. Antonia, ¿a qué te dedicas en tu tiempo libre?

⚫ CD1, TR 6

(Contd)

Antonia	Pues, tiempo libre tengo poquísimo, pues trabajo y además estoy casada y tengo dos hijos muy pequeños, pero, vamos, <u>cuando disponemos de algún tiempo</u>, mi marido y yo cogemos el coche y nos vamos con los chicos de paseo, pero eso no suele ocurrir muy a menudo. En verano sí, lo hacemos con más frecuencia. A veces nos vamos de camping. Hay un lugar muy bonito a pocos kilómetros de aquí que nos gusta mucho. Allí se está muy bien.
Presentador	Antonia, muchas gracias por estar con nosotros. Nuestro próximo invitado es Manuel Araya, de 55 años. Manuel, ¿qué prefiere hacer usted en sus ratos de ocio?
Manuel	Pues, yo soy un gran aficionado a la pintura, aunque mi trabajo habitual no tiene nada que ver con esto. Pero es una actividad que siempre me ha gustado y que he venido <u>desarrollando</u> desde que era muy joven. Cuando hay alguna exposición importante, nunca dejo de ir. Desgraciadamente, aquí la vida cultural es muy limitada y es poco lo que se puede aprender. Pero cuando voy a Madrid, voy siempre a algún museo. Prefiero el Museo del Prado, es el que más me gusta.
Presentador	Muchas gracias, Manuel, por haber venido.

(handwritten note:) When we have the time

Insight

Note the following two phrases in the interview: **con regularidad** (for **regularmente**) *regularly*, and **con más frecuencia** (for **frecuentemente**) *more frequently*. The overuse of adverbs ending in **-mente** is considered clumsy in Spanish, and phrases like these can avoid this.

ratos de ocio *(m pl)* leisure time
polideportivo *(m)* sports centre
disponer de tiempo to have time
paseo *(m)* drive, ride (in a car)

allí se está muy bien *it does us good to be there*
no tiene nada que ver con ... *it has nothing to do with* ...
por haber venido *for coming (Lit. for having come)*

··

Insight

Notice the use of the <u>imperfect tense</u> in:

Si *quería* **ir a la piscina.** *If I wanted to go to the swimming pool.*

Tenía que **ir a otro barrio.** *I had to go to another district.*

Tardaba **por lo menos** ... *It used to take me at least* ...

No lo *hacía* **muy a menudo.** *I didn't do it very often.*

For the formation and other uses of the imperfect tense see
Unit 5.

··

Language and comprehension check 2
Answer the following questions in Spanish.
 a José Ibáñez nadaba menos antes que ahora. ¿Por qué?
 b ¿Por qué no dispone de mucho tiempo libre Antonia
   Rodríguez?
 c ¿Qué hacen ella y su marido cuando están libres?
 d ¿Qué le gusta hacer a Manuel Araya en sus ratos de ocio?

──────────────────────────────

Key sentences

Making invitations and responding to an invitation
Tendrás que venir a verme   *You'll have to come and see*
 algún día. *(informal)*   *me some day.*
Gracias. Me gustaría mucho.   *Thank you. I'd like to*
 (formal/informal)   *very much.*

¿Quieres venir conmigo?
(very informal)

Do you want to come with me?

Vale. *(very informal)*

OK.

Other ways of making invitations

¿Por qué no viene/vienes a verme algún día?
(formal/informal)

Why don't you come and see me some day?

Ven/venga a verme algún día.
(informal/formal)

Come and see me some day.

Me gustaría invitarlo(a) a ...
(very formal)

I'd like to invite you to ...

Making suggestions

¿Qué te parece si vamos a verla ...? *(informal)*

What about going to see it ...? or
What if we go and see it ...?

Podemos regresar aquí ...

We can return here ...

Other ways of making suggestions

¿Qué le/te parece si ...?
(formal/informal)

What about ...?

¿Por qué no ...? *(formal/informal)*

Why don't you/we ...?

Le/te sugiero que *(followed by the present subjunctive, e.g.* **vaya/s,** *formal/informal)*

I suggest you (go).

Stating preferences

¿Qué prefiere hacer Vd.?

What do you prefer to do?

Prefiero ir mañana.

I prefer to go tomorrow.

Prefiero el Museo del Prado.

I prefer the Prado Museum.

Expressing likes and dislikes

¿Te gusta el cine?

Do you like going to the cinema?

A mí también me gusta.

I like it too.

Lo que más me gusta es nadar.

What I like most is swimming.

No me gusta.

I don't like it.

Grammar

1 Gustar *To like*

Remember that **gustar** is normally used in the third person singular or plural, and it may be followed by a noun (e.g. el museo *the museum*) or an infinitive (e.g. ir al cine *to go to the cinema*). In this construction, **gustar** is preceded by an indirect object pronoun:

me	**gusta(n)**	*I like it (them)*
te	**gusta(n)**	*you like it (them) (familiar)*
le	**gusta(n)**	*he or she likes it (them) you like it (them)*
nos	**gusta(n)**	*we like it (them)*
os	**gusta(n)**	*you like it (them) (familiar)*
les	**gusta(n)**	*they or you like it (them)*

For emphasis or to avoid ambiguity, as in **le gusta** (*he or she likes it* or *you like it*), use the following set of pronouns preceded by the preposition **a**:

a mí, a ti, a él, a ella, a usted, a nosotros/as, a vosotros/as, a ellos, a ellas, a ustedes.

Examples:

A **él le gusta el cine.**	*He likes going to the cinema.*
A *mí* **también me gusta.**	*I like it too.*
¿A Vd. **le gusta?**	*Do you like it?*
A *mí* **no.**	*I don't (like it).*

Negative sentences are formed by placing **no** before the indirect object pronoun.

No **me gustan.**	*I don't like them.*
A ella *no* **le gustan.**	*She doesn't like them.*

Encantar and **fascinar**, meaning *to love*, express stronger liking and are used in the same way as **gustar**.

Me encanta la música española.	*I love Spanish music.*
Me fascina viajar.	*I love travelling.*

2 Parecer *To seem, think*

Parecer is normally used in a construction similar to that of **gustar**.

¿Qué te parece si ...?	*What do you think if ...?*
Me parece bien.	*It seems all right (to me).*

3 Adverbs and adverbial phrases

Words such as **rápidamente** *quickly*, **inmediatamente** *immediately*, **fácilmente** *easily*, are known as adverbs. Excessive use of words ending in -mente is considered clumsy in Spanish, so these are sometimes replaced by adverbial phrases like the following: **de manera rápida** literally, *in a quick way*, **de forma inmediata** *immediately*, **de manera fácil** *in an easy way*. Words like **rápido**, **inmediato** and **fácil** are adjectives and the use of the feminine forms **rápida** and **inmediata** is due to the fact that **manera** and **forma** are feminine words. Some nouns can be used as adverbial phrases preceded by **con** with: **con rapidez** *quickly*, **con facilidad** *easily*, a construction which is less common and more restricted in use (see **con regularidad** and **con más frecuencia** in Dialogue 2).

Practice

1 Complete each blank space with one word only, using the informal form where appropriate.

  a ¿Qué ___ en tu tiempo libre, Carmen?

  b ___ gusta ver la televisión.

  c ¿Qué tipos de programas te ___?

  d ___ los programas deportivos, aunque también me ___ ver películas. ¿Y a ___ , qué te gusta hacer?

  e Me ___ los deportes, la televisión ___ me gusta nada.

  f ¿Qué deportes ___?

  g La natación, es lo que ___ me gusta.

  h ___ mí también. ¿Qué ___ parece si vamos a la piscina esta tarde?

  i ___ parece una excelente idea.

2 Study this dialogue between two friends.

José	¿Qué te parece si vamos al cine?
Elena	Vale, vamos. ¿Qué película te gustaría ver?
José	Podemos ver ¡Ay Carmela! ¿Qué te parece?
Elena	Bueno, la verdad es que ese tipo de película no me gusta nada. Yo prefiero ver Las cosas del querer. ¿Te parece bien?
José	De acuerdo. ¿Dónde la ponen?
Elena	En el cine Biógrafo. ¿A qué sesión prefieres ir? Hay una a las 7.00 y otra a las 9.00.
José	Prefiero ir a la de las 9.00.

Insight

Las cosas del querer (1989) is a musical film by the Spanish director Jaime Chavarri, which is set in post-Civil War Spain. *¡Ay Carmela!* (1990), set during the Spanish Civil War (1936–39), was directed by Carlos Saura. The cinema listing below features more recent films from Spain and Latin America.

Now make up a similar dialogue using the information in this advertisement.

sesión *(f) show (cinema)*

3 Imagine you are being interviewed on Spanish television. The presenter wants to know about your leisure activities.

Presentador	¿A qué se dedica usted en su tiempo libre?
Entrevistado(a)	*Say you have very little time. You work in an office from 9.00 to 5.00 and you are married and have three children. But when you can, you like to work in the garden and you also like to read. Now you are reading a novel by García Márquez, which you like very much. Ah, you are also studying Spanish, of course. You like Spanish a lot.*

Presentador	¿Y en sus vacaciones viene Vd. normalmente a España?
Entrevistado(a)	*Not always. Although you like Spain very much, it is an expensive country now, so you prefer to go somewhere cheaper.*
Presentador	Bueno, nuestro programa tiene una invitación especial para usted. Dos semanas de vacaciones para dos personas en el hotel y lugar de su elección.
Entrevistado(a)	*Wonderful! Thank you very much.*

4 You and your travelling companion decide to stay in your hotel room and watch television. Your friend is busy at the moment, so can you tell him/her:

a What sort of films are on?

b What they are about?

LA VIEJA MEMORIA
***

Documental. Esp. 1977. 2h. 45m.
Director: Jaime Camino.

Un eficaz documental en donde, a través de entrevistas y una buena labor de montaje, el director Jaime Camino profundiza en los antecedentes de la Guerra Civil española y en los sucesos ocurridos en Cataluña durante la República. Pese a resultar excesivamente larga, la película se sigue bastante bien. Una lección de historia a no olvidar.

A MÍ NO ME MIRE USTED
***

Comedia. Esp. 1941. 1h. 19m.
Director: J. L. Sáenz de Heredia.
Intérpretes: Valeriano León, Manuel Arbó y Rosita Yarza.

Una de las cintas más atípicas de Sáenz de Heredia en torno a un maestro rural que utiliza sus poderes hipnóticos para imponer orden en su clase. Una comedia con ribetes casi surrealistas.

(Guía del Ocio, Madrid)

antecedentes *(m pl)* background
suceso *(m)* event
cinta *(f)* film
en torno a *about*
maestro/a *(m/f)* teacher
ribetes *(m pl)* elements

5 A Spanish-speaking friend has sent you an email announcing that he/she will be passing through your home town. Write an email inviting your friend to stay with you for a few days. Here's what you want to say:
   a Say you have received his/her email and that you are glad he/she is coming to your home town.
   b Say you are sure he/she will like it very much.
   c Invite him/her to stay at your house for a few days.
   d Suggest he/she phones you to confirm his/her arrival.

alegrarse (de que ... *with the subjunctive)* *to be glad (that ...)*
estar seguro(a) *to be sure*
confirmar *to confirm*
llegada *(f)* arrival

6 ¡A escuchar!

◀) **CD1, TR 7**

   a The first exercise in this activity is centred on a commentary about a Latin American art exhibition in Madrid. Listen to the text if you have the recording or, alternatively, look at the transcript and use the text for reading comprehension, then answer the questions which follow.

asistencia *(f)* attendance
exposición *(f)* exhibition
asistentes *(m/f)* public
obra *(f)* work
connotado *famous*

28

pintores (mpl) painters
iberoamericano Latin American
proveniente from

    i How many works will the public be able to see?
    ii Where is the exhibition being held?
    iii Which are some of the countries represented?
    iv What expressions are used in the text to say: It is taking place, They will be able to see, It was opened by...?
  b The second piece is an announcement about a forthcoming cultural event taking place in Madrid. Once again, go through the text as suggested above, looking at the vocabulary first, then answer the questions below. The transcript is at the back of the book.

QUICK VOCAB

coloquio (m) talk
campo (m) field, area
acontecimiento (m) event
espectáculo (m) show
escenario (m) stage

    i What is the name of the festival being announced?
    ii What activities will it include?
    iii Which countries will be specially represented?

7 Leisure activities and sports can sometimes be a nuisance to others, as the person who wrote this letter to a Spanish newspaper seems to think. What does she complain about? Read it through and then say whether the statements which follow the text are true or false.

NO ME MEREZCO ESTO

Hace unos meses, y con mucho esfuerzo, compré un apartamento en el barrio de San Miguel. Buscaba la tranquilidad de un barrio alejado del centro de la ciudad, donde pudiera descansar y relajarme junto a mi familia después de una intensa semana de trabajo.

Creí que por fin había conseguido lo que tanto quería. Pero un buen día, en lo que antes era una tranquila esquina, justo enfrente de mi apartamento, se abrió una discoteca que no nos deja dormir por la noche. La música estridente y el constante ruido de quienes entran y salen empieza hacia la medianoche y no termina hasta el amanecer.

Yo no soy de las personas a las que les gusta quejarse por cualquier cosa, pero me parece que la autorización para la instalación de una discoteca en una zona netamente residencial es un disparate y atenta contra la salud mental de las personas.

Nuestras quejas al Ayuntamiento no han dado resultado. Las autoridades locales nos han ignorado, como suele ocurrir.

¿Qué podemos hacer para recuperar nuestra tranquilidad? ¿A quién podemos recurrir, que nos escuche y nos entienda? ¿O debemos irnos de aquí y dejar este lugar que tanto esfuerzo y dinero nos costó adquirir? ¡Ayúdennos, por favor!

Carmen Martínez
Sevilla

recuperar *to recover*
recurrir a *to turn to*
adquirir *to acquire, obtain*

¿Verdadero o falso?
  a Carmen quería un apartamento cerca del centro de la ciudad.
  b Enfrente del apartamento que compró había una discoteca.
  c A Carmen le molesta el ruido de la discoteca.
  d La música y el ruido continúan hasta la medianoche.
  e Carmen no suele quejarse.
  f El Ayuntamiento va a cerrar la discoteca.

TEST YOURSELF

1 How would you express the following in Spanish?
  a He likes theatre but she doesn't.
  b What we like most about this place is the people.
  c You like him? Well, I don't. I prefer Pablo. (informal)
  d What about going for a drink, Silvia? (informal)
  e It's all right with me. (use *parecer*)
  f They love watching this programme. Well, I don't like it at all.

2 Replace each of the adverbs ending in -**mente** in the following sentences by an adverbial phrase, using the words in brackets.
  a El trabajo avanza, pero muy lentamente. (*de manera muy ...*)
  b Mis amigos ingleses vienen a España frecuentemente. (*con ...*)
  c Carlos se comportó muy descortésmente. (*de forma muy ...*)
  d Sus padres nos recibieron muy amablemente. (*con mucha ...*)
  e Le expliqué claramente la situación a mi jefe. (*de manera ...*)
  f Te prestaré mi ordenador, pero tienes que tratarlo cuidadosamente. (*con ...*)

Although **gustar, parecer**, etc. in Test 1 constitute revision, the construction in which they occur is often a problem for English speakers. Check your answers in the Key to test yourself and see whether you got them right, otherwise go back to the grammar notes and practise writing your own examples. The importance of Test 2 is that it focuses on phrases which are commonly used in the spoken and written language. If your answers were right go on to Unit 3.

3

¡A trabajar!
To work!

In this unit you will learn how to:
- **Describe your job**
- **Discuss working conditions**
- **Say what you like or dislike about your job**
- **Refer to events which began in the past and which are still in progress**

1 Hablando de trabajo *Talking about work*

En un vuelo hacia un país de habla española, dos extraños hablan sobre su trabajo.

Señor	¿Adónde va usted?
Señora	Voy a Lima. ¿Y usted?
Señor	Yo voy a Santiago de Chile.
Señora	¿Va de vacaciones?
Señor	No, voy por negocios. Soy representante de una empresa de maquinaria agrícola. ¿Y usted va de vacaciones?
Señora	No, yo también voy por razones de trabajo, aunque también me tomaré unos días de vacaciones. Pero, principalmente voy de compras. Tengo una tienda de artesanía y en Perú compramos muchos de los artículos que vendemos. También en México. Tienen una artesanía maravillosa.

(Contd)

CD1, TR 8

Señor	Vd. es peruana, ¿verdad?
Señora	Sí, soy peruana, pero vivo en España desde hace muchos años. ¿Y usted ha estado antes en Sudamérica?
Señor	Solamente en Venezuela y en Colombia. Conozco muy bien Venezuela. Trabajé dos años allí en una empresa de petróleo …
Señora	Le gusta viajar, supongo.
Señor	Bueno sí, es una de las cosas que más me gusta de mi trabajo. Viajo constantemente.
Señora	A mí me encanta viajar, pero no lo hago muy a menudo. Esta es una excepción. Normalmente las compras las hace mi socio, pero esta vez me ha tocado a mí. Además, necesitaba un descanso.
Señor	¿Cuánto tiempo va a quedarse en Perú?
Señora	Dos semanas solamente. Dedicaré una semana a mis compras y luego me iré por una semana a Arequipa a visitar a mis padres.

Insight

Note the word order in the following sentence: **Normalmente las compras las hace mi socio** *The buying is normally done by my partner*. The focus in this sentence is on **mi socio**. A different word order can shift the emphasis to another word: **Mi socio hace normalmente las compras** (this could imply *I do something else*). You will find more information on word order in the Grammar section.

QUICK VOCAB

voy por negocios *I am going on business*
maquinaria agrícola *(f) agricultural machinery*
artesanía *(f) handicrafts*
suponer *to suppose*
socio *(m) partner*
esta vez *(f) this time*
tocar *to be one's turn*

Insight

Notice the indirect object pronouns **me, le, nos** in **Me ha tocado a mí** *It has been my turn*, **Le ha tocado a él/ella/usted** *It has been his/her/your turn*, **Nos toca a nosotros** *It is our turn*. Note also **¿A quién le toca?** *Whose turn is it?*

Language and comprehension check 1

i Fill in the blanks with a suitable preposition.

a ¿Viaja usted _____ vacaciones o _____ negocios?

b Soy representante _____ una empresa _____ productos agrícolas.

c Voy _____ compras _____ dos semanas solamente.

d Ellos viven _____ Madrid _____ hace mucho tiempo.

e Me iré _____ unos días al campo _____ visitar a mi familia.

f Mi padre tiene una tienda _____ artículos eléctricos.

ii Which of the following information is not expressed in the dialogue?

a Represento a una empresa de maquinaria agrícola.

b Vendo artesanía en una tienda que tengo en España.

c No llevo mucho tiempo viviendo en España.

d Estuve un par de años trabajando en Venezuela.

e Detesto viajar, aunque no es algo que haga con frecuencia.

f Normalmente me toca a mí hacer las compras fuera de España.

2 ¿En qué trabajas? *What work do you do?*

Mercedes y Paloma acaban de conocerse en casa de un amigo común. Las dos chicas hablan sobre sus actividades.

Mercedes	¿En qué trabajas tú?
Paloma	Trabajo en la oficina de turismo.
Mercedes	¡Qué bien! Es un trabajo interesante, ¿no?

(Contd)

CD1, TR 9

Paloma	Pues sí, lo que pasa es que llevo mucho tiempo allí y estoy un poco aburrida. Pero, vamos, tampoco me puedo quejar. El sueldo no está nada mal y tengo un mes de vacaciones al año.
Mercedes	¿Cuánto tiempo hace que trabajas allí?
Paloma	Casi cinco años. Al principio me gustaba mucho, especialmente el contacto con el público. Eso era lo que más me gustaba, pero luego te das cuenta de que el trato es más bien impersonal y estás repitiendo casi siempre lo mismo …, que dónde está esto, dónde está lo otro, que si tiene usted un mapa, y cosas por el estilo … Bueno, ¿y tú qué haces?
Mercedes	Soy profesora. Enseño español a extranjeros en un instituto de idiomas.
Paloma	¿Y qué tal? ¿Te gusta?
Mercedes	Pues, enseñar sí me gusta, lo que no me gusta es el sueldo. Nos pagan muy poco.
Paloma	¿Por qué no pides un aumento?
Mercedes	¡Vamos, que la cosa no es tan fácil!
Paloma	¿Cuánto tiempo llevas trabajando allí?
Mercedes	Un año solamente, pero espero cambiarme pronto.
Paloma	Bueno, ¡que tengas suerte!
Mercedes	Gracias, tú también.

Insight

Note the use of **llevar** with a time phrase in **Llevo mucho tiempo allí** *I've been there for a long time*, where **estar** *to be* is understood. Compare this with the alternative construction with **hacer: Hace mucho tiempo que estoy allí**. Later in the dialogue you find **¿Cuánto tiempo hace que trabajas allí?** *How long have you been working there?* and the alternative **¿Cuánto tiempo llevas trabajando allí?**

aburrido(a) *bored*
quejarse *to complain*
al principio *(m) in the beginning*
darse cuenta *to realize*
trato *(m) relationship*
cosas por el estilo *things like that*
extranjero *(m) foreigner*
¡que tengas suerte! *I hope you are lucky!*

Insight

Lo que can translate *what* or *the thing that*. Note its use in:
lo que pasa es que ... *what happens is that ...*, **lo que más me gustaba ...** *what I liked most ...* , **lo que no me gusta ...** *what I don't like ...*

Language and comprehension check 2

i Answer the following questions in Spanish.

  a ¿Qué siente Paloma en relación con su trabajo?
  b ¿Qué dice sobre su sueldo?
  c ¿Cuánto tiempo hace que trabaja en el mismo lugar?
  d ¿Qué es lo que más le gustaba cuando empezó a trabajar?
  e ¿A qué se dedica Mercedes?
  f ¿Le gusta su trabajo? ¿Y el sueldo?

ii Give the English for the following sentences.

  a Tampoco me puedo quejar.
  b El sueldo no está nada mal.
  c Al principio me gustaba mucho.
  d El trato es más bien informal.
  e Enseñar sí me gusta.
  f ¡Vamos, que la cosa no es tan fácil!

Key sentences

Describing your job

Tengo una tienda de artesanía.	*I have/own a handicraft shop.*
Soy profesora.	*I am a teacher.*
Trabajo en la oficina de turismo.	*I work in the tourist office.*

Discussing working conditions

El sueldo no está nada mal.	*The salary is not bad at all.*
Tengo un mes de vacaciones al año.	*I have a month's holiday a year.*

Saying what you like or dislike about your job

Es una de las cosas que más me gusta de mi trabajo.	*It is one of the things I like most about my job.*
Me gusta enseñar.	*I like teaching.*

Referring to events which began in the past and which are still in progress

¿Cuánto tiempo llevas trabajando allí?	*How long have you been working there?*
¿Cuánto tiempo hace que trabajas allí?	*How long have you been working there?*
Llevo mucho tiempo allí.	*I have been there for a long time.*

Grammar

1 Llevar *Followed by gerund*

This construction is used to refer to events which began at some point in the past but which are still now in progress. Consider again the sentences in **Dialogue 2** and these further examples.

¿Cuánto tiempo *llevas viviendo* **en este piso?**	*How long have you been living in this flat?*

Llevo **dos años** *viviendo* **aquí**.	*I have been living here for two years.*
¿Lleváis **mucho tiempo** *trabajando* **juntos?**	*Have you been working together for a long time?*
Llevamos **seis meses** *trabajando* **juntos.**	*We have been working together for six months.*

If the context makes it clear, as with **vivir** and **trabajar,** the gerund **viviendo, trabajando** may be omitted. For example:

¿Cuánto tiempo *llevas* **en Barcelona?**	*How long have you been (living) in Barcelona?*
Él *lleva* **cinco años en esta empresa.**	*He has been (working) in this company for five years.*

Llevar may also be used in the imperfect tense to refer to an action which began in the past and which continued until some point in the past. For example:

María *llevaba* **diez años** *(trabajando)* **en esa firma cuando cerró.**	*Maria had been (working) in that firm for ten years when it closed.*

To form the gerund add **-ando** to the stem of **-ar** verbs and **-iendo** to that of **-er** and **-ir** verbs. e.g. trabajar, trabajando, vivir, viviendo.

2 Hace + *time phrase followed by* **que** + *present tense*

An alternative to the construction above is this one with **hace** in the third person. Consider again the example in **Dialogue 2** and then these further examples:

¿Cuánto tiempo *hace* **que vives en España?**	*How long have you been living in Spain?*
Hace **un año que** *vivo* **en España.**	*I have been living in Spain for a year.*

or

*Vivo **en España** desde hace*   *I have been living in Spain for*
  un año.   *a year.*

Notice also the use of **hacer** in the imperfect tense:

*Hacía **tres años que yo no la** veía. I hadn't seen her for three years.*

Compare this sentence with:

*Hace **tres años que yo no la** veo.   I have not seen her for three years.*

3 Word order

Word order within sentences is much more flexible in Spanish than in English. In statements focusing on more than one element, the part of the sentence you want to highlight may be placed in final position.

La compra la hace *María.*   *It is María who does the shopping.*
El problema lo solucionó *José.*   *It was José who solved the*
                                     problem.

The subject of the sentence, María in the first example, José in the second, has been placed in final position. This deviates from the normal word order pattern, which is subject + verb:

María hace la compra.   *María does the shopping.*
José solucionó el problema.   *José solved the problem.*

In short sentences, the tendency is to place the verb before the subject.

Salió el avión.   *The plane left.*
Llamó Andrés.   *Andrés phoned.*

Within a clause, the verb is normally placed before the subject.

Lo que quiere mi madre es que   *What my mother wants is not to*
  no la dejemos sola.   *be left alone.*

Practice

1 How would you ask Antonio how long he has been d...
each of the following and how would he reply? Use the
construction with **llevar** with an appropriate verb: jugar, hac...
yoga, estudiar, tocar, vivir, trabajar.

a
Tres años

b
Dos años y medio

c
Cinco años

d
Cuatro años

e
Seis meses

f
Tres semanas

2 Can you now say how long Antonio has been doing each of
these activities? This time use the alternative construction with
hace + time phrase.

3 Complete the blanks in this passage with the appropriate
words.

Me llamo Martín Iglesias, _____ hace cuatro años trabajo _____
administrativo en una agencia _____ empleos. Es mi primer
_____ y estoy bastante contento con _____, ya que tengo la _____
de relacionarme con mucha gente _____, especialmente gente
joven que _____ trabajo por primera vez. Eso es _____ que más
me gusta.

Mi ____ de trabajo no está mal, pues ____ a las 9.00 de
_____ mañana y termino a las 6.00. Los sábados ____ tengo
libres. Mis vacaciones ____ de tres semanas.

Mi ____ no es muy bueno, ya que ahora sólo ____ 1.200 euros
al mes, pero _____ que a comienzos del año que ____ me den
un aumento.

Lo único que no me ____ de mi trabajo es que tengo que viajar
mucho, pues ____ bastante lejos del barrio ____ vivo, pero en
el futuro espero ____ a un lugar más cercano.

4 You will be spending six months at a language school in Spain
and you wish to do some part-time work to earn some money
and have contact with Spanish people. Two job advertisements
in a newspaper attract your attention.

**PERSONA MAYOR
DE 23 AÑOS
90 EUROS DIARIOS
SUPERABLES**

Llamar de 9.00 a 14.00 horas y
de 16.00 a 19.30 horas.

**TELS.: 91 471 14 00 y
91 462 79 00**

PREGUNTAR POR LA SRTA. TOÑI

¡¡OPORTUNIDAD ÚNICA!!
**PERSONAS MAYORES
DE 23 AÑOS**

Empresa líder Ofrece:
TRABAJO 3 HORAS DIARIAS

– Formación a nuestro cargo
– 1,700 euros mensuales

TELEF.: 91 361 25 88

superables *and more*
formación a nuestro cargo *training to be provided by us*

You decide to telephone to get more information on the jobs.
Here is your first telephone conversation:

Telefonista	Hispánica, buenos días. ¿Dígame?
Tú	*Good morning. Say you are calling about the advertisement in the newspaper and that you would like to speak to señorita Toñi.*
Telefonista	Un momento, por favor. No cuelgue. *(pausa)* ¿Oiga?
Tú	*Yes?*
Telefonista	La extensión de la señorita Toñi está comunicando. ¿Quiere Vd. esperar?
Tú	*It's all right. You'll wait. (pausa)*
Telefonista	¿Oiga? Le pongo con la señorita Toñi.
Srta. Toñi	¿Sí, dígame?
Tú	*Say good morning, give your name and say you have seen the advertisement in the newspaper and that you would like to have more information about the job.*
Srta. Toñi	Bueno, se trata de una editorial y necesitamos vendedores a domicilio para ofrecer nuestra nueva enciclopedia. ¿Tiene Vd. experiencia en este tipo de trabajo?
Tú	*Yes, you worked as a salesman/woman for a time although you have never sold books. But you are willing to learn. You are living in Spain now (don't say it's only for six months) and you need to earn some money and this is the sort of job you are looking for. You are very interested in it.*
Srta. Toñi	Bueno, nosotros daremos entrenamiento al personal que seleccionemos. Si Vd. quiere le puedo enviar un folleto informativo sobre la empresa, nuestros productos y las condiciones de trabajo. Le incluiremos, además, una solicitud, y si a Vd. le interesa el puesto puede rellenarla y enviarla con una fotografía reciente. ¿Me da su nombre y dirección, por favor?
Tú	*Give your name and address.*

anuncio *(m) advertisement*
no cuelgue *don't hang up*
le pongo con ... *I'll put you through to ...*
vendedor(a) a domicilio *door to door salesman (woman)*
estar dispuesto a *to be willing to*
entrenamiento *(m) training*
solicitud *(f) application form*
rellenar *to fill in*
está comunicando *it is engaged*

5 Roberto Urrutia from Chile needed a letter from his boss to get a loan. This is part of the letter written by Roberto's boss to the company that requested the references.

García y Cía.
Calle Miraflores 546, Santiago, Chile
Santiago, 4 de octubre de 2010

Señora Carmen Aldunate
Gerente PROCASA S.A.
Avenida El Bosque 321, Las Condes, Santiago

Estimada señora:
En respuesta a su carta del 15 del corriente, me es muy grato confirmar que el señor Roberto Urrutia trabaja como jefe de ventas en nuestra empresa desde hace cinco años. El señor Urrutia gana actualmente un sueldo bruto de ochocientos mil pesos mensuales.

Forms of address in letter writing
Formal

Muy señor mío:	*Dear Sir,*
Muy señora mía:	*Dear Madam,*
Muy señores míos:	*Dear Sirs,*
Estimado señor:	*Dear Sir,*
Estimada señora:	*Dear Madam,*

Less formal

Estimado señor Díaz/Juan:	*Dear Mr Díaz/Juan,*
Estimada señorita Pérez/Ana:	*Dear Miss Pérez/Ana,*

Informal

Querido Carlos:	*Dear Carlos,*
Querida María:	*Dear Maria,*

Introductory phrases

En respuesta a …	*In reply to …*
Me es muy grato …	*I am pleased to …*
Acuso recibo de su carta de fecha …	*I acknowledge receipt of your letter of …*
En contestación a su carta de fecha …	*In answer to your letter of …*
… de fecha (12 de marzo)/ (10) del corriente/de los corrientes	*… of (12th March)/(10th) of the current month*
El objeto de la presente es …	*This is to …*

Formal

Atentamente or Le(s) saluda (muy) atentamente	*Yours truly or Yours sincerely*

Less formal

Un cordial/afectuoso saludo (de) …	*Best wishes (from) …*

Informal

Un (fuerte) abrazo (de) …	*Love (from) …*

Insight

Note that Spanish uses a colon instead of a comma after phrases such as **Muy señor mío** *Dear Sir*. The words **señor, señora** and **señorita** are usually found in their abbreviated form, each followed by a full stop: **Sr., Sra., Srta.** The word **Estimado/a** is preferred when the name of the person is known. You can use this with the surname or even with the first name when the relationship is more informal. With friends, however, use **Querido/a** or simply **Hola** (Diego/Teresa).

Imagine your boss is giving similar information about you. Write the letter you are likely to get. Give your own or an imaginary occupation and salary.

6 ¡A escuchar!

◀ CD1, TR 10

Hablando de trabajo: A journalist from a Spanish magazine conducted a series of interviews with people at work. Here are two of those interviews. If you have the recording, you can treat this as a listening comprehension exercise, following the suggestions given in the introduction to the book and in previous units. If you do not have the recording, you can use the transcripts of the interviews for reading comprehension. In either case, refer to the notes and questions below.

María del Carmen Salas

This is the first interview. As you listen (or read) fill in the form below with the information given by María del Carmen. If you are using the recording and have difficulty in understanding, listen again as many times as you need. Then you'll be able to check the transcript before you go back to the recording again.

publicarse *to be published*
artículo *(m) article*
agradar *to like*
terreno *(m) field*
lectora *(f) reader*
satisfacer *to satisfy*
exigir *to demand*
estar dispuesta a *to be ready or willing to*

MARÍA DEL CARMEN SALAS

Edad: ....

Profesión: ....

Deberes: ....

Aspectos que considera positivos en su profesión: ....

....

....

Aspectos que considera difíciles en su profesión: ....

....

....

....

Now listen to (or read) the interview once more and, as you do so, give the Spanish for the following phrases used by María del Carmen and the interviewer.

a Could you tell me what you do for a living?
b I am in charge of ...
c What do you like most about your profession?
d Field work.
e That is what I like most.
f Is there anything you don't like about your work?
g They are very demanding.
h You have to renew yourself constantly.

Javier Molina

In the second interview, Javier Molina talks about his job at the tourist information office in Alicante. Listen to (or read) the interview and then answer the questions below in Spanish.

funcionario *(m) official*
tener suerte *to be lucky*
propiedad *(f) property*
seguro *safe (adjective)*

Answer the following questions in Spanish.

  a ¿Cuánto tiempo hace que trabaja Javier en la Oficina de Turismo de Alicante?
  b ¿Dónde trabajaba antes?
  c ¿Por qué decidió cambiarse?
  d ¿Cómo describe su nuevo puesto?
  e ¿En qué consiste su trabajo?
  f ¿Qué tipo de información piden los turistas?

7 Rephrase the following sentences using an alternative word order, making any changes that are necessary. Give two alternatives for each. Remember that changes in word order may affect the emphasis you give to different elements within the sentence.

  a Fue María la que me lo dijo.
  b Llegó a Madrid el viernes por la tarde.
  c Su madre le llamó por teléfono a las cinco de la mañana.
  d El teléfono móvil lo dejé en el restaurante donde comimos.
  e La noticia la supimos por Pepe, que nos llamó.
  f Antonia recibió el email de César el sábado.

8 The following text looks at youth unemployment in Spain through the story of María Soledad, one of thousands of young people who are looking for their first job. Read the text and answer the questions that follow.

LA BÚSQUEDA DEL PRIMER EMPLEO

María Soledad P. tiene 23 años, una licenciatura en traducción e interpretación de una universidad madrileña, que completó hace dos años con excelentes resultados. Domina perfectamente el inglés y el francés, pero María Soledad, como muchos otros jóvenes españoles, no ha podido encontrar trabajo en su especialidad. Actualmente trabaja vendiendo libros a domicilio y sus ingresos, escasos y fluctuantes, no le permiten alquilar un piso y vivir independientemente, lo que la obliga a seguir viviendo en casa de sus padres, donde comparte con dos de sus hermanos.

El caso de María Soledad no es único, puesto que son miles los jóvenes españoles que se encuentran en similar situación. El paro, que en el último tiempo ha alcanzado niveles nunca antes vistos, afecta mayormente a los jóvenes y a las mujeres. El haber hecho estudios universitarios no es garantía de que se pueda conseguir un empleo estable y bien remunerado.

Las posibilidades de que esta situación cambie son escasas por ahora, y María Soledad quizá deba seguir esperando un tiempo largo antes de que consiga un trabajo que tenga relación con lo que estudió. Mientras tanto, y día a día, sigue mirando los anuncios de trabajo del periódico y enviando su currículum con la esperanza de que la llamen al menos para una entrevista. El día que ello suceda, María Soledad sabe que deberá enfrentarse a una dura competencia con tantos otros que, como ella, buscan cambiar su situación.

a What did María Soledad study?
b What does she do at present?
c Who is she living with and why?
d What does she do day by day?
e How are the following expressed in the text?: 'she's completely fluent in English and French', 'she works selling

books door-to-door', 'having done university studies', 'in the hope that she may at least be called for an interview'.

f Can you find expressions meaning the following in the text? una universidad de Madrid, ya que, obtener un trabajo, con un buen sueldo/salario, cuando esto ocurra.

g There are a few present subjunctive verbs in the text. Can you identify them? Give their infinitives too.

QUICK VOCAB

licenciatura *(f) degree*
ingresos *(mpl) income*
escasos *low, poor, scarce*
paro *(m) unemployment*
el anuncio *(m) advertisement*

TEST YOURSELF

1 How would each of the following people say what their occupation is and what it is they do? Look up the occupations in your dictionary if necessary, and fill in the blank spaces with an appropriate verb: fabricar, cuidar, enseñar, conducir, construir, dirigir, apagar, repartir.

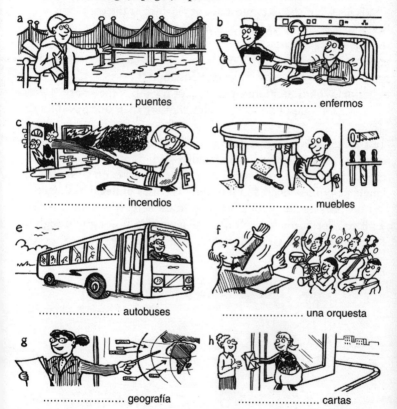

a .... puentes

b .... enfermos

c .... incendios

d .... muebles

e .... autobuses

f .... una orquesta

g .... geografía

h .... cartas

2 How would you express the following in Spanish?

    a They have been living on the Costa del Sol for five years. (use *llevar*)

    b How long have you been working for this company? (informal, use *hace*)

    c Victoria is going to New York on business but I'm going on holiday. I'm also going shopping.

    d What she likes most about teaching is the contact with people. She's been teaching Spanish for a long time. (use *llevar*)

    e It's normally my boss who does the buying but today it's my turn. (more than one possibility)

    f What I don't much like about my job is the salary, although I do like travelling. (more than one possibility)

Test 1 checks language related to professions and occupations that you are probably already familiar with. If not, this is a good chance to increase your vocabulary. Test 2 focuses on a number of language points covered in this unit. The uses of **llevar** and **hace** in time phrases are particularly important here. If you are satisfied with your performance go on to the next unit, if not go through the Key sentences and Grammar notes once again.

4

De vuelta al colegio
Back to school

In this unit you will learn how to:
- *Talk about your studies*
- *Say what languages you speak*
- *Refer to past events*
- *Say how long ago something happened*
- *Make enquiries*

1 Usted habla muy bien español
You speak Spanish very well

En una reunión social en un país de habla española, hablan dos desconocidas, Francisca Bravo y Sarah Parker.

Francisca	Vd. es inglesa, ¿verdad?
Sarah	Sí, soy inglesa, de Bath. ¿Conoce Vd. Inglaterra?
Francisca	Sí, estuve en Londres con mi marido hace un par de años. Nos gustó mucho. Es una ciudad muy bonita. Me gustaría mucho volver. ¿Y Vd. está aquí de vacaciones?
Sarah	No, mi marido ha sido enviado aquí por su empresa y nos quedaremos tres años.
Francisca	¡Estupendo!, Vd. habla muy bien español.
	(Contd)

🎧 CD1, TR 11

Sarah	Gracias. Estudié español en la escuela y antes de venirme hice un curso intensivo de tres meses. Pero todavía me falta mucho por aprender. Espero tomar algún curso en una escuela de idiomas. ¿Y Vd. habla inglés?
Francisca	¡Uy! Lo hablo, pero muy mal. Me da vergüenza decirlo. Mi marido sí, él habla inglés bastante bien. Lo aprendió en Estados Unidos. Vivió allí antes de que nos casáramos. También habla algo de alemán, y el francés lo domina perfectamente. Su madre es francesa.
Sarah	¡Qué bien! A mí me encantan los idiomas.

Insight

Note the following two constructions: **antes de** + infinitive
(**antes de venirme** *before coming away*), and **antes de que** +
subjunctive (**antes de que nos casáramos** *before we got
married*). The use of a preposition, **de** in this case, requires
the use of the infinitive, while **que** calls for the use of the
subjunctive. The verb form **casáramos** is the imperfect
subjunctive. There is more on this in Unit 9.

QUICK VOCAB

ha sido enviado *he has been sent*
un par *(m) a couple*
todavía me falta mucho por aprender *I (still) have a lot to learn*
me da vergüenza *I feel ashamed.*
lo domina perfectamente *he is perfectly fluent*

Language and comprehension check 1
¿Verdadero o falso?
a Francisca está en Londres con su marido desde hace un par de años.
b Londres les agradó mucho.
c El marido de Sarah es empresario.
d Los primeros estudios de español de Sarah los hizo en la escuela.

e Francisca vivió en Estados Unidos antes de que se casara.

f Su marido domina el inglés, el alemán y el francés.

2 Pidiendo información *Asking for information*

Sarah Parker pide información sobre cursos de español en una escuela de lenguas.

◈ CD1, TR 12

Secretaria	Buenos días. ¿Qué desea?
Sarah	Buenos días. ¿Podría darme información sobre los cursos de español para extranjeros?
Secretaria	¿Quiere usted pasar a la oficina número veinte, por favor? Allí le darán toda la información que necesite. Está al final del pasillo.
Sarah	Gracias.
	(En la oficina No. 20)
Encargado	Buenos días, ¿dígame?
Sarah	Buenos días. He venido a pedir información sobre los cursos de español para extranjeros.
Encargado	¿Vd. es profesora de español? Se lo pregunto porque para profesores extranjeros de español tenemos cursos especiales.
Sarah	No, no, estoy interesada en un curso general.
Encargado	Bueno, en ese caso le puedo recomendar el curso general que empieza el 31 de julio y termina el 26 de agosto.
Sarah	¿Del 31 de julio al 26 de agosto me ha dicho?
Encargado	Exactamente. Son cuatro semanas en total. También tenemos un curso intensivo que va del 3 al 29 de julio y un curso abreviado del 28 de agosto al 16 de septiembre.
Sarah	Prefiero el curso general. No dispongo de mucho tiempo como para hacer el curso intensivo y el curso abreviado no es suficiente. ¿Cuál es el horario de clases?
	(Contd)

Encargado	Bueno, en el caso del nivel superior, que es el que le correspondería a Vd. por su nivel de español, las clases de lengua son de 9.00 a 1.00. Y por la tarde, de 5.00 a 7.00, hay un ciclo de conferencias sobre cultura y civilización hispánicas.
Sarah	Perdone, no he entendido lo último que me ha dicho.
Encargado	He dicho que entre las 5.00 y las 7.00 de la tarde hay una serie de conferencias sobre cultura y civilización.
Sarah	¿Y ... puede decirme cuánto cuesta la matrícula?
Encargado	Un momento, por favor, le daré un folleto informativo que incluye los precios y el boletín de inscripción. También tiene aquí información sobre alojamiento en caso de que lo necesite.
Sarah	Muchas gracias.

Insight

Note the use of **me, le, lo, se lo** in **¿Podría darme ...?** *Could you give me ...?*, **Allí le darán ...** *There they'll give you ...* , **... en caso de que lo necesite ...** *in case you need it*, **Se lo pregunto ...** *I'm asking you (about it) ...* These words are called object pronouns. Can you identify other such words in the dialogue? Their use is explained in the Grammar section.

QUICK VOCAB

al final del pasillo *at the end of the corridor*
curso abreviado *(m) short course*
no dispongo de ... *I haven't got ...*
nivel superior *(m) advanced level*
matrícula *(f) registration*
folleto informativo *(m) information brochure*
alojamiento *(m) accommodation*

Language and comprehension check 2
Answer the following questions in Spanish.

a ¿Por qué le pregunta el encargado a Sarah si ella es profesora de español?

b ¿Qué duración tiene el curso general? ¿Y el curso abreviado?

c ¿Por qué no desea hacer el curso intensivo Sarah?

d ¿Qué le da el encargado a Sarah?

Key sentences

Saying what you have studied and what languages you speak

Estudié español en la escuela.	*I studied Spanish at school.*
Lo hablo (el inglés), pero muy mal.	*I speak it, but very badly.*
Él habla inglés bastante bien.	*He speaks English very well.*

Referring to past events

Estudié español.	*I studied Spanish.*
Lo aprendió en EE. UU.	*He learnt it in the United States.*
Vivió allí antes de que nos casáramos.	*He lived there before we got married.*

Saying how long ago something happened

Estuve en Londres con mi marido hace un par de años.	*I was in London with my husband a couple of years ago.*

Making enquiries

¿Podría darme información sobre los cursos de español?	*Could you give me information about the Spanish courses?*
¿Puede decirme cuánto cuesta la matrícula?	*Can you tell me what the registration fees are?*

Grammar

1 The preterite tense

Usage

To refer to events which are past and complete and to events which lasted a definite period of time and ended in the past, you use the preterite tense or simple past tense. For example:

Lo *aprendió* **en Estados Unidos.**   *He learnt it in the United States.*
Estudié **español durante dos años.**   *I studied Spanish for two years.*

Formation

The preterite tense has two sets of endings, one for -ar verbs and another one for -er and -ir verbs. Here are two fully conjugated verbs: **estudiar** *to study* and **aprender** *to learn*.

estudié	*I studied*	**estudiamos**	*we studied*
estudiaste	*you studied (familiar)*	**estudiasteis**	*you studied (familiar)*
estudió	*he/she/you studied*	**estudiaron**	*they/you studied*

aprendí	*I learnt*	**aprendimos**	*we learnt*
aprendiste	*you learnt*	**aprendisteis**	*you learnt (familiar)*
aprendió	*he/she/you learnt*	**aprendieron**	*they/you learnt*

For irregular verbs in the preterite, such as **hacer** *to do, make,* **hice, hiciste, hizo …**, **estar** *to be,* **estuve, estuviste, estuvo …**, see the Irregular verbs section.

2 Hace *Ago*

With a verb in the preterite tense, **hace** translates into English as *ago*.

Estuve **en Londres con mi**   *I was in London with my*
  marido *hace* **un par de años.**   *husband two years ago.*

Compare this construction with the one you learnt in Unit 3, such as:

Hace **un año que vivo en Madrid.**   *I have been living in Madrid for*
a year.

3 Direct object pronouns

The word **lo** in **lo hablo** *I speak it*, **lo aprendió** *he learnt it*, is
a direct object pronoun. You use a direct object pronoun to
avoid the repetition of a noun, in this case the word **el inglés,**
English.

¿Y usted habla inglés?	*And do you speak English?*
Lo hablo, pero muy mal.	*I speak it, but very badly.*

Here is the complete set of direct object pronouns:

Singular		Plural	
me	*me*	**nos**	*us*
te	*you (familiar)*	**os**	*you (familiar)*
lo	*you, him, it (m)*	**los**	*you, them (m)*
la	*you, her, it (f)*	**las**	*you, them (f)*

Here are some further examples:

La **vi ayer.**	*I saw her/it yesterday.*
Nos **llamó.**	*He/she called us.*

In Madrid and in some regions of central Spain you are more
likely to hear **le, les**, instead of **lo, los**, for human males – singular
and plural respectively – all of which are considered correct.
It may be easier for you to memorise the following simple rule
when using the masculine form of direct object pronouns: use **lo**
and **los** *for things* and **le** and **les** *for people.*

¿Conoces a Juan?	*Do you know Juan?*
Sí, *le* **(or** *lo***) conozco.**	*Yes, I know him.*

4 Indirect object pronouns

To say *to/for me*, *to/for you*, *to/for him*, *her*, etc., you use the following set of words which are called indirect object pronouns.

Singular	Plural
me me, to me, for me	**nos** us, to us, for us
te you, to you, for you (familiar)	**os** you, to you, for you (familiar)
le you, him/her, to you, him/her, for you, him/her	**les** you, them, to you, them, for you, them

Examples:

¿Podría dar*me* información ...?   *Could you give me information...?*

Allí *le* darán toda la información ...   *There they will give you all the information ...*

If you have two object pronouns, one direct and one indirect, the indirect one comes first.

Él *me* lo explicó.   *He explained it to me.*

When the indirect object **le** (or **les**) precedes **lo**, **la**, **los** or **las**, the indirect object becomes **se**. For example:

Le pregunto.	*I ask you.*
Lo pregunto.	*I ask about it.*
Se lo pregunto.	*I ask you (about it).*

Notice that object pronouns normally precede the verb, but in phrases where a verb precedes an infinitive, the object pronouns may either precede the main verb or be attached to the infinitive. For example: ¿Podría dar*me* información ...? or ¿**Me** podría dar información?

Practice

1 Read this extract from a letter written by Alfonso to his pen friend in England and complete each blank space in the letter with a verb from the box. Use the preterite tense.

> *Querida Bárbara:*
>
> .... *mucho de recibir carta tuya nuevamente y de saber que te* ....
> *bien en tus exámenes. Por lo que me cuentas, el curso que* .... *era*
> *bastante difícil.*
>
> *Me preguntas si he estudiado inglés. Bueno, la verdad es que lo* ....
> *durante varios años, pero nunca* .... *hablarlo correctamente. Creo que*
> *no* .... *un buen profesor y además éramos muchos en la clase y no*
> *teníamos oportunidad de practicarlo. Pero hace unos seis meses* ....
> *a un curso intensivo en una escuela de lenguas que se* .... *aquí en*
> *Segovia y* .... *bastante.* .... *estudiar mucho, pues teníamos seis horas*
> *diarias de clases, pero creo que* .... *la pena, ya que ahora al menos*
> *puedo comunicarme y entiendo casi todo. Espero que cuando te visite en*
> *Inglaterra me puedas ayudar ...*

estudiar	aprender	asistir
abrir	alegrarse	merecer
conseguir	ir	tener que
tener	hacer	

2 Complete the blank spaces below with the correct object pronouns: **me, te, lo, le**, etc.

    a '¿___ puedes explicar lo que significa esta frase? No entiendo muy bien el español.' 'Por supuesto, yo ___ ___ explicaré'.

    b '¿Habla Vd. español?' '___ hablo, pero no muy bien.'

    c Carlos habla demasiado rápido. No ___ entiendo casi nada.

d 'Por favor, cuando llegue María diga___ que ___ llame. Necesito preguntar___ algo'. 'Muy bien, ___ ___ diré'.

e 'Por favor, ¿podría dar___ información sobre los cursos de español?' 'Un momento, por favor, ___ ___ daré en seguida, y ___ daré también un folleto informativo'.

3 At a conference in a Spanish-speaking country you engage in informal conversation with one of the participants.

Señor	Vd. habla muy bien español.
Tú	*(Thank him. Say that is very kind of him.)*
Señor	¿Dónde lo aprendió?
Tú	*(Say you learnt it at school, but you also spent six months in Spain. Ask him if he speaks English.)*
Señor	Lo hablo, pero bastante mal. Lo encuentro muy difícil. Pero el francés sí lo hablo muy bien.
Tú	*(Ask him where he studied French.)*
Señor	Bueno, mis padres vivieron en París cuando yo era pequeño. Lo aprendí allí. ¿Y Vd. habla francés?
Tú	*(Yes, you did several years of French at school and you had an excellent teacher. And you also go to France every summer. Last year you were in Cannes. You liked it very much.)*
Señor	Sí, a mí me encanta Cannes también. Mi mujer y yo estuvimos allí hace unos cinco años. Lo pasamos estupendamente.

4 You are going to make enquiries about Spanish courses at a language school in Spain. Write the necessary questions to get the information you need.

a Ask if they do summer courses in Spanish.

b Ask when they start.

c Ask what levels they offer.

d Ask how much they cost.

e Ask about the timetable.

f Ask if they can help you find accommodation.

5 Pamela Johnson wrote to a school in Malaga asking for information about Spanish courses. This is her letter. Translate it into your own language.

> 26 Devonshire Street
> Londres W3 7HF
> Inglaterra
>
> 26 de mayo de 2010
>
> Señor Director de Estudios
> Cursos para extranjeros
> Universidad de Málaga
> San Agustín 6
> 29080 – Málaga
> España
>
> Muy Señor mío:
> El objeto de la presente es solicitar a Vd. que me envíe información sobre los cursos de español para extranjeros que ofrecerá la Universidad de Málaga este verano.
>
> Le ruego que me dé información detallada sobre las fechas en que estos se realizarán, los niveles que se ofrecen, el horario de clases y el valor de la inscripción.
>
> Le agradeceré además que me informe sobre la posibilidad de conseguir alojamiento a través de ustedes con una familia española.
>
> En espera de sus gratas noticias, le saluda atentamente,
>
> Pamela Johnson

What information did Pamela ask for in the letter?

el objeto de la presente es ... *This is to...*
en espera de sus gratas noticias *I look forward to hearing
from you*

6 Here is part of the information Pamela Johnson received from
the school of languages in Malaga. Read it through and make
a note in English of the following points:
  a How can you register?
  b What certificates or diploma can you obtain?
  c What sort of accommodation can they help you
    find?
  d How are the students grouped?
  e How many hours a week do you have to attend?
  f What activities can students take part in during the
    course?

CURSOS DE ESPAÑOL PARA EXTRANJEROS
CURSO DE VERANO

El Curso se dirige a extranjeros que deseen iniciar o ampliar sus conocimientos en lengua y cultura españolas.

Duración
Se desarrolla en tres ciclos, pudiéndose inscribir en uno, dos o los tres.

Ciclo I	03.07 – 30.07
Ciclo II	01.08 – 30.08
Ciclo III	02.09 – 27.09

Inscripción y matrícula
El Curso de verano es un curso abierto: no es necesario ningún título académico para inscribirse, sólo se precisa tener 16 años.

Enviar a la Secretaría la ficha de inscripción, dos fotografías y fotocopia del documento de pago.

Exámenes y certificados
Los exámenes son obligatorios sólo para los alumnos que deseen obtener uno de estos títulos:
- ▶ **Certificado de Lengua Española;**
  Permanencia mínima: un mes.
- ▶ **Diploma de Estudios Hispánicos;**
  Permanencia mínima: dos meses.

Alojamiento
La Secretaría del Curso facilitará direcciones de familias o apartamentos a los alumnos inscritos que lo soliciten.

Horario de clases y niveles
Los alumnos se dividen en niveles según sus conocimientos de lengua: básico, intermedio y superior. Se imparten cuatro clases diarias de lunes a viernes desde las 9.00 a las 13.15.

(Contd)

Otras actividades

Durante el curso se organizan conciertos, espectáculos y sesiones de cine. Asimismo hay visitas a los principales monumentos de la ciudad y excursiones a ciudades de interés (Granada, Córdoba, Sevilla y Ronda).

También se organiza un viaje a Marruecos. Durante el mes de agosto son las fiestas de la ciudad con actos folklóricos y culturales de gran interés.

7 In a Spanish magazine, you see the following courses advertised and you decide to write making enquiries about one of them.

GRADUADO ESCOLAR

Preparación para la obtención del Titulo del Estado.

CULTURA GENERAL

Los conocimientos que toda persona debe poseer hoy.

DECORACIÓN

Podrás decorar desde una habitación de niños a una tienda.

GUITARRA

Método seguro. Por solfeo o por cifra. Incluye cassettes.

ORDENADORES Y BASIC

Lograrás un conocimiento completo de lo que da de sí un Ordenador Personal y su programación.

CONTABILIDAD

Muy sencillo y práctico. Diploma de Contable.

Follow this guideline:

a Say you have seen the advertisement for courses offered by the Centro de Estudios Eva and state which course you are interested in.

b Ask them to send you all the relevant information about the course, including the date when it is held, registration fees, timetable and how you can register.

c Ask them to send you the information as soon as possible.

For other standard words and phrases used in formal letter writing see the letter in Exercise 5 above and that in Unit 3. Here are some key words.

anuncio (m) advertisement
ofrecer to offer
información referente a ... relevant information about ...
realizarse to be held
inscribirse to register
lo antes possible as soon as possible
estar interesado(a) to be interested

8 ¡A escuchar!

◄) **CD1, TR 13**

Recuerdos: In an interview on the subject of education, Gloria Díaz from Spain talked about the school she went to. Listen to the conversation if you have the recording, or alternatively, use the transcript for reading comprehension. First study these key words, then look at the questions and answer them as you read or listen to the conversation.

recuerdos (m) memories
olvidado forgotten
disfruté I enjoyed it
nos llevábamos mal. we didn't get on
simpatiquísima very nice
asignatura (f) (school) subject
suspendí I failed
guardar to keep

¿Verdadero o falso?

a Hace casi dos años que Gloria está en el colegio.
b Gloria estudió en un colegio religioso para chicas.
c Ella fue allí porque prefería estar sólo con chicas.
d La profesora que más le gustaba era la de matemáticas.
e Con la profesora de historia se llevaba muy bien.
f Sus asignaturas favoritas eran Matemáticas y Ciencias.

9 Five writers talk about some of their childhood experiences. Look at the vocabulary first, then read the texts and answer the questions which follow them.

QUICK VOCAB

tirar *to throw away*
mono/a *pretty*
engañar *to deceive*
aguantar el llanto *to hold back one's tears*
enfermizo/a *unhealthy, morbid*
autoestima *(f) self-esteem*
amenazado/a *threatened*
reponerse *to recover*
quiebra *(f) bankruptcy*
redundar en *to have as a consequence*
huellas profundísimas *(f pl) deep marks*
Edad Dorada *(f) Golden Age*

a Rosa Montero, Spain

De pequeña, cuando tenía cinco años, me enfermé de tuberculosis. Estuve en casa sin ir al colegio durante muchos años. Entonces mi distracción era leer y escribir muchísimo. La escritura era un juego: empezaba una novela del Oeste o de asesinatos y al día siguiente la tiraba y escribía otra. A los nueve o diez años, cuando volví al colegio, mi sorpresa fue descubrir que las demás niñas no jugaban a eso.

b Ana María Matute, Spain

Me sentía fea... ¡Y no lo era! Era muy mona. Digo, las fotografías no engañan, ¿no?

Pero mis hermanas eran unas bellezas... Así, yo vivía en mi soledad, tranquila, tímida, aguantándome siempre el llanto.

c Isabel Allende, Chile

Yo tuve una infancia bien infeliz. Llena de terrores, de preguntas sin respuestas. Con una sensibilidad enfermiza y un orgullo ilimitado, que provenía de una muy baja autoestima y de sentirme muy amenazada, muy vulnerable.

d Mario Benedetti, Uruguay (1920–2009)

A mi padre le fue mal con una farmacia que había comprado en Tacuarembó y durante años no pudimos reponernos de esa quiebra. Eso redundó en una infancia sin juguetes, y eso nunca fue un buen recuerdo.

e Mario Vargas Llosa, Perú

La peor marca quedó a partir de los diez años, cuando conocí a mi padre, en una relación espantosa que me dejó huellas profundísimas. Pero, tal vez, también me marcaron esos primeros diez años vividos con la familia de mi madre, que son algo así como la Edad Dorada.

(*Revista de Libros, El Mercurio, Chile*)

Insight

Ana María Matute (Barcelona, 1926), a well-known Spanish novelist, was only ten years old at the outbreak of the Spanish Civil War (1936–39). The war and life in post-war Spain had a profound influence on her writing. Rosa Montero (Madrid, 1951), a journalist and writer, is the author of a number of successful books, including several novels. Mario Benedetti (Uruguay, 1920–2009), a journalist, novelist and poet, was one of the most outstanding writers in the Hispanic world. Mario Vargas Llosa (Peru, 1936), a novelist, essayist and playwright, is renowned internationally for his works of fiction. Isabel Allende (Peru, 1942), a Chilean and best-selling novelist, has done most of her writing in the United States.

Now answer these questions:
  a What did Rosa Montero do during her illness, and what did she discover when she returned to school?
  b How does Ana María Matute describe herself in her childhood?
  c What does Isabel Allende say about her childhood?
  d What event marked Mario Benedetti's life?
  e How does Mario Vargas Llosa describe the relationship with his father? And with his mother's family?

TEST YOURSELF

1 Complete each sentence with the preterite tense of the verb in brackets.

 a Cristóbal ____ sus estudios en Madrid, Alberto y Mercedes los ____ en Barcelona. Yo también los ____ allí. (*hacer*)

 b Esteban ____ cinco días en París y Luis y yo ____ en Londres una semana. (*estar*)

 c (Yo) le ____ a Gloria que viniera, pero (ella) me ____ que no podía. (*decir*)

 d – ¿Dónde (tú) ____ mi libro? – (Yo) lo ____ en tu biblioteca. (*poner*)

 e Jorge ____ un buen estudiante, Marta y Paca también lo ____, pero nosotros ____ los mejores. (*ser*)

 f José ____ en el coche, Sara y Ramón ____ en el autobús y yo ____ en la bici. (*venir*)

2 How would you express the following in Spanish?

 a Could you give me information about the Spanish summer courses, please?

 b Will you send us information about accommodation too? We'll give you our emails.

 c I feel ashamed to say it, but my Spanish is not as good as my French, although I studied it for a year.

 d My son is completely fluent in French and Spanish. He learnt them at school and also spent some time in France and Spain.

3 The following phrases are typical of formal letter writing. What do they mean?

 a El objeto de la presente es pedir un folleto informativo ...

 b Le ruego que me indique cuál es el valor de la inscripción ...

 c Les agradeceré que me consigan alojamiento con una familia española ...

 d En espera de sus gratas noticias ...

Did you manage to get all the verb forms right in Test 1? If you did, congratulations! These verbs are very common. If you are still uncertain about them, check the Irregular verbs section. Don't be discouraged if you made a few mistakes in Tests 2 and 3. Communication is the first step, accuracy will follow.

5

De vacaciones
On holiday

In this unit you will learn how to:
- *Describe places and people you knew in the past*
- *Express hope*
- *Express intentions*
- *Talk about the future*
- *Talk about the weather*
- *Express regret*

1 Un viaje a Cuba *A journey to Cuba*

Pablo Dávila y Ana Ramírez hablan de sus últimas vacaciones.

Pablo	¿El año pasado también viniste aquí de vacaciones?
Ana	No, el año pasado fui a Cuba con unas amigas. Estuvimos en La Habana y en Varadero.
Pablo	¿Y qué tal?
Ana	Nos gustó muchísimo. Estuvimos tres días en La Habana y una semana en Varadero. Varadero es un lugar muy bonito y tiene unas playas estupendas. Y el hotel donde nos quedamos era excelente. Estaba a cinco minutos de la playa. Tenía piscina, discoteca …
Pablo	¿Fuisteis a través de alguna agencia de viajes?

CD1, TR 14

(Contd)

Ana	Sí, porque de otra manera nos habría resultado demasiado caro. Mereció la pena, y la gente del grupo era muy maja, la mayoría era gente joven.
Pablo	La verdad es que a mí los viajes organizados no me gustan nada. Prefiero viajar por mi cuenta.

Insight

In Ana's account of her holiday the *preterite* is used for the actions that took place at some point in the past, **El año pasado fui a Cuba** *Last year I went to Cuba*, while the imperfect tense forms provide the background description for the actions expressed by the preterite, **El hotel donde nos quedamos era excelente** *The hotel where we stayed was excellent*.

agencia de viajes *(f) travel agency*
majo(a) *nice (Spain)*
por mi cuenta *by myself, independently*

Insight

¿Y qué tal? Notice this colloquial phrase which has different translations in English, depending on the context. Here it means *And how was it?* or *How did it go?* with reference to the holiday Ana is talking about. Note also the use of **resultar**, which normally translates as *to be*, **Nos habría resultado caro** *It would have been expensive for us.*

Language and comprehension check 1
Answer the following questions in Spanish.

a ¿Dónde pasó sus vacaciones Ana el año pasado?
b ¿Cuánto tiempo estuvo allí?
c ¿Qué dice Ana del hotel?
d ¿Fue por su cuenta? ¿Por qué sí/no?
e ¿Cómo describe Ana a la gente con que viajó?

f ¿Qué dice Pablo de los viajes organizados?

g ¿Qué expresiones se usan en el diálogo para decir lo siguiente?
through, otherwise, it was worth it.

2 Espero ir a México *I hope to go to Mexico*

Pablo y Ana hablan de sus planes para las próximas vacaciones.

Ana	¿El año que viene vendrás aquí otra vez?
Pablo	No, el próximo verano espero ir a México. Un amigo mexicano que conocí en Salamanca me ha invitado a su casa. Pienso irme hacia finales de julio y me quedaré allí todo el mes de agosto. Él tomará sus vacaciones en la misma fecha y viajaremos juntos. Así podré conocer un poco del país.
Ana	¡Estupendo! Te gustará mucho. Mi hermana estuvo en México hace un par de años y me contó maravillas de los sitios que visitó y de la gente.
Pablo	Bueno, ¿y tú que harás? ¿Volverás aquí otra vez?
Ana	No lo creo. Espero ir a algún lugar diferente. Hay unos viajes al oriente que me entusiasman mucho y que no son nada caros. Ya veremos. Aún falta mucho tiempo …

◆ CD1, TR 15

espero ir *I hope to go*
pienso irme *I'm thinking of going*
hacia finales de *towards the end of*
así podré conocer … *that way I'll be able to see … (Lit. to know)*
… que me entusiasman … *which I am very tempted by*
ya veremos *we'll see*

QUICK VOCAB

Insight

a **Me contó maravillas de…** *She spoke wonderfully about … The expression is* **contar** *or* **decir maravillas de …,** *to speak wonderfully of …* (people or things).

(Contd)

b Aún falta mucho tiempo. *There is still a long time to go.*
In this construction, the verb **faltar** is used in the third
person singular or plural. Look at these other examples:
Falta **mucho para mi cumpleaños** *My birthday is a long way
off*, *Faltan* **dos meses para la Navidad** *There are two months
to go to Christmas*.

Language and comprehension check 2

Complete these phrases with information from the dialogue.

a El próximo verano Pablo irá de vacaciones a ____
b Él ha sido invitado por ____
c Piensa viajar en (mes) ____
d Estará allí todo el mes de (mes) ____
e Viajará con ____
f A Ana le gustaría ir a (lugar) ____

3 Hablando del tiempo *Talking about the weather*

En la recepción del Hotel El Conquistador, dos turistas
sudamericanos hablan del tiempo.

CD1, TR 16

Señor	¿Sigue lloviendo?
Señorita	Lamentablemente sí, no ha parado de llover en toda la noche. Está lloviendo a cántaros en este momento.
Señor	¡Qué lástima! Y yo que pensaba salir de paseo. Tendré que quedarme en el hotel.
Señorita	¡Es una pena! Pero probablemente mañana hará buen tiempo.
Señor	¡Ojalá!

y yo que pensaba ... *and I was thinking of ...*
hará buen tiempo *the weather will be good*
lamentablemente *unfortunately*

QV

Language and comprehension check 3
What phrases are used in the dialogue to say the following?
  a Is it still raining?
  b It hasn't stopped raining.
  c It's pouring with rain.
  d What a pity!
  e It's a pity.
  f I hope so.

Key sentences

Describing places and people you knew in the past

El hotel era excelente.	*The hotel was excellent.*
Tenía piscina.	*It had a swimming pool.*
La gente era muy maja.	*The people were very nice.*
La mayoría era gente joven.	*The majority were young people.*

Expressing hope

Espero ir a México.	*I hope to go to Mexico.*
¡Ojalá!	*I hope so.*

Expressing intentions

Pienso irme hacia finales de julio.	*I intend to go towards the end of July.*
Yo pensaba salir de paseo.	*I was thinking of going out.*

Talking about the future

Me quedaré allí todo el mes de agosto. — I will stay there for all of August.

Él tomará sus vacaciones en la misma fecha. — He will take his holidays on the same date.

Other ways of talking about the future

Voy a viajar a España. — I am going to travel to Spain.

Vamos a quedarnos aquí. — We are going to stay here.

Mañana salgo para Londres. — I am leaving for London tomorrow.

Talking about the weather

Está lloviendo a cántaros. — It's pouring with rain.

Mañana hará buen tiempo. — The weather will be good tomorrow.

Other ways of talking about the weather

Hace frío/calor. — It is cold/warm.

Hace buen/mal tiempo. — The weather is good/bad.

Está despejado. — It is clear/cloudless.

Llueve/Está lloviendo. — It rains, it is raining.

Hace viento/sol. — It is windy/sunny.

Hace bueno. — The weather is good.

Está nublado. — It is cloudy/overcast.

Está nevando. — It is snowing.

Nieva. — It snows, it is snowing.

Expressing regret

Lamentablemente sí. — Unfortunately/regrettably yes!

¡Qué lástima! — What a pity!, What a shame!

¡Es una pena! — It is a pity!, It is a shame!

Other ways of expressing regret

Desafortunadamente .../ Desgraciadamente ... — Unfortunately ...

¡Qué desgracia! — What a shame!

Insight

In exclamations such as **¡Qué lástima/pena/desgracia!**
Spanish does not use the equivalent of *a* (as in the English
What a pity/shame!). Exclamations which use *how* in English
also translate in Spanish with **qué: ¡Qué terrible/difícil/
increíble!** *How terrible/difficult/incredible!*

Grammar

1 Looking ahead

To refer to the future you can use:

a the future tense:

Me quedaré allí todo el mes.	*I'll stay there the whole month.*
¿Vendrás aquí otra vez?	*Will you come here again?*

b the construction **ir** with **a** and the infinitive:

Va a llover.	*It's going to rain.*
¿Qué vas a hacer?	*What are you going to do?*

c the present tense, particularly with verbs which indicate
movement:

Él llega mañana.	*He's arriving tomorrow.*
Esta tarde voy a Madrid.	*I'm going to Madrid this afternoon.*

2 The future tense

Formation
The future tense is formed with the whole infinitive, to which
the endings are added. The same endings are used for the three
conjugations: **-ar, -er** and **-ir** verbs. Here is an example:

tomar *to take*	
tomaré	*I will take*
tomarás	*you will take (familiar)*
tomará	*he, she, it, you will take*
tomaremos	*we will take*
tomaréis	*you will take (familiar)*
tomarán	*they, you will take*

A few verbs, such as **venir** *to come*, are irregular in the future tense: **vendré, vendrás, vendrá, vendremos, vendréis, vendrán**. For other irregular verbs in the future see the Irregular verb section.

3 The imperfect tense for past description

To describe places or people you knew in the past, you normally use the imperfect tense, for example:

El hotel era excelente.	*The hotel was excellent.*
Estaba a cinco minutos de la playa.	*It was five minutes away from the beach.*
La gente era muy maja.	*The people were very nice.*

Formation
There are two sets of endings for the imperfect tense, one for **-ar** verbs and another one for **-er** and **-ir** verbs. Here are two examples:

estar *to be*	
estaba	*I was*
estabas	*you were (familiar)*
estaba	*he, she, it was, you were*
estábamos	*we were*
estabais	*you were (familiar)*
estaban	*they, you were*

tener *to have*	
tenía	*I had*
tenías	*you had (familiar)*
tenía	*he, she, it, you had*
teníamos	*we had*
teníais	*you had (familiar)*
tenían	*they, you had*

Ser *to be*, is irregular in the imperfect tense: **era, eras, era, éramos, erais, eran.** For other irregular verbs in the imperfect tense, see the Irregular verb section.

4 Expressing hope

Notice the use of infinitive after **esperar** *to hope* when expressing hope not involving others or something outside ourselves.

Espero ir a México.	*I hope to go to Mexico.*
Esperamos volver pronto.	*We hope to come back soon.*

Practice

1 Put the infinitives into the correct form of the future tense.

Querida Paloma:

Te escribo para contarte que el lunes que viene John y yo (**viajar**) a España. (**Salir**) de aquí a las 2.00 de la tarde y (**llegar**) a Madrid a las 5.00. Aún no sabemos cuánto tiempo (**quedarse**), pero esperamos estar allí por lo menos dos semanas. ¿(**Poder**) venir a vernos al hotel el lunes por la noche? (**Estar**) en el Hotel Gran Vía. Tengo un regalo para ti de Paul y te lo (**dar**) cuando nos veamos ... A propósito, ¿qué (**hacer**) tú en tus próximas vacaciones? Nos gustaría mucho que vinieras a Inglaterra ... .

2 Change the infinitives in brackets into the right form, the preterite or the imperfect.

  a El año pasado Isabel y Javier (**ir**) al Perú. (**Estar**) allí diez días en total.

  b (**Ser**) la primera vez que (ellos) (**ir**) allí y ambos (**estar**) fascinados con la idea de conocer Cusco y Machu Picchu.

  c El vuelo desde Madrid les (**resultar**) bastante largo, pero el avión (**llegar**) a la hora. En el aeropuerto les (**esperar**) Antonio, un amigo de Javier que (**vivir**) desde hacía dos años en Lima.

  d Los primeros dos días los (**pasar**) en Lima donde Javier, que (**conocer**) bien la ciudad les (**llevar**) a conocer los principales sitios de interés.

  e Al tercer día Isabel y Javier (**tomar**) *u*n vuelo a Cusco. La llegada a la ciudad les (**parecer**) espectacular. (**Ser**) mediodía cuando el avión aterrizó.

  f La estancia en la ciudad y la posterior visita a Machu Picchu (**ser**) los momentos culminantes de un viaje que ambos (**soñar**) con realizar desde hacía mucho tiempo.

3 A Spanish friend asks you about your last holiday. Answer his questions.

Él ¿Dónde pasaste tus últimas vacaciones?

Tú *(Say you spent them in San Sebastián, in northern Spain.)*

Él ¿Y qué tal? ¿Te gustó?

Tú *(Say you liked San Sebastián very much. It is a very nice town, and the hotel where you stayed was excellent. It was opposite the beach, it had a swimming pool and an excellent restaurant. And you were very lucky with the weather. It wasn't too hot.)*

Él ¿Con quién fuiste?

Tú *(Say you went with some friends. You got on very well together, they were very nice people.)*

Él ¿Y cuánto tiempo estuvisteis allí?

Tú *(Say you didn't stay long. Unfortunately, you all had to come back to work.)*

4 You are going on holiday to Mexico. The holiday, which starts in Madrid, will take you to Cancún and Mexico City (México D.F.). Read the programme sent to you by the travel agency.

CANCÚN/MÉXICO D.F.

DIA 1.° MADRID-CANCÚN
Presentación en salidas internacionales del aeropuerto de Barajas en el mostrador de Club Vacaciones, dos horas antes de la salida del vuelo. Viajarás en Boeing 767 de la compañía Spanair en vuelo sin escala a Cancún. A la llegada te espera personal de nuestra organización que te trasladará en autobús privado al hotel. Alojamiento.

DIAS 2.° AL 6.°: CANCÚN
Estancia en los hoteles en el régimen de pensión elegido, atendidos por nuestro personal que te informará además de las excursiones facultativas que puedes hacer durante tu permanencia.

DIA 7.°: CANCÚN/MÉXICO D.F.
Recogida en el hotel y traslado al aeropuerto para salir en avión a México D.F. Llegada y traslado en autobús privado al hotel. Alojamiento.

DIAS 8.° AL 13.°: MÉXICO D.F.
Estancia en los hoteles en régimen de alojamiento. Posibilidad de excursiones facultativas.

(Contd)

DIA 14.° MÉXICO D.F./CANCÚN

Recogida en el hotel y traslado al aeropuerto para salir hacia Cancún. Traslado al hotel y alojamiento.

DIA 15.° CANCÚN/MADRID

Recogida en el hotel y traslado al aeropuerto a la hora que te indique nuestro personal, para embarcarte en un Boeing 767 de la compañía Spanair hacia Madrid donde finaliza nuestro servicio.

Your travelling companion wants to know the following:

a Which airline are we flying with?
b Is there a stopover on the way to Cancún?
c How are we getting from Cancún airport to the hotel?
d How are we travelling from Cancún to Mexico City?
e How long are we staying in Mexico City?
f Are we flying back to Madrid from Mexico City?

mostrador *(m) counter, flight desk*
escala *(f) stopover*
estancia *(f) stay*
facultativo *optional*
recogida *(f) pick-up*

5 You are talking about your next holiday in Mexico with a Spanish-speaking friend. Answer your friend's questions.

a ¿A qué parte de México irás?
b ¿Qué lugar visitarás primero?
c ¿Cuántos días te quedarás en total?
d ¿Te quedarás en casa de amigos?

Insight

With just over 100 million people, Mexico is the largest Spanish-speaking country in the world, and Mexico City, which Mexicans normally call **México** or **el D.F.** (**Distrito Federal** *Federal District*), is one of the largest cities in the whole world. In terms of the number of tourists, with over 20 million visitors per year, Mexico is one of the ten most popular destinations worldwide.

6 During a flight to Madrid you are given a Spanish newspaper which has a weather chart for the whole of Spain and the forecast for the following day. What will the weather be like in Madrid? Study the following information and then answer the questions.

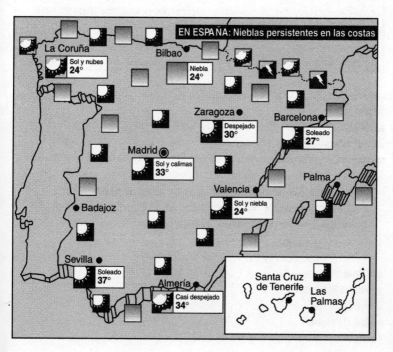

EN ESPAÑA: Nieblas persistentes en las costas

La Coruña — Sol y nubes 24°
Bilbao — Niebla 24°
Zaragoza — Despejado 30°
Barcelona — Soleado 27°
Madrid — Sol y calimas 33°
Palma
Valencia — Sol y niebla 24°
Badajoz
Sevilla — Soleado 37°
Almería — Casi despejado 34°
Santa Cruz de Tenerife
Las Palmas

EL TIEMPO EN MADRID

MAÑANA

Área urbana: (Máxima: 33 / Mínima: 18). Cielo despejado. Calimas. Neblinas a primeras horas y calimas posteriormente. Sin cambios térmicos.

Área de la Sierra: Despejado por la mañana con nieblas a primeras horas. Algo nuboso por la tarde con nubes altas. Ventolinas del suroeste.

CONTAMINACIÓN

Los índices de contaminación se mantienen relativamente bajos. La contaminación, por tanto, estacionaria.

El sol saldrá hoy domingo a las 7 horas y 48 minutos y se pondrá a las 20 horas y 36 minutos. La luna saldrá a las 7 horas y 46 minutos y se pondrá a las 20 horas y 20 minutos.

Fase de la luna: Estamos en luna nueva.

(Diario El Mundo, Madrid, Spain)

Insight

Word formation. Note the ending **-oso** in **nuboso** *cloudy*, an adjective derived from **nube** *cloud*. A number of Spanish adjectives can be formed in the same way: **caluroso** *warm* (from **calor**), **ruidoso** *noisy* (from **ruido**), **amoroso** *loving*, *affectionate* (from **amor**). Like all adjectives, such words will agree in gender and number with the noun that they go with: **una noche calurosa** *a warm night*, **unos vecinos ruidosos** *noisy neighbours*.

---

a Will it be overcast in Madrid tomorrow?

b What will the weather be like early in the morning? And later on in the day?

c If you wanted to drive up to the Sierra, what will the weather be like there early in the morning? And in the afternoon?

d With all the traffic that there is in Madrid, the air becomes very polluted at times. What will the situation be like tomorrow?

e If you spend the day at the Sierra tomorrow, you want to return to the city before sunset, as you don't like driving at night. What time will the sun set?

7 ¡A escuchar!

◄) **CD1, TR 17**

El pronóstico del tiempo: Now that you are familiar with some of the terminology used in Spanish weather forecasts, you will have a chance to hear a recording about the weather in Santiago de Chile. If you do not have the recording, you can use the transcript for reading comprehension. First, familiarize yourself with some words and phrases which did not appear in the previous exercise. Then, as you listen to the recording or read the text, answer in Spanish the questions which follow.

llovizna (f) drizzle
grado (m) degree
nubosidad (f) cloudiness
humedad (f) humidity

a ¿Cómo estará el tiempo hoy en Santiago, según la Dirección Meteorológica de Chile?

b ¿Cuál será la temperatura mínima probable? ¿Y la máxima?

c ¿Cuáles fueron las temperaturas mínima y máxima ayer en la capital? ¿A qué hora fueron?

d ¿Cuáles son las perspectivas para el viernes 21 de febrero?

e ¿Cuál es la temperatura del momento?

8 What sort of holidays do most people in your country prefer, organized tours or independent travel? And what do they like to do when they go on holiday? Read the following passage and compare their preferences with those of Spaniards, and then answer the questions below.

No nos gusta ir todo el día detrás de un guía

A los españoles nos encanta el viaje organizado, pero mucho menos que al resto de los europeos. Buscamos la seguridad de que alguien se responsabilice de nosotros, aunque los paquetes turísticos ofertados a los españoles son bastante abiertos: dejan tiempos libres y dan opciones diferentes dentro de un mismo viaje, porque se sabe que nuestra idiosincrasia hace que no nos guste ir a todas horas detrás de un guía. Por otra parte, a los españoles nos interesa visitar monumentos, museos, parques naturales … Hay una inquietud cultural manifiesta.

(Revista Quo)

---

a ¿Qué prefieren los españoles, el viaje organizado o el viaje independiente?

b ¿Qué prefieren hacer en sus vacaciones?

TEST YOURSELF

1 Change the verbs in brackets into the appropriate forms of the future tense.

   a Andrés _____ sus vacaciones en Italia, Sofía y Julio las _____ en Egipto, y yo _____ todo el verano en casa. (*pasar*)

   b El pronóstico del tiempo dice que hoy _____ mucho calor. Adela y yo _____ una excursión a la sierra para escapar de la ciudad. (*hacer*)

   c Debido a la enfermedad de su madre Sandra _____ que cancelar el viaje y lamentablemente (*yo*) _____ que viajar solo. (*tener*)

   d – ¿Dónde _____ (*vosotros*) el regalo que os hizo Elena?
   – Creo que (*nosotros*) lo _____ en el salón. (*poner*)

   e – ¿(*Tú*) le _____ a Paco lo que ocurrió?
   – Yo no se lo _____ , pero seguramente Victoria se lo _____ . (*decir*)

   f David y Lucía _____ a pasar sus vacaciones con nosotros, pero su hijo Pablo no _____ . ¿(*Tú*) _____ conmigo al aeropuerto a recogerlos? (*venir*)

2 How would you express the following in Spanish?

   a The hotel where they stayed was excellent. It wasn't far from the beach and it also had a swimming pool, but unfortunately it poured with rain most of the time.

   b But it was worth going. The town was interesting, although it was a bit noisy.

   c We're thinking of travelling to Brazil next year. Patricia was there two years ago and she told me wonderful things about Rio.

   d No, we're not taking an organized tour. We prefer to travel independently, otherwise it will be too expensive. We'll book our tickets through a travel agency.

   e Well, I hope to go on holiday at the end of August. There are some holidays in the Caribbean which are not at all expensive. We'll see. It's still a long way off.

f – Is it still raining?
  – Unfortunately, yes. It hasn't stopped raining since we got up.
  – What a pity! I was thinking of playing tennis.

The main focus in these tests is verbs, the future tense in Test 1 and the imperfect, preterite and future tenses in Test 2. Note that all but one of the verbs in Test 1 is irregular. For their full forms see the Irregular verbs section. Test 2 also assesses your knowledge of the vocabulary and expressions from Dialogues 1–3. Go back to the dialogues and Key phrases if necessary, or continue your progress by going on to Unit 6.

6

Un lugar donde vivir
A place to live

In this unit you will learn how to:
* *Ask for information about accommodation*
* *Book into a hotel*
* *State requirements*
* *Describe a place*
* *Ask and say what something costs*

1 Reservando una habitación *Booking a room*

🔊 **CD1, TR 18**

Martin Baron, su mujer Susan y sus dos hijos están de vacaciones en España. Desde Madrid, Martin llama por teléfono al Hotel San Marcos de Marbella para reservar una habitación.

HOTEL SAN MARCOS

COMODIDAD, ELEGANCIA Y DISTINCIÓN EN PLENO CENTRO DE MARBELLA Y A SOLO CINCUENTA METROS DE LA PLAYA

▶ Habitaciones individuales y dobles (Descuentos especiales para niños)
▶ Media pensión o pensión completa

(Contd)

- ▶ Aire acondicionado
- ▶ TV color vía satélite
- ▶ Tres grandes piscinas
- ▶ Discoteca
- ▶ Tiendas para uso exclusivo de nuestros clientes

PARA INFORMACIÓN Y RESERVAS LLAME AL TELÉFONO 95 83 41 02
DE MARBELLA O CONSULTE A SU AGENCIA DE VIAJES

Recepcionista	Hotel San Marcos, ¿dígame?
Martin	Buenos días. ¿Podría decirme si tiene habitaciones disponibles para la última semana de agosto?
Recepcionista	Sí, señor, sí tenemos. ¿Qué tipo de habitación desea Vd.? ¿Individual o doble?
Martin	Perdone, pero no se oye bien. ¿Podría repetir?
Recepcionista	Le pregunto si quiere una habitación individual o doble.
Martin	Bueno, somos dos adultos y dos niños pequeños. Necesitamos una habitación con una cama de matrimonio y dos camas individuales para los chicos.
Recepcionista	Perfectamente.
Martin	Tengo entendido que hay un descuento especial para los niños. ¿No es así?
Recepcionista	Sí, efectivamente, hacemos un descuento del 25 por ciento por cada niño. En total, incluido el descuento, la habitación le saldría a 80 euros.
Martin	¿El desayuno está incluido en el precio de la habitación?
Recepcionista	No, señor, el desayuno se paga aparte. El desayuno continental vale seis euros. Y también tenemos un servicio de restaurante en caso de que Vd. prefiera tomar media pensión o pensión completa.
Martin	No, sólo tomaremos la habitación con desayuno.
Recepcionista	Muy bien, ¿y para qué fecha la quiere Vd.?
Martin	A partir del 24 de agosto.
Recepcionista	¿Y para cuántas noches?

Martin	Siete noches en total. Hasta el 30 de agosto inclusive.
Recepcionista	Del 24 ... al ... 30 de agosto ... ¿Me dice su nombre, por favor?
Martin	Martin Baron.
Recepcionista	Perdone, ¿cómo ha dicho?
Martin	Martin Baron.
Recepcionista	¿Cómo se escribe, por favor?
Martin	B-a-r-o-n, Baron.
Recepcionista	Muy bien, señor Baron.
Martin	Ah, ¿oiga?
Recepcionista	Sí, ¿dígame?
Martin	¿Tienen Vds. aparcamiento en el hotel? Vamos a viajar en coche.
Recepcionista	Sí, señor, tenemos un aparcamiento para uso exclusivo de los clientes.
Martin	¡Estupendo! Adiós, muchas gracias.
Recepcionista	De nada, adiós.

QUICK VOCAB

disponible *available*
tengo entendido que ... *I understand that* ...
descuento *(m) discount*
a partir de ... *starting on* ...

Insight

Notice this special use of the verb **salir,** here *to come to, to cost.*

Le *saldría* **a ochenta euros.** *It would cost you 80 euros.*

Me *salió* **muy caro.** *It cost me a lot of money.*

¿Cuánto *sale*? *How much does it come to?*

La cena *salió* **a 35 euros.** *Dinner came to 35 euros.*

Language and comprehension check 1

i Answer the following questions in Spanish.
    a ¿Qué tipo de habitación necesita Martin Baron?
    b ¿Para cuándo quiere la habitación y para cuánto tiempo?
    c ¿Cuánto cuesta la habitación?
    d ¿Está incluido el descuento para los niños?

ii How is the following expressed in the dialogue?
    a No oigo bien.
    b Entiendo que ...
    c No está incluido.
    d Si usted prefiere ...
    e Desde el 24 de agosto.
    f ¿Cómo se llama usted?

2 Buscando un apartamento *Looking for an apartment*

Elizabeth Reed trabaja para una empresa multinacional en Barcelona. Elizabeth necesita alquilar un apartamento y llama por teléfono a una inmobiliaria.

CD1, TR 19

Empleada	Sí, ¿dígame?
Elizabeth	Buenas tardes. He visto en *La Vanguardia* un anuncio de un apartamento que se alquila en la calle Pelayo. ¿Podría decirme si está disponible todavía?
Empleada	Sí, ¿quiere esperar un momento, por favor? Ahora le pongo con la persona encargada.
Empleado	Sí, ¿diga?
Elizabeth	Buenas tardes, llamo por el anuncio del apartamento que se alquila en la calle Pelayo. ¿Estará disponible todavía?
Empleado	Sí, un momento, por favor ... pues, tal como pone el anuncio, es un apartamento muy pequeño, de veinticinco metros cuadrados, tiene un aseo con ducha y cocina americana. Y está amueblado. Está muy bien de precio, cuatrocientos cuarenta euros solamente.

Elizabeth	Es justamente lo que busco. Necesito algo que no sea demasiado caro y que esté cerca de mi oficina. Yo trabajo en el centro. ¿En qué piso está?
Empleado	Está en el cuarto piso, pero tiene ascensor. Es un apartamento muy bonito, es exterior y está en perfecto estado. Lo acaban de pintar. Tiene agua caliente, teléfono …
Elizabeth	¿Sería posible verlo esta misma tarde?
Empleado	Sí, no creo que haya problema. ¿Por qué no pasa Vd. por aquí entre las tres y las cuatro y la acompañaré yo mismo? ¿Tiene Vd. nuestra dirección?
Elizabeth	Sí, sí, la tengo, gracias.

Insight

Note the use of the present subjunctive in **Necesito algo que no sea demasiado caro y que esté cerca …** *I need something which is not too expensive and which is near …* and **No creo que haya problema** *I don't think there'll be any problem.* In the first sentence the subjunctive is determined by a main verb expressing need followed by **que**; in the second one, by a verb denoting doubt or uncertainty. (See Unit 1.)

alquilar *to rent*
inmobiliaria *(f) accommodation agency, estate agent*
encargado(a) *person in charge*
tal como pone el anuncio *just as the advertisement says*
aseo *(m) small bathroom*
cocina americana *(f) open plan kitchen*
amueblado *furnished*
estado *(m) condition*
pasar por *to come round*

QUICK VOCAB

Language and comprehension check 2
i ¿Verdadero o falso?
  a El apartamento de la calle Pelayo está alquilado.
  b El apartamento tiene un gran baño.

c Tiene una cocina con muebles americanos.

d El apartamento da a la calle.

e Está en el centro de Barcelona.

ii What phrases are used in the dialogue to say the following?

a I'm calling/phoning about the advertisement.

b Is it available? (2 phrases)

c I'll put you through to … right now.

d It's a very good price.

e It's just what I'm looking for.

f They have just painted it.

Key sentences

Asking for information about accommodation

¿Podría decirme si tiene habitaciones disponibles …?	*Could you tell me if you have rooms available?*
¿Podría decirme si está disponible todavía?	*Could you tell me if it is still available?*
¿Estará disponible todavía?	*Is it still available?*

Booking into a hotel

Tomaremos la habitación con desayuno.	*We'll take the room with breakfast.*
¿Para qué fecha?	*For what date?*
A partir del 24 de agosto.	*Starting on 24th August.*

Stating requirements

Necesitamos una habitación con una cama de matrimonio.	*We need a room with a double bed.*
Necesito algo que no sea demasiado caro.	*I need something which is not too expensive.*

Describing a place

Está en el cuarto piso.	*It is on the fourth floor.*
Es un apartamento muy pequeño.	*It is a very small apartment.*
Tenemos un aparcamiento.	*We have a car park.*

Asking and saying how much something costs

Vale seis euros. *It costs 6 euros.*
Le saldría a ochenta euros. *It would come to/cost 80 euros.*

Other ways of asking and saying what something costs	
¿Cuánto cuesta/vale?	*How much does it cost?*
¿Qué precio tiene?, ¿Cuál es el precio?	*What is the price?*
Cuesta/vale 100 libras.	*It costs £100.*
¿Cuánto sale?	*How much does it come to?*

Grammar

1 Ser and estar

Observe the use of **ser** in these sentences from the dialogues:

To denote characteristics:

Es **un apartamento pequeño.** *It is a small apartment.*

With impersonal expressions such as **es posible, es mejor, es difícil:**

¿Sería **posible verlo?** *Would it be possible to see it?*

With figures:

Somos **dos adultos.** *We are two adults.*

Consider now the use of **estar** in these sentences:

To indicate position:

Está **en el cuarto piso.** *It is on the fourth floor.*

To denote a temporary state or condition:

*Está **en perfecto estado.***   *It is in perfect condition.*

Before a past participle to denote a condition resulting from an action:

*Está **amueblado.***   *It is furnished.*

2 *Use of* se

Notice how **se** has been used in the dialogues.

In a passive sentence:

El desayuno *se* **paga aparte.**   *Breakfast is paid for separately.*

In passive sentences with **se**, the verb agrees in number (singular or plural) with the subject. Compare the previous sentence with this one:

Las bebidas *se pagan* **aparte.**   *The drinks are paid separately.*

In an impersonal sentence:

No *se* **oye bien.**   *One can't hear well.*

3 **Para** *and* **por**

Observe the use of **para** in these phrases from the dialogues.

To denote length of time:

*¿Para **cuántas noches?***   *For how many nights?*

With time phrases:

*¿Para **qué fecha?***   *For what date?*

To indicate destination:

Dos camas *para* **los chicos.**   *Two beds for the children.*

Notice how **por** has been used in these phrases:

With the meaning of *per*:

Un descuento del 25% *por* **cada niño.**   *A 25% discount per child.*

With the meaning of *about*:

Llamo *por* **el anuncio.**   *I am calling about the advertisement.*

To indicate movement:

¿*Por* **qué no pasa Vd. por aquí?**   *Why don't you come round?*

Practice

1   ¿Ser o estar?

Select the correct verb and its form.

El Hotel Doña Bárbara (**es/está**) situado en pleno centro de Caracas y (**es/está**) uno de los mejores de la ciudad. El Hotel Doña Bárbara (**es/está**) dotado de todo lo necesario para el turista exigente. El servicio de restaurante y de bar (**es/está**) de excelente calidad y a pesar de su elegancia, sus precios (**son/están**) relativamente módicos para el turista europeo. En el Hotel Doña Bárbara le (**será/estará**) posible disfrutar de un verdadero descanso y si Vd. (**es/está**) acompañado de sus hijos, la dirección del hotel le ofrecerá generosos descuentos para ellos.

2 ¿Por o para?

Choose **por** or **para** from the brackets.

> **A** Buenos días. Llamo *(por/para)* reservar una habitación *(por/para)* este fin de semana.
>
> **B** ¿Es *(por/para)* una persona solamente?
>
> **A** No, quiero una habitación doble.
>
> **B** ¿*(Por/para)* cuántas noches la quiere?
>
> **A** *(Por/Para)* tres noches solamente, de viernes a domingo. Llegaremos allí el viernes *(por/para)* la tarde. ¿Tienen Vds. aparcamiento *(por/para)* los clientes?
>
> **B** No, nosotros no tenemos. Pero enfrente del hotel hay un aparcamiento. Me parece que vale siete euros *(por/para)* día ...
>
> **A** ¿Y cuánto cobran Vds. *(por/para)* la habitación doble con media pensión?
>
> **B** Ciento veinte euros *(por/para)* persona ...

3 Carol Wilson sent an email to the Hotel Don Quijote in Gandía to book a room. Read her email and then use it as a model to make your own hotel booking using some of the words and phrases opposite.

Estimados señores:

El objeto de la presente es solicitar a Vds. la reserva de una habitación doble, con dos camas y con baño, a partir del sábado 28 de agosto próximo y hasta el 13 de septiembre inclusive. Les ruego que me confirmen la reserva a la brevedad posible. Les saluda muy atentamente.

Carol Wilson

Insight

Les ruego que me confirmen ... *Please confirm* (literally, *I beg you that you confirm* ...). The verb following **Les ruego que** ... goes in the present subjunctive. In letter or email writing **que** is sometimes omitted: **Les ruego confirmen** ... Note also the phrase **a la brevedad posible** *as soon as possible*. Alternative phrases with the same meaning are **lo más pronto posible** and **cuanto antes**.

> Useful words and phrases
> **una habitación doble/individual**   *a double/single room*
> **con cama de matrimonio/cama**   *with a double bed/single beds*
>   **doble/camas individuales**
> **con/sin (cuarto de) baño**   *with/without bathroom*
> **una habitación exterior/con**   *a room with a view/with a sea*
>   **vistas al mar/con terraza**   *view/with balcony*

4 You and some friends would like to spend a month in Fuengirola. In a local newspaper you see this advertisement and you decide to phone to ask for more information.

> FUENGIROLA Alquilo, por meses o larga temporada, o vendo apartamento Paseo Marítimo (Torreblanca), 2 dormitorios, baño, gran salón-comedor.
> Teléfono (952) 473078

Señora	¿Dígame?
Tú	*(Say you are ringing about the ad in the newspaper.)*
Señora	Ah, por el apartamento.
Tú	*(That's it. Say you are looking for something to rent. Ask her to give you more information about the apartment.)*
Señora	Pues, es un apartamento nuevo, con vistas al mar y muy tranquilo. Tiene dos habitaciones, además del salón-comedor, la cocina y el baño.
Tú	*(Say you need something which is available immediately.)*
Señora	El apartamento está disponible ahora mismo.
Tú	*(Well, you are also looking for something which is not too expensive. Ask how much the monthly rent is.)*
Señora	Bueno, es un precio muy razonable. Mil ciento cincuenta euros por mes.
Tú	*(Thank her and say that is too much for you.)*

5 Tony, a student from London, received the following letter from his Spanish correspondent in Barcelona. Read the letter and then answer the questions.

Querido Tony:

En mi carta anterior te escribí sobre mi familia. Hoy te contaré algo sobre el lugar donde vivimos, que es muy especial.

Como te decía, vivo con mis padres y mis dos hermanos menores. Tenemos un piso muy grande y muy antiguo en el Paseo de Gracia, una de las calles principales de Barcelona, en pleno centro de la ciudad. Aquí vivió mi padre cuando era niño y aquí he vivido siempre.

El piso está en un edificio muy bonito, de principios del siglo pasado, que está muy bien conservado. Tiene un gran salón, un comedor también muy grande, y cinco habitaciones más. Una de ellas la utiliza mi padre como despacho. Mis dos hermanos comparten uno de los dormitorios, yo tengo mi propia habitación y para cuando tú vengas a Barcelona, tenemos una habitación para las visitas también.

El salón da a la calle, una calle muy ruidosa, pero con una arquitectura muy interesante. Mi habitación, afortunadamente, es interior, de manera que no me despierta el ruido del tráfico por la mañana. Los fines de semana suelo dormir hasta muy tarde.

En el barrio tenemos todo lo que necesitamos: supermercados, tiendas de ropa, grandes almacenes —el Corte Inglés está muy cerca de aquí-, buenos restaurantes, cafés, etc. En la esquina hay una estación de metro, la de Paseo de Gracia, donde cojo el metro para ir al instituto. Allí también cogemos el tren para ir a Sitges el fin de semana. Te llevaré allí cuando vengas a verme. Estoy seguro de que te gustará. ¡Tiene mucha marcha!

Me preguntas si seguiré viviendo con mi familia cuando vaya a la universidad. Por cierto que me gustaría mucho vivir independientemente, pero no creo que pueda hacerlo ya que aquí alquilar un piso cuesta una fortuna. No es como en Inglaterra. Aquí no tenemos más alternativa que seguir viviendo con la familia. Cuando trabaje, quizá sí, entonces tendré dinero suficiente para alquilar mi propio piso o compartir con *algún amigo, pero de momento no. Tampoco me puedo quejar puesto que en casa estoy muy bien.*

¿Y tú, qué tal? Me dices que el próximo año te irás a vivir fuera de Londres y que tendrás que encontrar un lugar donde vivir. Espero que tengas suerte. Algún día iré a visitarte. Mientras tanto, escríbeme y cuéntame de ti.

Un abrazo
Paco

....

Insight

Note the use of the present subjunctive in: **Cuando tú vengas a Barcelona** *When you come to Barcelona*, **Cuando vengas a verme** *When you come and see me*, **Cuando vaya a la universidad** *When I go to university*, **Cuando trabaje ...** *When I work ...* The subjunctive is used here because in this context **cuando** refers to an action which is not yet a reality. The subjunctive is also needed in **No creo que pueda hacerlo** *I don't think I'll be able to do it* (uncertainty) and **Espero que tengas suerte** *I hope you are lucky* (hope).

....

en pleno centro *right in the centre*
siglo pasado *last century*
bien conservado *well preserved*
grandes almacenes *(m pl) department store*
tiene mucha marcha *there's a lot going on there*
por cierto *of course, naturally*
puesto que *as*

QUICK VOCAB

Answer the following questions in Spanish.
  a ¿Con quién vive Paco?
  b ¿Cómo es el piso donde vive?
  c ¿Cómo es el edificio?

d ¿Cuántas habitaciones tiene?

e ¿Comparte habitación Paco?

f ¿Cómo es la calle donde vive?

g ¿Dónde está la estación de metro más cercana?

h ¿Por qué seguirá viviendo con su familia Paco cuando vaya a la universidad?

6 ¡A escuchar!

◀ **CD1, TR 20**

a **Un nuevo piso:** Pablo is going to share a flat with some friends. In a conversation with Soledad he described the place where he is going to live. A rather inaccurate description of Pablo's flat made later that day by Soledad to a friend follows. Can you correct it? Listen to the dialogue if you have the recording or read the transcript.

'Pablo se ha mudado a un piso estupendo a sólo veinticinco minutos de la Plaza Mayor. Es un piso de dos habitaciones, pero no tiene vistas. Va a compartirlo con un amigo y van a pagar doscientos sesenta euros mensuales.'

búsqueda (f) search
mudado moved (house)

◀ **CD2, TR 1**

b **Hotel O'Higgins:** The Hotel O'Higgins in Viña del Mar, Chile, is announcing a special offer. Listen to this radio advertisement, if you have the recording, or read the transcript, and then answer the questions which follow. Here are some key words.

impuesto (m) tax
merecido deserved

¿Verdadero o falso?

i   La oferta especial es válida para niños menores de doce años.

ii   Los niños se pueden quedar con dos adultos por la mitad del precio.

iii   La oferta es válida sólo por tres noches.

iv   El desayuno y el impuesto están incluidos en el precio.

7   A group of young Europeans were asked why many of them continued living with their parents after leaving school.

Can you think of some reasons why young people might stay at home? Try listing them in Spanish in order of importance and then compare your answers with those in the following chart.

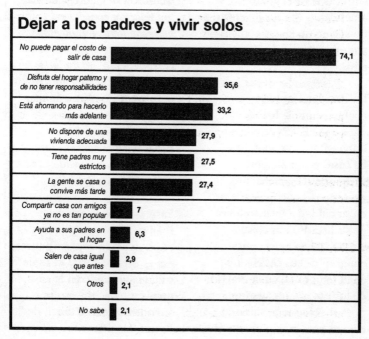

Dejar a los padres y vivir solos

No puede pagar el costo de salir de casa	74,1
Disfruta del hogar paterno y de no tener responsabilidades	35,6
Está ahorrando para hacerlo más adelante	33,2
No dispone de una vivienda adecuada	27,9
Tiene padres muy estrictos	27,5
La gente se casa o convive más tarde	27,4
Compartir casa con amigos ya no es tan popular	7
Ayuda a sus padres en el hogar	6,3
Salen de casa igual que antes	2,9
Otros	2,1
No sabe	2,1

(El Mercurio, Chile)

The following article looks at this issue from the point of view of young Spanish people. Why do you think many of them continue living with their parents well into their twenties? Read and find out.

VIVIR CON MAMÁ A LOS 30, UNA MODA IMPUESTA POR LAS CIRCUNSTANCIAS

En España es muy normal que los jóvenes de 25 a 30 años e incluso de más edad vivan aún con los padres, hecho insólito para otras culturas como la europea o americana. Allí los jóvenes no suelen quedarse con sus padres más allá de los 20 años.

En Estados Unidos, cuando el chico cumple los 18 años e inicia sus estudios universitarios se marcha de casa. Normalmente suele matricularse en una universidad que queda lejos de su ciudad e incluso fuera de su Estado. Las chicas y muchachos americanos emigran de sus casas a una edad temprana, en la mayoría de los casos para siempre, pues si acaso regresan a su ciudad para trabajar, vivirán solos en un apartamento, o en el peor de los casos compartiéndolo con algún amigo.

En España esa mentalidad independentista se inició años atrás, pero se ha truncado. Alfonso de Hohenlohe, 30 años, aristócrata y conspicuo representante de la *jet* española, piensa que vivir con los padres resulta más cómodo. Él aún comparte techo con su madre y afirma, *'mi relación con ella es perfecta, tiene una mentalidad jovencísima y es fácil convivir con ella, si no, no dudaría en vivir solo. Desde luego es más cómodo vivir en familia porque no te tienes que ocupar de nada, ahorras y tienes independencia, como es mi caso. La casa además es amplia y confortable'.*

Para el español Alfonso Ibáñez, administrativo, 33 años viviendo con sus padres, esa es otra historia. Él sigue todavía viviendo en la casa que le vio nacer y eso le supone una carga difícil de llevar. *'La situación – dice – es a menudo exasperante, notas una asfixia que impide desarrollar tu personalidad. No se trata, por supuesto, de que a mis 33 años me limiten la libertad, sino que uno necesita más que un cuarto de tres por dos en donde tener su propia intimidad.'*

Y es que en España las cosas son diferentes. Para asombro de extraños, es muy normal encontrar en este país hombres y mujeres que, superada ampliamente ya la etapa de juventud, aún comparten vivienda con sus progenitores. '*Ahora* (señala el sociólogo Amando de Miguel) *se ha invertido la tendencia que se daba en los años sesenta y principios de los setenta cuando los jóvenes buscaban su independencia y marchaban a vivir solos o en grupos de amigos en viviendas de alquiler. La vocación emancipadora se ha roto y se ha reinstaurado la costumbre de no salir de la casa paterna hasta el casamiento.'*

La cuestión económica es la principal responsable de esta situación. Los jóvenes son los principales afectados por el paro y sin un salario mensual y estable es imposible vivir independientemente.

(Revista Tiempo No 316, España)

Insight

Word formation. The suffix **-miento** serves to form nouns from verbs: **casar (se)** *to marry* – **casamiento** *marriage* (see the text above), **aparcar, estacionar** *to park* – **aparcamiento** (see Dialogue 1), **estacionamiento** *car park*, **almacenar** *to store* – **almacenamiento** *storage*, etc. The suffix **-ario/a** added to a noun indicating a place designates an occupation: **universidad** *university* – **universitario/a** *university student* (see above), **biblioteca** *library* – **bibliotecario/a** *librarian*, **parlamento** *parliament* – **parlamentario/a** *member of parliament*, etc.

---

insólito *unusual*
si acaso *if*
en el peor de los casos *at worst*
truncarse *to cut short*

QUICK VOCAB

ahorrar *to save*
carga *(f) burden*
doloroso(a) *painful*
asombro *(m) surprise*
progenitores *(m pl) parents*
romperse *to break*

i Read the text again and see how the following phrases have been used. For each of them write an alternative phrase expressing the same idea. In the answer key you will find some examples.

   a Comparte techo con su madre.
   b Emigran de sus casas a una edad temprana.
   c Mi relación con ella es perfecta.
   d No te tienes que ocupar de nada.
   e La casa que le vio nacer.
   f Aún comparten vivienda con sus progenitores.
   g La vocación emancipadora se ha roto.

ii How are the following expressed in the text?

   a They don't normally stay.
   b beyond the age of 20
   c He usually registers at a university.
   d forever
   e if they return to their (home) town
   f Of course, it's not a question of ... but ...

TEST YOURSELF

1 Complete the sentences with **por** or **para**, as appropriate.
   a Llamo ____ el anuncio de su página web. Queremos una habitación ____ tres personas, ____ cinco días, ____ el 10 de julio.
   b Una habitación individual ____ nuestro hijo y una doble ____ nosotros.
   c ¿Cuánto es ____ día?
   d ¿El precio que se paga es ____ persona o ____ la habitación?
   e – Y ____ llegar allí, ¿qué carretera tenemos que tomar? Pueden venir ____ la A45.
   f Podemos confirmar su reserva ____ correo electrónico o ____ fax, o ____ teléfono, si prefiere.

2 Choose between **ser** and **estar** and fill in the Spanish for the words in brackets.
   a El apartamento (*which is for rent*) on Pelayo Street, ¿es/está (*still available*)?
   b Es/Está un apartamento (*furnished*).
   c Es/Está (*in very good condition*) y es/está (*very nice. They have just painted it*).
   d Es/Está (*facing onto the street*).
   e Es/Está (*just what I'm looking for*).
   f ¿(*On which floor*) es/está? No soy/estoy seguro, pero (*I'll put you through to the person in charge now*).

Por, para, ser, estar, and some of the expressions from Dialogues 1–2 are the focus of these tests. Even if you did well, make sure you understand why you used one form instead of another before you go on to the next unit. Most grammar books will have references to such words.

7

¿Por dónde se va?
Which way is it?

In this unit you will learn how to:
- **Ask how to get to a place**
- **Give directions**
- **Ask and give information about transport**

1 ¿Qué línea tengo que tomar? *What line do I have to take?*

Mark Johnson, un turista de visita en Madrid, pregunta cómo ir a la estación de Chamartín. Mark está en la estación de metro Sol.

CD2, TR 2

Mark	Perdone, ¿qué línea tengo que tomar para ir a la estación de Chamartín?
Empleado	Coja la línea 1 hasta Plaza de Castilla y allí cambie a la línea 8 en dirección a Fuencarral.
Mark	Gracias.
Empleado	De nada.

QV

línea *(f) line*
coger *to take*

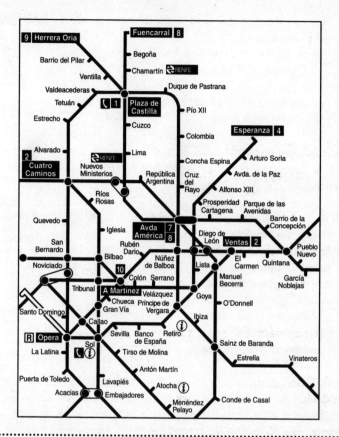

Insight

Coger and **tomar** *to take*, are interchangeable in this context. **Coger**, however, seems to be more frequent in Spain. In certain Latin American countries, notably Argentina, **coger** is a taboo word and it is better to avoid it. **Tomar** will be understood everywhere.

Language and comprehension check 1

i ¿Verdadero o falso?

    a Mark desea ir a la estación de Chamartín.

    b La línea 1 va directo a Chamartín.

    c Mark tiene que cambiar a la línea 8 en Fuencarral.

ii What expressions are used in the dialogue to say the following?

    a Take line 1.
    b as far as ...
    c Change onto line ...

2 ¿A qué hora llega el expreso? *What time does the express train arrive?*

Mark ha ido a la estación de Chamartín a buscar a un amigo que viene de Zaragoza. En información Mark pregunta por la llegada del tren.

◆ CD2, TR 3

Mark	Por favor, ¿a qué hora llega el expreso que viene de Zaragoza?
Empleada	La hora de llegada es a las catorce treinta, pero hoy viene con veinte minutos de retraso. Llegará a las catorce cincuenta.
Mark	¿A qué andén llega?
Empleada	No lo sé, tiene que mirar el tablero de llegadas.
Mark	Gracias.
Empleada	De nada.

Insight

Rail travel has changed considerably in Spain in the last few years. The **AVE** (**Alta Velocidad Española**, literally *Spanish High Speed*), a fast-speed train, links Madrid with some major cities such as Seville, Zaragoza and Barcelona. Travelling to Seville on the **AVE** takes about two and a half hours and to Barcelona about three hours. The **AVE**, which can reach a speed of 300 km per hour, is operated by **RENFE** (**Red Nacional de los Ferrocarriles Españoles**), the Spanish state-owned railway company.

QUICK VOCAB
llegada *(f)* arrival
retraso *(m)* delay
andén *(m)* platform
tablero *(m)* board

Language and comprehension check 2

i Answer the following questions in Spanish, using the 12-hour
clock.

   a ¿A qué hora llega normalmente a Madrid el expreso de
Zaragoza?

   b ¿Con cuántos minutos de retraso llegará hoy?

   c ¿A qué hora llega?

ii What phrases are used in the dialogue to say the following?

   a the arrival time

   b Which platform does it arrive at?

   c the arrivals board

3 Sigan todo recto *Go straight ahead*

Mark y su amigo Robert están en un hotel en la calle de la
Magdalena. En su segundo día en Madrid deciden visitar el Museo
del Prado. En la recepción del hotel preguntan cómo llegar hasta allí.

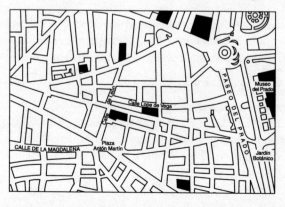

Robert	Buenos días.
Recepcionista	Buenos días, señor. Dígame.
Robert	Por favor, ¿nos puede decir por dónde se va al Museo del Prado?
Recepcionista	Sí, miren, al salir del hotel tuerzan ustedes a la derecha y vayan hasta la Plaza Antón Martín que está a cien metros de aquí. Allí cojan la calle de León que está a la izquierda y sigan hasta la calle Lope de Vega. Sigan todo recto por Lope de Vega hasta llegar al Paseo del Prado. Al otro lado del Paseo está el Museo.
Robert	Muchas gracias. Dígame, ¿hay alguna oficina de correos por aquí?
Recepcionista	No, por aquí no. Pero si es para comprar sellos, en la Plaza de Antón Martín hay un estanco. Allí venden sellos.
Robert	Gracias, adiós.
Recepcionista	Adiós, buenos días.

sigan todo recto *go straight on*
tuerzan (torcer) *turn (to turn)*
hasta llegar a *until you get to*
estanco *(m) tobacco shop*

Insight

Note the following phrase: **¿Por dónde se va a ...?** *Which is the way to ...?* (Lit. *Which way does one go to ...?*) This is an impersonal expression and a very useful form of asking the way.

Language and comprehension check 3

i After leaving the hotel, Robert repeated the directions given by the receptionist to Mark in English. Complete Robert's version of the directions: 'First we have to turn ...'.

ii What expressions are used in the dialogue to say the following?

    a ¿Qué desea?/¿En qué puedo ayudarle?
    b ¿Puede decirnos ...?
    c Cuando salgan ...
    d Giren a la derecha.
    e Sigan de frente.
    f ... hasta que lleguen ...

4 Se puede ir en tren o en autocar *You can go by train or coach*

Mark y Robert quieren viajar a Toledo, ciudad que está a 70 km de Madrid. En una agencia de viajes piden información.

Empleada	Buenos días, ¿qué desean?
Mark	Por favor, ¿podría decirnos cómo podemos viajar a Toledo?
Empleada	A Toledo se puede ir en tren o en autocar. Los trenes salen de la estación de Atocha y los autocares de la estación Sur, en la calle Canarias.
Mark	¿Sabe usted cuál es el horario de los trenes?
Empleada	Hay trenes cada hora, a la hora exacta, a partir de las siete de la mañana y hasta las veintitrés horas.
Mark	¿Dónde está la estación de Atocha?
Empleada	Pues, tienen que coger la línea 1 del metro. Pueden cogerla aquí en Sol. Les llevará directo.
Mark	¿Tiene usted un folleto informativo sobre Toledo?
Empleada	No, de Toledo no nos queda ninguno, pero en la estación quizá puedan conseguir uno.
Mark	Muchas gracias. Adiós.
Empleada	No hay de qué.

◆ CD2, TR 5

autocar *(m) coach*
folleto informativo *(m) information brochure*
quedar *to be left*
no hay de qué *you're welcome*

QUICK VOCAB

> **Insight**
>
> Note the impersonal construction **Se puede ir en tren ...**,
> literally *One can go by train ...* Compare this with **Pueden
> ir en tren ...** *You can go by train ...* Note also **Quizá puedan
> conseguir uno** *Perhaps you can get one ...* Because **quizá(s)**
> expresses uncertainty, **poder** is in the present subjunctive.

Language and comprehension check 4

i Complete these phrases with information from the dialogue:

  a A Toledo se puede ir en (means of transport) ...
  b Los trenes salen de (name of station) ...
  c Los autocares salen de (name of coach station) ...
  d Hay trenes (frequency) ...
  e El primer tren sale a las (time) ...
  f El último tren sale a las (time) ...

ii What phrases are used in the dialogue to say the following?

  a Could you tell us ...?
  b the train timetable
  c every hour on the hour
  d from 7 o'clock in the morning
  e We don't have any left.

Key sentences

Asking the way

¿Dónde está ...?	*Where is it?*
¿Nos puede decir por dónde se va a ...?	*Can you tell us how we can get to ...?*

Other ways of asking the way	
¿La ruta/carretera/autopista para ... por favor?	*The road/highway/motorway for ... please?*
¿En qué dirección está...?	*In which direction is ...?*

Giving directions

Tuerza/doble a la derecha.	*Turn right.*
Vaya hasta ...	*Go as far as ...*
Siga hasta la calle ...	*Continue as far as ... street.*
Siga todo recto	*Go straight on/ahead*
Tome/coja ...	*Take ...*

Other ways of giving directions	
Suba/baje por esta calle.	*Go up/down this road.*
Está al lado de/junto a ...	*It is next to ...*
Está en la esquina.	*It is on the corner.*
Cruce ...	*Cross ...*
Está al lado	*It is next door*
Está enfrente de ...	*It is opposite ...*
Está entre ... y ...	*It is between ... and ...*

Asking and giving information about transport

¿Qué línea tengo que tomar/ coger?	*What line do I have to take?*
Tome/coja la línea 1.	*Take line 1.*
Cambie/transborde a ... en ...	*Change on to ... at ...*
¿Podría decirme/nos cómo puedo/podemos viajar a ...?	*Can you tell me/us how I can/ we can travel to ...?*
¿A qué hora llega el expreso?	*What time does the express train arrive?*
La hora de llegada es a las ...	*The arrival time is ...*
Llega/llegará a las ...	*It arrives/it will arrive at ...*
Sale(n) de ...	*It leaves/they leave from ...*
Hay (trenes) cada hora.	*There are (trains) every hour.*

Grammar

1 The imperative – giving directions

Directions are normally given with the imperative, e.g. **cruce la calle** *cross the street*, **suba por esta avenida** *go up along this* *avenue.* The imperative is the same as the third person singular of the present subjunctive (see Unit 1). As with the subjunctive, you use the stem of the first person singular of the present tense plus the appropriate ending. In Spanish, you use different imperative forms depending on who you are talking to (polite or familiar) and whether you are speaking to one, or more than one, person (singular or plural).

a Polite imperatives
Here are the polite imperatives of three regular verbs: **doblar** *to turn*, **retroceder** *to go back*, **subir** *to go up*:

Present tense *(1st person)*	Imperative	
doblo	dobl**e**	*turn (sing)*
	dobl**en**	*turn (pl)*
retrocedo	retroced**a**	*go back (sing)*
	retroced**an**	*go back (pl)*
subo	sub**a**	*go up (sing)*
	sub**an**	*go up (pl)*

The negative imperative is formed by placing **no** before the verb, e.g. **no** doble aquí *don't turn here*. As the imperative is formed with the stem of the 1st person singular of the present tense, verbs which are irregular or stem-changing in the present are also irregular or stem-changing in the imperative, e.g. **vengo** *I come*, **venga** *come*, **vuelvo** *I come back*, **vuelva** *come back*.

b Positive familiar imperatives
Familiar imperatives have different positive and negative forms:

Present tense *(yo)*	Imperative *(tú/vosotros)*	
doblo	dobl**a/d**	*turn*
retrocedo	retroced**e/d**	*go back*
subo	sub**e/id**	*go up*

Irregular forms: di (decir), haz (hacer), ve (ir), oye (oír), pon (poner), sal (salir), ten (tener), ven (venir), sé (ser).

c Negative familiar imperatives

Present tense (yo)	Imperative (tú/vosotros)	
doblo	no dobl**es**	*don't turn*
	no dobl**éis**	*don't turn*
retrocedo	no retroced**as**	*don't go back*
	no retroced**áis**	*don't go back*
subo	no sub**as**	*don't go up*
	no sub**áis**	*don't go up*

Latin Americans do not use the **vosotros** forms of the imperative: **hablad – no habléis; subid – no subáis,** etc. The **ustedes** form of the imperative is used in formal and informal address: **hablen – no hablen, suban – no suban,** etc. In the River Plate area (Argentina, Uruguay and Paraguay), where **vos** replaces **tú,** positive informal imperative forms are: **doblá, retrocedé, subí.** Negative informal forms are: **no doblés, no retrocedás, no subás.** Plural forms are as above.

d Pronouns with imperatives

If the imperative includes a pronoun, this must go at the end of the positive form but before the negative one. Positive imperatives which carry a pronoun may need to add an accent, e.g. **bajarse** to get off: **bájese** *get off,* **no se baje** *don't get off.*

When the pronoun **-os** is added to the **vosotros** form of the imperative, the final **-d** of the imperative is dropped: **cuidarse** *to take care,* **cuidaos** *take care of yourselves;* **callarse** *to be quiet,* **callaos** *be quiet.* In colloquial speech, however, imperative forms such as these are often replaced by the infinitive: **cuidaros, callaros.**

2 Using the present tense to give directions

Directions can also be given with the present tense, using the usted or the tú form of the verb, as appropriate.

Sigue todo recto por la calle Mayor y luego toma la segunda a la izquierda. (formal)	*You go straight on along the high street and then you take the second turning on the left.*

Sigues todo recto hasta el parque, cruzas el parque y luego tomas la primera calle a la derecha. (informal)

You go straight on as far as the park, you go across the park and then you take the first street on the right.

The present tense seems to be just as frequent as the imperative in giving directions and it is a useful alternative to know if you have difficulty using the different imperative forms. You must, however, make an effort to understand directions or instructions given to you in forms other than the present tense.

Practice

1 Change the imperatives into the familiar form.
Para llegar a mi oficina **coja** el autobús número 4 y **bájese** en la plaza Isabel La Católica. **Cruce** la plaza en dirección a la Catedral y **suba** por la calle de la Catedral hasta el primer semáforo. La empresa donde trabajo está justo en la esquina. **Suba** en el ascensor hasta la quinta planta. Al salir del ascensor hay un pasillo. **Siga** por el pasillo hasta el fondo. Mi oficina es la 510 y está a la mano izquierda.

2 You have been in Madrid for a few days and you are now familiar with the underground system (**el metro**). Someone you have met at your hotel near the Opera metro, who does not speak English, needs your help. Look at the map of the Madrid underground in Unit 7, section 1 and answer his questions.

Conocido	Buenos días, ¿cómo está Vd.?
Tú	*(Reply to his greeting.)*
Conocido	Muy bien, gracias. Hoy tengo que ir a visitar a unos amigos que viven cerca de la estación de Goya. ¿Sabe Vd. qué línea tengo que tomar?
Tú	*(Study the map of the underground and tell him how to get there.)*

Conocido	¿Va directo?
Tú	*(Tell him whether it does or not.)*
Conocido	Gracias. Y después tengo que ir a una tienda que está cerca de la estación de Colombia. ¿Podría decirme qué línea tengo que tomar para ir allí desde la estación de Goya?
Tú	*(Study the map and tell him how to get there.)*
Conocido	Muchas gracias. Aún no entiendo el metro de Madrid. ¿Y Vd. qué planes tiene para hoy?
Tú	*(Say you are going to the Prado Museum and then you'll have lunch with a Spanish friend.)*
Conocido	Bueno, espero que nos veamos esta noche. Podríamos salir a tomar una copa, ¿qué le parece?
Vd.	*(Why not! You'll be back at the hotel about 7.00.)*

Note: There is no one way to give the directions above. The **Key to the exercises** provides a model.

3 With the help of the map overleaf, try building up simple dialogues showing different ways of asking and giving directions. Use some of the words and phrases from the introductory dialogues and from the **Key sentences** section.

   a You get out of the metro station at Nuñez de Balboa (No. 9 on the map) and someone stops you to ask the way to the Banco Central (No. 4 on the map).

   b You have been to a museum (No. 1) and as you go out, omeone stops you to ask the way to the Hotel Plaza (No. 6).

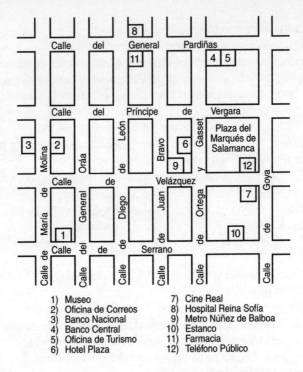

1) Museo
2) Oficina de Correos
3) Banco Nacional
4) Banco Central
5) Oficina de Turismo
6) Hotel Plaza
7) Cine Real
8) Hospital Reina Sofía
9) Metro Núñez de Balboa
10) Estanco
11) Farmacia
12) Teléfono Público

4 Someone who is visiting a South American country received this letter with directions. Complete it with the most appropriate word. Notice it is a formal letter.

Estimada señora Peña:

El objeto de la presente es explicarle brevemente cómo llegar hasta nuestras oficinas desde su hotel.

Al ____ del hotel ____ a la derecha y ____ hasta la estación de metro ____ próxima, que es la estación de Moneda. Allí ____ la línea 1 que va en ____ a Las Condes y ____ en la estación de Pedro de Valdivia que ____ en la Avenida Providencia. A dos ____ de allí, en ____ oriente, está la calle Concepción. Allí ____ a la izquierda y ____ por esa misma calle ____ el final. Nuestra oficina se encuentra justo en la ____ a la mano derecha. Atentamente,

Julián García

5 Christine lives in London and today her friend Antonio is coming to visit her. This is the note Christine sent to Antonio with directions to get to her place. First study the note and make sure you understand the directions. Then do the exercise below.

¡Hola Antonio!

Te envío esta nota para decirte cómo llegar a mi casa desde la estación Victoria. Yo vivo cerca de la estación de metro de Hammersmith. Al llegar a Victoria tienes que buscar la estación de metro y preguntar por la 'District line'. Coge esa línea en dirección a Richmond o a Ealing Broadway y bájate en Hammersmith. Al salir de la estación de Hammersmith cruza la calle por el paso subterráneo hasta Shepherd's Bush Road. Sigue todo recto por Shepherd's Bush Road hasta llegar a un pequeño parque que verás a tu derecha. Ése es Brook Green. Sigue por el lado derecho del parque hasta Luxemburg Gardens, que es donde yo vivo. Es la segunda calle viniendo de Shepherd's Bush Road. Allí tuerces a la derecha. Mi casa tiene el número 25 y está en la esquina.

Espero que no te pierdas.

Un abrazo

Christine

Imagine the directions are for somebody much older than Christine whom she doesn't know well. She would need to use the polite form. Rewrite the note using the polite imperative, making other necessary changes.

6 A tourist phones a travel information centre in Madrid to ask about train travel to Paris. The following are the answers given to him/her. What were his/her questions?
   a El Eurocity a París sale de la estación de Chamartín.
   b Sale de Madrid a las 19:35.
   c Hace cinco paradas.
   d Tarda trece horas en total.

e Llega a París a las 8:30 de la mañana del día siguiente.
f Llega a la estación de Austerlitz.
g Sí, sí, se puede reservar por teléfono con su número de tarjeta.

MADRID	IRÚN	PARÍS

TIPO DE TREN	Estrella	EC
ORIGEN		
MADRID-CHAMARTIN	18.15	19.35
ARANDA DE DUERO	20.38	I
BURGOS	21.48	22.12
MIRANDA DE EBRO	23.16	I
GASTEIZ/VITORIA	23.43	I
DONOSTIA/SAN SEBASTIÁN	1.35	I
IRÚN	2.03	1.23
HENDAYA (Transbordar)	2.08	1.39
HENDAYA	3.36	1.59
HENDAYA	5.59	3.57
PARÍS-AUSTERLITZ	10.30	8.30
DESTINO		

HORARIO DE TRENES

MADRID -PARIS- LISBOA

2 DE JUNIO AL 28 DE SEPTIEMBRE **26**

RENFE

EC *(m) Eurocity*
RENFE (Red Nacional de los Ferrocarriles Españoles) *Spanish railways*

7 ¡A escuchar!

◄) **CD2, TR 6**

En viaje al aeropuerto: Here is some more practice in understanding directions. Listen to the recordings or alternatively read the transcripts, and take notes in English of the directions given by each speaker.

8 Your Spanish-speaking friend wants to take a holiday abroad. What advice would you give him/her to travel cheaply? Read the article which follows and see if you can find suggestions you did not think of.

TRUCOS PARA HACER TURISMO SIN ARRUINARTE

▶ Viaja fuera de las fechas que se consideran temporada alta. Un par de días de diferencia pueden significar precios más baratos.

▶ Elige agencias especializadas en el destino escogido. Además de conocer todas las tarifas, y acceder a precios más baratos, te ayudarán a planear mejor el viaje. Las oficinas de turismo de cada país tienen listados de estas agencias.

▶ Pide los precios por separado si prefieres contratar un paquete turístico (viaje, traslados con guía y alojamiento): a veces la tarifa global oculta que te cobran a precio de oro los transportes del aeropuerto al hotel, y viceversa. En estos casos, ir en taxi te puede salir mucho más económico.

▶ La fórmula más barata suele ser 'avión + alojamiento'. Si eres un viajero experimentado y sabes moverte con soltura en otros países, no dudes en contratarla.

▶ Haz tu reserva con antelación y, para mayor tranquilidad, contrata en la propia agencia un seguro de cancelación del viaje.

▶ Aprovecha las ofertas de última hora si tienes la suerte de no tener que ajustar tus vacaciones a unas fechas determinadas. Pero ten en cuenta que, contratando una semana antes de salir, difícilmente podrás elegir el destino que más te guste.

▶ Si quieres hacer un 'tour' por varios países, siempre te saldrá más económico contratar un viaje organizado que ir por libre.

(Revista Quo)

> **Insight**
>
> **Word formation.** A number of Spanish adjectives are formed from verbs by adding **-ado** (**-ar** verbs) or **-ido** (**-er** and **-ir** verbs) to them. Like all adjectives, these must show agreement in number and gender with the noun they qualify. Examples in the text are **agencias especializadas** *specialized agencies*, **destino escogido** *chosen destination*, **viajero experimentado** *experienced traveller* and **viaje organizado** *organized trip*.

a precio de oro *a fortune*
con antelación *in advance*
por libre *independently*

Now read the article again and:
  a Find all the imperative forms used in the passage and list them with their corresponding infinitive.
  b Find the equivalent of the following words and phrases:

> tener acceso planificar lista separadamente
> el precio total con facilidad/sin dificultad

  c Find the Spanish for:
   high season; a package tour; It can be much more economical for you; Don't hesitate to ...; cancellation insurance; Take advantage of last minute offers; But bear in mind that ...

TEST YOURSELF

1 Fill in the blanks with a verb from the list using the imperative corresponding to usted.

girar – seguir – coger – cruzar – mirar – bajarse

a _____ la línea 2.

b _____ el tablero de llegadas.

c _____ a la izquierda.

d _____ todo recto.

e _____ en la estación de metro Sol.

f _____ al otro lado de la calle.

2 Make the following sentences negative.

a Dáselos.

b Díselo.

c Ponedla aquí.

d Por favor, hazlo.

e Envíasela por email.

f Bájate aquí.

Don't be discouraged if you made a few mistakes. The different forms of the imperative in Spanish require a lot of practice. The most important thing is that you are able to understand people when they give you directions or instructions. But when it comes to being the active participant and you need to tell others what to do, the present tense is just as appropriate and common as the imperative in this context.

8

Servicios y comunicaciones
Services and communications

In this unit you will learn how to:
- *Refer to the recent past*
- *Use indirect speech*
- *Make complaints*
- *Give advice and recommendations*
- *Give instructions*
- *Express certainty and uncertainty*

1 Una reclamación *A complaint*

Pamela Miles ha pedido una transferencia de dinero desde su banco en Inglaterra, pero la transferencia aún no ha llegado.

◆ CD2, TR 7

Pamela	Buenos días.
Empleado	Buenos días. ¿Dígame?
Pamela	He pedido una transferencia de dinero a mi banco en Inglaterra y quisiera saber si ha llegado.
Empleado	¿Su nombre, por favor?
Pamela	Pamela Miles. M-i-l-e-s. Miles.
Empleado	Un momento, por favor. Veré si ha llegado.
(El empleado revisa la documentación y se dirige a la clienta.)	
	Aún no ha llegado. ¿Cuándo la pidió usted?
Pamela	La pedí hace una semana. Me dijeron que la enviarían inmediatamente y que tardaría sólo dos días. ¿Está seguro de que no hay nada?

Empleado	Estoy completamente seguro. He revisado todas las transferencias que han llegado en los últimos días y la suya no está.
Pamela	¡No es posible! ¿Qué puedo hacer? Necesito ese dinero urgentemente.
Empleado	Pues, lo siento mucho, pero lamentablemente yo no puedo hacer nada. ¿Por qué no vuelve Vd. mañana sobre el mediodía para ver si la hemos recibido? Y si no ha llegado, es mejor que llame Vd. por teléfono o escriba a su banco en Inglaterra para saber qué ha ocurrido.
Pamela	Bien, volveré mañana. Adiós.
Empleado	Adiós. Buenos días.

Insight

There are a number of perfect tense forms in the dialogue, all linking the present with the recent past: **He pedido una transferencia** *I've asked for a transfer*, **Quisiera saber si ha llegado** *I'd like to know if it has arrived*, etc. Note also the use of the conditional in indirect speech: **Me dijeron que la enviarían ... y que tardaría sólo dos días** *They told me they'd send it ... and that it would only take two days.*

reclamación *(f) complaint*
estar seguro *to be sure*

QV

Language and comprehension check 1

How are the following expressed in the dialogue?

a It hasn't arrived yet.
b Are you sure?
c I'm completely sure.
d I've checked all transfers.

e tomorrow about midday
f You'd better phone or write to your bank.

2 Una llamada telefónica *A telephone call*

En un locutorio de la Compañía Telefónica, Pamela Miles pregunta a la telefonista cómo llamar a Inglaterra.

CD2, TR 8

Pamela	Por favor, ¿podría decirme qué prefijo tengo que marcar para llamar a Londres?
Telefonista	Primero tiene que marcar el cero siete que es internacional y espere un segundo tono. Después marque el cuarenta y cuatro que corresponde a Inglaterra.
Pamela	Cero siete, cuarenta y cuatro ...
Telefonista	Luego marque el siete uno u ocho uno de Londres*, y el número del abonado.
Pamela	Vale. Gracias.
Telefonista	Pase a la cabina siete.

Insight

The international direct dial access code in Spain is now oo. This must be followed by the country code (44 for the United Kingdom), the area code and the phone number. London numbers are now '020 7' or '020 8'. You should drop the 'o' before the area code.

prefijo *(m) code*
marcar *to dial*
abonado *(m) subscriber*

Insight

Observe the change from **c** to **qu** in the imperative (and present subjunctive) form in verbs ending in **-car: marcar**

130

(*to dial*) – **marque** (*dial*); verbs ending in **-gar** change **g** to **gu**: **llegar** (*to arrive*) – **llegue** (*arrive*); verbs ending in **-ger** or **-gir** change **g** to **j**: **coger** (*to take*) – **coja** (*take*), **corregir** (*to correct*) – **corrija** (*correct*); verbs ending in **-guir** take **g**: **seguir** (*to continue, go on*) – **siga** (*continue, go on*); and the **z** of **-zar** becomes **c**: **cruzar** (*to cross*) – **cruce** (*cross*). These changes allow such verbs to preserve the sound of the infinitive.

Language and comprehension check 2

i List all the verbs from the dialogue which are used to express instructions, e.g. **llame** *call*, and give the infinitive corresponding to each one, e.g. **llamar** *to call*.

ii What words and phrases are used in the dialogue to say the following?

    a What code do I have to dial?
    b dialling tone
    c the subscriber's number
    d telephone booth

3 En correos *At the post office*

Robert Davies, un hombre de negocios, desea enviar unas muestras desde Bilbao a Madrid. En Correos pide información.

Sr. Davies	Buenos días. Quisiera enviar unas muestras a Madrid. ¿Qué servicio me recomienda? Las necesitan con urgencia.	CD2, TR 9
Empleada	Pues, en ese caso le recomiendo que utilice el servicio **postal express**. Es un servicio de urgencia y además tiene la ventaja de que el envío es certificado. Es el servicio más seguro y rápido que tenemos.	
Sr. Davies	¿Y lo llevan a domicilio?	
Empleada	Sí, la entrega se hace a domicilio. Es un poco más caro que los otros servicios, pero en este caso creo que es lo que más le conviene.	
Sr. Davies	Gracias. Este es el paquete que quiero enviar.	

hombre de negocios (m) businessman
muestra (f) sample
envío (m) package, parcel
domicilio (m) home, address
entrega (f) delivery

Insight

Le recomiendo que utilice ... *I recommend you use ...* After **recomendar**, when the subject of the main clause (**Yo le recomiendo ...**) is different from the subject of the subordinate clause (**...que Vd. utilice ...**) you need to use the subjunctive. Here, the verb **utilizar** is in the present subjunctive.

Language and comprehension check 3

Study the dialogue once more and try to memorize some of the key words and phrases used in it, then complete this passage with the most suitable words and phrases. Try not to look at the text while you work through it.

El señor Davies va a ____ porque quiere enviar unas ____ a Madrid. La empleada le ____ que utilice el servicio ____ express, porque este es un servicio de ____ y además tiene la _____ de que el envío es ____. Por otra parte, la ____ se hace a domicilio. Este servicio es más ____ que los otros, pero, en este caso, cree la empleada, es lo que más le ____ al señor Davies.

4 Una queja *A complaint*

John y Helen Brown, dos turistas de vacaciones en España, han alquilado un coche a través de una agencia en Inglaterra. Al llegar al aeropuerto en Palma de Mallorca, John y su mujer se dirigen al mostrador de la agencia de alquiler.

Sr. Brown	Buenas tardes.
Empleada	Buenas tardes.
Sr. Brown	Me llamo John Brown. Hemos alquilado un coche a través de su agencia en Manchester. ¿Dónde podemos recogerlo?
Empleada	¿Cómo me ha dicho que se llama?
Sr. Brown	John Brown. B-r-o-w-n. Brown.
Empleada	Un momento, por favor. … Sí, aquí tenemos una reserva a su nombre, pero es para el día quince y hoy estamos a catorce.
Sr. Brown	¿Cómo? ¿Para el día quince ha dicho Vd.? Mire Vd., yo mismo hice la reserva y no me cabe duda que era para el catorce. ¡Esto es el colmo de la incompetencia! Exijo que me entreguen el coche que pedí inmediatamente.
Empleada	Lo siento, pero en este momento no tenemos ningún coche disponible.
Sra. Brown	¡Es increíble! Es la primera vez que nos sucede algo así.
Empleada	Pues, les aconsejo que hablen con el encargado. A lo mejor él les puede solucionar el problema. Yo no puedo hacer nada. ¿Quieren esperar un momento, por favor? Iré a buscarle.

Insight

Note the use of the present subjunctive in **Exijo que me entreguen el coche …** *I demand that you hand me the car …*, **Les aconsejo que hablen con el encargado …** *I suggest (literally, I advise you …) you speak to the manager.*

recoger *to pick up, collect*
yo mismo *I … myself*
no me cabe duda … *I have no doubt …*
es el colmo (de) … *it's the height of, it's the limit …*
exigir *to demand, insist*
aconsejar *to advise*

Language and comprehension check 4

Answer the following questions in Spanish.

a ¿Dónde alquilaron el coche los Brown?

b ¿Para qué día hicieron la reserva?

c ¿Quién hizo la reserva?

d ¿Para qué día tenía la reserva la agencia en Palma de Mallorca?

e ¿Por qué no puede darle otro coche la empleada?

f ¿Qué les aconseja la empleada?

Key sentences

Referring to the recent past

He pedido una transferencia. — *I've asked for a transfer.*

Aún no ha llegado. — *It hasn't arrived yet.*

Using indirect speech

Me dijeron que la enviarían inmediatamente. — *They told me they would send it immediately.*

Me dijeron que tardaría solo dos días. — *They told me it would take only two days.*

Making complaints

¡No es posible! — *That's impossible!*

¡Es increíble! — *It's incredible!*

¡Esto es el colmo de la incompetencia! — *This is the height of inefficiency!*

Other ways of making complaints	
Quiero hacer una reclamación.	*I want to make a complaint.*
Tengo una queja.	*I have a complaint.*
Quisiera quejarme de ...	*I'd like to complain about ...*

Giving advice and recommendations

Es mejor que llame Vd. por teléfono a su banco.
You'd better telephone your bank.

Le recomiendo que utilice el servicio postal express.
I recommend you use the postal express service.

The verbs most frequently used to give advice and recommendations are **aconsejar** to *advise*, **recomendar** to *recommend*, **sugerir** to *suggest*.

Giving instructions

Primero tiene que marcar el 00. *First you have to dial 00.*
Espere un segundo tono. *Wait for a second dialling tone.*

Insight

In writing, instructions and procedures are often expressed with the infinitive, e.g. **levantar el auricular** *lift up the receiver*, **depositar una moneda de … euros** *insert a coin of … euros.*

Expressing certainty and uncertainty

¿Está seguro/a de que no hay nada?
Are you sure there is nothing?

Estoy (completamente) seguro/a. *I'm (absolutely) sure.*

Other ways of expressing certainty and uncertainty	
Me parece que …	*I think (that) …*
Creo que …	*I think (that) …*
No creo que … (plus the subjunctive)	*I don't think (that) …*

Grammar

1 The perfect tense

This is used to refer to the recent past and to events which have happened in a period of time which includes the present.

Sentences such as:

He pedido una transferencia.   *I have asked for a transfer.*
Hemos alquilado un coche.   *We have hired a car.*

refer to the recent past and are normally expressed in Spanish in the perfect tense.

Events which have happened in a period of time which includes the present, e.g. **hoy** *today*, **esta mañana** *this morning*, **esta semana** *this week* **todavía**, **aún** *still, yet*, **ya** *already*, etc., are also normally expressed in the perfect tense, as in:

Hoy he hablado con él.   *Today I've spoken to him.*
Aún no ha llegado.   *It hasn't arrived yet.*

- **a** In Latin America and in the North-Western regions of Spain, notably Galicia and Asturias, the preterite tense, e.g. **Hoy hablé con él** *Today I spoke to him*, is much more common than the perfect tense.
- **b** The Spanish perfect tense often translates into English as simple past, e.g. **Lo he llamado hace un rato.** *I phoned him a while ago.*

Formation

To form the perfect tense you use the present tense of **haber** *to have* followed by a past participle which does not change. The past participle of -**ar** verbs ends in -**ado** while -**er** and -**ir** verbs form the past participle by adding -**ido** to the stem. Here are two verbs, **llegar** *to arrive*, and **pedir** *to ask for* in the perfect tense.

he llegado	*I have arrived*
has llegado	*you have arrived (familiar)*
ha llegado	*he/she/it has arrived, you have arrived*
hemos llegado	*we have arrived*
habéis llegado	*you have arrived (familiar)*
han llegado	*they/you have arrived*

he pedido	*I have asked (for)*
has pedido	*you have asked (for) (familiar)*
ha pedido	*he/she/it has asked (for), you have asked (for)*
hemos pedido	*we have asked (for)*
habéis pedido	*you have asked (for) (familiar)*
han pedido	*they/you have asked (for)*

2 The conditional tense in indirect speech

Compare these sentences:

La enviaremos inmediatamente.	*We'll send it immediately.*
Me han dicho/Dicen que la enviarán inmediatamente.	*They've told me/They say they will send it immediately.*
Me dijeron que la enviarían inmediatamente.	*They told me (that) they would send it immediately.*

The first sentence is a direct statement while the other two are indirect ones. Verbs like **decir** *to say*, **prometer** *to promise*, and **asegurar** *to assure*, are often used in indirect statements. As in English, there is no fixed way in which to make an indirect statement, but *normally*, if the direct statement is in the future tense, as above, the indirect one can start with a verb in the present, the perfect or the preterite tense. With the first two, the verb in the second clause will *not* normally change tense, but if the indirect statement is introduced by the preterite, the second verb will be in the conditional tense.

Tardará sólo dos días.	*It will only take two days.*
Me dijeron que tardaría solo dos días.	*They told me it would only take two days.*
Os devolveré el dinero la semana que viene.	*I'll return the money to you next week.*
Nos prometió que nos devolvería el dinero la semana que viene.	*He/she promised us to return the money to us next week.*

Note the similarity between Spanish and English when reporting a direct statement that refers to the past:

La enviamos ayer. *We sent it yesterday.*
Dicen que la enviaron ayer. *They say they sent it yesterday.*
Me dijeron que la habían *They told me they had sent*
  enviado ayer. *it yesterday.*

Formation of the conditional tense

Like the future tense, the conditional is formed with the infinitive, to which the endings are added. The endings of the three conjugations are the same as those of the imperfect tense of -**er** and -**ir** verbs (see Unit 5). Here is the conditional tense of a regular verb, **enviar** *to send*.

enviaría	*I would send*
enviarías	*you would send (familiar)*
enviaría	*he/she/you would send*
enviaríamos	*we would send*
enviaríais	*you would send (familiar)*
enviarían	*they/you would send*

Note that -**er** and -**ir** verbs have the same endings as -**ar** verbs.

Practice

1 Complete this note with the correct form of the perfect tense of the verb shown:

Antonio:

Esta mañana te (llamar) Ricardo. Dice que él y su mujer (llegar) hoy a Madrid y que (reservar) una habitación en el Hotel El Escorial. Volverá a llamar esta tarde. Yo (ir) a Correos a echar unas cartas, pero espero volver antes de las 2.00. Te (dejar) la comida en la nevera. No te olvides de que mi madre nos (invitar) a cenar esta noche.

Mari Carmen

2 Make indirect statements using the introductory phrases given:

   a **La transferencia llegará mañana.** El empleado me dijo que ...

   b **Tardará una semana.** Ella me aseguró que ...

   c **La carta estará allí el lunes.** En Correos me dijeron que ...

   d **Les entregaremos el coche esta tarde.** En la agencia nos prometieron que ...

   e **Le repararemos el coche ahora mismo.** El mecánico me prometió que ...

   f **Te llamaré por teléfono esta noche.** Alfonso me dijo que ...

3 You arrive in a hotel in a Spanish-speaking country and you are told that there is no record of your booking and that there are no rooms available. How would you say the following in Spanish?

   a I made the reservation myself. (Use the perfect tense.)

   b I have no doubt it was for today.

   c Are you sure there isn't any reservation in my name?

   d This is the height of inefficiency!

   e This is incredible!

   f I demand that you give us a room immediately.

   g Well, I'd like to make a complaint.

   h It's the first time something like this has happened to us. (Use the present tense for the second verb.)

4 Rosa had many reasons to complain about the apartment she rented. Can you match the complaints with the drawings overleaf?

   a Uno de los cristales está roto.

   b La nevera no funciona.

   c Hay una gotera en el techo.

   d El vecino hace mucho ruido.

   e La bañera está atascada.

   f Uno de los grifos está estropeado.

5 A Spanish-speaking friend is visiting you at home and you
have gone out together for the day. Your friend wants to
telephone his/her parents in Barcelona from a public phone
box. He/she has never used a public telephone in your country.
Tell him/her what to do using the phrases in the box. The code
for Barcelona from the United Kingdom is oo 3493.

> **Amigo(a)** Dime, ¿qué tengo que hacer para llamar a Barcelona
> desde un teléfono público?
>
> **Tú** ___ ___ ___ ___ ___ ___ ___

levantar/descolgar el auricular *to pick up the receiver*
la ranura *slot*
poner monedas de ... *insert coins of ...*

Note that **descolgar** changes the **o** of the stem (**descolg-**) into **ue**.

6 ¡A escuchar!

🔊 **CD2, TR 11**

a **¡Dígalo por la PR!** This is the title of a public announcement from *Radio la Romántica*, XHPR, in Veracruz, Mexico. Listen to the announcement, or alternatively, read the transcript of the text, and then explain:

   i What kind of service does *Radio la Romántica* offer its listeners?

   ii How does this service operate?

b **¡Quejas y más quejas!** Some people like to complain! Listen to these complaints, or alternatively read the transcript, and then say where each of the complaints takes place and what they are about.

7 Have you ever written a letter of complaint to a newspaper or magazine? Here are two letters sent by people in Chile and Spain. What are they complaining about? Read the letters and find out and then write a brief summary of their content in Spanish.

Sobreventa en línea aérea

Hace unos días mi mujer y yo íbamos a viajar a Londres vía Nueva York, pero al presentarnos en el mesón de Aerosur, nos informaron que no podríamos viajar, ya que el vuelo estaba completo, hecho insólito, ya que habíamos hecho y pagado nuestras reservas hacía un mes.

Nos quejamos al encargado de la línea aérea en el aeropuerto, pero sin éxito. Después de esperar más de dos horas, este prometió enviarnos en un vuelo que salía al día siguiente.

Regresamos a nuestra casa, y al otro día, antes de iniciar nuestro viaje al aeropuerto, llamamos por teléfono a la línea aérea para reconfirmar nuestras reservas. Grande fue nuestra sorpresa e indignación al enterarnos de que sólo estaba confirmado el vuelo hasta Nueva York, y que en el vuelo

(Contd)

---

de conexión de Nueva York a Londres estábamos en lista de espera. ¡No podíamos creerlo! Nunca nos había sucedido una cosa así, por lo que decidimos anular nuestras reservas y viajar en otra empresa.

La sobreventa, según nos hemos enterado, es una práctica habitual en Aerosur. Ello nos causó grandes molestias y pérdida de tiempo y dinero. Aparte de eso, el trato que recibimos por parte del personal de la línea aérea fue descortés y su actuación incompetente. No volveremos a utilizar sus servicios.

Juan Carlos Reyes,
Santiago de Chile

Insight

Word order. The position of **grande** and **nunca** in initial position in the following sentences serves to highlight their meanings: **Grande fue nuestra sorpresa, Nunca nos había sucedido.** More usually, you would say **Nuestra sorpresa fue grande, No nos había sucedido nunca.**

El inglés en Ibiza

Es el colmo que en España no nos permitan leer en nuestro propio idioma.

Este verano pasé mis vacaciones en un hotel en Ibiza, y todas la indicaciones estaban en inglés. Me pareció increíble. Me dio la impresión de que estaba en Inglaterra o en Estados Unidos en lugar de España. Estoy segura de que esto no sucede en otros países. Al menos en mis viajes nunca lo había experimentado. Sentí que era una suerte de discriminación ejercida contra los españoles en su propio país. ¿Dónde están las autoridades que no hacen nada al respecto? Debería haber una ley que prohibiera situaciones como ésta. Defendamos nuestra lengua.

María de la Luz García, Madrid

Insight

The concern expressed by the person who wrote this letter reflects the feelings of many Spanish people who live in or travel to popular tourist destinations. Like some hotels, Spanish restaurants often have signs or list their menus in other languages, with waiters often speaking to customers in English.

Read the letters again and find the expressions which mean the following:

- **a** puesto que
- **b** raro, extraño
- **c** presentamos una queja
- **d** empezar, comenzar
- **e** rabia, ira
- **f** poco cortés, poco amable
- **g** nunca me había pasado
- **h** una especie de

sobreventa *(f) overbooking*
mesón *(m) counter*
enterarse *to find out*
ley *(f) law*

TEST YOURSELF

1 Change the verbs in brackets into an appropriate form. For some of the sentences there is more than one possibility.

   a Marta aún no (*volver*). Dijo que (*venir*) sobre las seis.

   b Le he (*escribir*) un email a Pablo y le he (*aconsejar*) que lo (*hacer*) lo antes posible.

   c Me han (*recomendar*) que (*contratar*) un seguro de viaje, y así lo he (*hacer*).

   d – Es mejor que Vd. mismo se lo (*decir*).
      – Se lo he (*decir*) hace un momento.

   e Exijo que Vds. me (*entregar*) el dinero ahora mismo. Vds. me dijeron que lo (*hacer*).

   f Para llamar a Inglaterra (*marcar*) Vd. el oo 44. ¿Me ha (*entender*)?

2 Fill in the blanks with a suitable word from the list:
seguro, encargado, tono, cabina, reserva, prefijo, entrega, reclamación, ventaja

   a ¿Cuál es el ____ para llamar a Nueva York?

   b Espera el ____ de marcar y después marcas el oo.

   c El servicio postal express es un servicio ____ y la ____ se hace a domicilio. Esa es una gran ____.

   d – ¿Tiene Vd. una ____ disponible? Quería llamar a Irlanda.
      – Sí, pase Vd. a la seis, esa está libre.

   e Estoy muy descontento con la atención y quiero hacer una ____. ¿Me puede poner con el ____, por favor?

   f La ____ está a mi nombre. Yo mismo la he hecho.

Test 1 focuses on the use of the perfect tense, the conditional in indirect speech and the subjunctive after certain verbs. In Test 2 the main focus is on vocabulary. Check your answers in the key to Test yourself and go on to the next unit if most of your answers were correct. Don't be discouraged if you made a few mistakes, as the important thing is that you are able to communicate.

9

Usted, el consumidor
You, the consumer

In this unit you will learn how to:
- *Ask for something in a shop and enquire about forms of payment*
- *Describe things*
- *Express open and remote conditions*
- *Express obligation and needs*
- *Express surprise*

1 En una tienda de artículos de piel *In a leather shop*

Una señora entra en una tienda de artículos de piel para comprar un regalo para su hija.

Clienta	Buenas tardes. Quisiera comprar un bolso. Es para regalo.
Dependienta	¿Es para una persona joven?
Clienta	Sí, es para mi hija que está de cumpleaños.
Dependienta	¿Cuánto desea gastar aproximadamente?
Clienta	Unos cien euros.
Dependienta	Pues, tenemos estos que están de oferta y están muy bien de precio. Los tenemos a ochenta y cinco euros. Este marrón, por ejemplo, es muy bonito y es de muy buena calidad. Mire Vd.
	(Contd)

CD2, TR 12

Clienta	Sí, es precioso. Pero no creo que a mi hija le guste ese color. Prefiero llevar uno blanco. Aquel, por ejemplo, ¿vale lo mismo?
Dependienta	Sí, tiene el mismo precio. Y si no le gusta puede cambiarlo, pero deberá traer la factura.
Clienta	De acuerdo. Me lo quedo.
Dependienta	¿Va a pagar en efectivo?
Clienta	No, ¿puedo pagar con tarjeta de crédito?
Dependienta	Sí, sí, claro.
Clienta	¿Me lo puede envolver para regalo, por favor?
Dependienta	Sí, por supuesto.

Insight

One of the main grammatical points in this unit is conditional sentences. Note the following example in Dialogue 1: **Si no le gusta, puede cambiarlo** *If you don't like it, you can change it.* For an explanation of this see the Grammar section.

piel (f) *leather*
bolso (m) *handbag*
gastar *to spend*

Language and comprehension check 1

There are a number of words and phrases related to shopping in this dialogue. Can you find the Spanish for the following?

 a It's for a present.
 b They are on offer.
 c You can change it.
 d You must bring the receipt.
 e I'll take it.
 f To pay cash
 g to pay with a credit card
 h Can you wrap it up for me?

Can you think of other expressions related to the theme of shopping?

146

2 Describiendo un coche *Describing a car*

Javier y su amiga Trini hablan de coches.

● CD2, TR 13

Javier	¿Sabes que Cristóbal va a vender su coche?
Trini	¿De veras? Es un coche estupendo y está casi nuevo. ¿Por qué lo piensa vender?
Javier	Se ha ganado una beca para Estados Unidos y necesita el dinero.
Trini	¡No me digas! ¿Y sabes tú cuánto pide por él?
Javier	Tres mil euros.
Trini	¡Hombre! ¡Y con las ganas que tengo yo de tener un coche! Si tuviera dinero se lo compraría.

Insight

Si tuviera dinero, se lo compraría *If I had money I'd buy it* is also a conditional sentence, but different from the one you encountered in Dialogue 1. See the Grammar section for an explanation of this.

QUICK VOCAB

¿de veras? *really?*
beca *(f) scholarship*
¡no me digas! *you don't say!*
¿cuánto pide por él? *how much is he asking for it?*
tener ganas *to want, be longing to*

Language and comprehension check 2
¿Verdadero o falso?

a Cristóbal ha vendido su coche.
b Critóbal necesita el dinero para obtener una beca.
c El coche está bien de precio.
d Trini piensa comprar el coche de Javier.

3 En un taller de reparaciones *In a repair shop*

Un cliente lleva su televisor a un taller de reparaciones.

CD2, TR 14

Cliente	Buenas tardes. ¿Podría repararme este televisor?
Empleado	¿Qué le pasa?
Cliente	La imagen no se ve muy bien.
Empleado	Bien, pero habrá que revisarlo primero y después le daré un presupuesto por la reparación. Y si Vd. está conforme haremos el trabajo.
Cliente	De acuerdo. ¿A qué hora puedo volver?
Empleado	Vuelva Vd. esta tarde después de las seis.

Insight

Habrá que revisarlo *We'll have to check it* is an impersonal sentence expressing need, and using the verb **haber** *to have*, here in the future tense. You may be familiar with the present tense form **hay que**: **Hay que repararlo** *We need to repair it.*

QUICK VOCAB

taller de reparaciones *(m)* repair shop
imagen *(f)* picture (TV)
presupuesto *(m)* estimate
estar conforme to be in agreement

Language and comprehension check 3
Answer the following questions in Spanish.
  a What's the trouble with the television set?
  b What's the employee going to do before repairing it?
  c What is the condition for carrying out the work?

Key sentences

Asking for something in a shop and enquiring about forms of payment

Quisiera comprar un bolso.	*I'd like to buy a handbag.*
¿Va a pagar en efectivo?	*Are you going to pay cash?*
¿Puedo pagar con tarjeta de crédito?	*May I pay with a credit card?*

Describing things

Es muy bonito y es de muy buena calidad.	*It is very nice and the quality is very good.*
Es un coche estupendo y está casi nuevo.	*It is an excellent car and it is almost new.*

Expressing open and remote conditions

Si no le gusta puede cambiarlo (open condition).	*If you don't like it you can change it.*
Si tuviera dinero se lo compraría (remote condition).	*If I had money I would buy it from him.*

Expressing obligation and needs

Deberá traer la factura.	*You'll have to bring the receipt.*
Habrá que revisarlo.	*It will be necessary to check it.*

Expressing surprise

¿De veras?	*Really?*
¡No me digas!	*You don't say!*
¡Hombre!	*Good heavens!, I never!*

....

Insight

The word **¡Hombre!** used as an exclamation is extremely common in most social contexts in Peninsular Spanish and it has a number of meanings depending on the context: other than those above it can also be used to mean *Of course!, You bet!, (Oh) come on!, Oh please!, Hey!, Dear oh dear!,* etc.

....

Grammar

1 Conditional sentences

Open conditions
These are sentences in which the condition may or may not be
fulfilled, as in:

Si Vd. está conforme, haremos el *If you are in agreement we shall*
trabajo. *do the job.*

The combination of tenses used in these sentences is the same as it
is in English, e.g. present tense plus future tense, as in the previous
sentence, present tense plus present tense, as in:

Si llueve, es mejor no ir. *If it rains it is better not to go.*

Notice that **si** is followed by a verb in the indicative, not the
subjunctive.

Remote conditions
Most sentences of this type express a condition which is contrary
to fact, that is, which may not be fulfilled, as in:

Si tuviera dinero, se lo compraría. *If I had money I would buy it*
from him.

The verb which follows **si** must be in the imperfect subjunctive while the verb in the second clause is normally in the conditional (for the conditional tense see Unit 8).

This same construction is sometimes used to express conditions which may be fulfilled (as in open conditions). Consider, for example:

Si fueras ahora, la verías.   *If you went now, you would see her.*

which is practically equivalent to:

Si vas ahora, la verás.   *If you go now, you will see her.*

2 Imperfect subjunctive tense

Formation
The imperfect subjunctive, used in remote conditions, can be formed in two ways. The first is directly derived from the third person plural of the preterite (see Unit 4), for example:

Infinitive	Preterite	Imperfect subjunctive (1st and 3rd person sing)
comprar *to buy*	compr**aron**	compr**ara**
vender *to sell*	vend**ieron**	vend**iera**
escribir *to write*	escrib**ieron**	escrib**iera**

The same derivation occurs with irregular and stem-changing verbs:

tener *to have*	tuvier**on**	tuvier**a**
ser/ir *to be/go*	fuer**on**	fuer**a**
querer *to want*	quisier**on**	quisier**a**

Verbs of the second and third conjugation (**-er** and **-ir**) form the imperfect subjunctive in the same way. First conjugation verbs (**-ar**) have a different set of endings. Here are two examples:

comprar:	(sing)	comprara compraras comprara
	(pl)	compráramos comprarais compraran
vender:	(sing)	vendiera vendieras vendiera
	(pl)	vendiéramos vendierais vendieran

The imperfect subjunctive has a second set of endings which appear to be less frequent than the first. The two forms are generally interchangeable. Again, -er and -ir verbs share the same endings.

comprar:	(sing)	comprase comprases comprase
	(pl)	comprásemos compraseis comprasen
vender:	(sing)	vendiese vendieses vendiese
	(pl)	vendiésemos vendieseis vendiesen

Sequence of tenses with the imperfect subjunctive

Other than in remote conditions such as the above, the imperfect subjunctive normally occurs in sentences which carry a main clause in the:

a Imperfect:

Él *quería* **que yo lo** *comprara*.   He wanted me to buy it.

b Preterite:

Ella me *pidió* **que lo** *cambiara*.   She asked me to change it.

c Pluperfect:

Yo le *había pedido* **que me** *diera* **un presupuesto.**   I had asked him to give me an estimate.

d Conditional:

Me *gustaría* **que lo** *hicieras*.   I'd like you to do it.

e Perfect conditional:

Yo habría preferido que lo *hicieras*.   I'd have preferred you to do it.

3 Verbs which express obligation and needs

Tener que *to have to*

Tendré que venderlo.	*I will have to sell it.*

Deber *to have to, must*

Deberá traer la factura.	*You'll have to bring the receipt.*

Ser necesario *to be necessary*

¿Crees que es necesario?	*Do you think it is necessary?*
No es necesario esperar.	*We don't need to wait.*
No es necesario que esperes.	*You don't need to wait.*

Necesitar *(to need)*

Necesito un coche.	*I need a car.*
Necesito comprar un regalo.	*I need to buy a present.*
Necesito que me ayudes.	*I need you to help me.*

Hacer falta *to be necessary*

¿Hace falta tener visado?	*Does one need a visa?*
No hace falta que me lo digas.	*You don't need to tell me.*

Note again the use of the subjunctive in the subordinate clause in
the second example.

Hay que *it is necessary – one has to, you/we have to*

Hay que hacerlo.	*One has to do it.*

Hay derives from **haber** (auxiliary verb *to have*), and it can be used
in tenses other than the present tense.

Habrá que revisarlo.	*It will be necessary to check it.*
Hubo que repararlo.	*It was necessary to repair it.*
Habría que venderlo.	*It would be necessary to sell it.*

Practice

1 Follow the example and express remote conditions.
   Ejemplo: No iré porque no tengo dinero.
              Si tuviera dinero, iría.
   a No viajaré a España porque no tengo vacaciones.
   b No compraré el coche porque está en mal estado.
   c No lo haremos reparar porque no merece la pena.
   d No se quedarán porque tienen que volver al trabajo.
   e No los recibiré porque estoy ocupado.
   f Ella no le entiende porque él no habla bien español.

2 Say what you have or need to do. Follow the example.

Ejemplo: ¿Qué necesitas comprar? (**un regalo**)
   Necesito comprar un regalo.

   a ¿Qué tuviste que hacer? (**vender el piso**)
   b ¿Qué tenías que decirme? (**algo importante**)
   c ¿Qué hay que hacer? (**nada**)
   d ¿Qué debes llevar? (**el pasaporte**)
   e ¿Qué necesitabas comprar? (**una maleta**)
   f ¿Qué habrá que traer? (**algo para beber**)

3 You go into a shop to buy yourself a pair of trousers. Play the part of the customer in this conversation with the shop assistant.

Dependiente(a) ¿En qué puedo servirle?

   a Tú   *I'd like to buy some trousers. Have you got any on offer? I don't want to spend too much.*

Dependiente(a) Sí, tenemos dos o tres modelos de oferta. Son para usted, ¿verdad?

   b Tú   *Yes, they are for me. I'm looking for something of good quality.*
   Dependiente(a)   Tenemos estos de algodón, son de muy buena calidad y están de moda. ¿Qué le parecen?

   c Tú   *Yes, they are nice. I like them very much. Have you got them in black?*

Dependiente(a) Sí, y también en marrón y en gris. ¿Qué talla tiene Vd.?

   d Tú   *I'm size 46. Have you got any in that size?*

Dependiente(a) Sí, este es el último pantalón que nos queda en esa talla.

e Tú I'd like to try them on. Where's the fitting room?

Dependiente(a) Está al fondo a la derecha.

(Coming back to the sales person)

f Tú They fit very well. How much are they?

Dependiente(a) Cuestan cuarenta y ocho euros.

g Tú They are a little expensive, but I like them. I'll take them. Do you accept credit cards? I haven't got any cash.

Dependiente(a) Sí, por supuesto.

> **pantalón/pantalones** *(m sing/pl) trousers*
> **probarse** *to try on*
> **quedar bien** *to fit*

....

Insight

Quedar has a number of meanings: **Me/Nos queda uno/ quedan dos** *I/We have one/two left;* **Me queda grande** *It's too big for me;* **Estos zapatos me quedan bien** *These shoes fit (me) well;* **¿Dónde queda Andorra? Queda entre España y Francia** *Where's Andorra? It's between Spain and France;* **He quedado con Paco** *I've agreed to meet Paco.*

....

4 A friend of yours, who has just started learning Spanish, has asked you to translate the postcard below which she received from someone in Venezuela.

Querida Pat:

¡Qué sorpresa recibir carta tuya otra vez! Me alegro de que estés bien y espero que te vaya estupendamente en tus exámenes finales.

Te agradezco mucho tu invitación para este verano, pero desgraciadamente no tengo suficiente dinero para viajar. Si pudiera, naturalmente que iría a verte. ¡No sabes cómo me gustaría! El próximo año quizás, pero tendré que trabajar mucho para ahorrar dinero ya que el viaje es muy caro. Tú también tendrás que venir a Venezuela algún día. No hace falta que te invite formalmente. Te estaré esperando.

Un abrazo
Raúl

5 ¿Qué harías si te ganaras la lotería?

Ana, Luis, and Raquel each commented on what they would do or buy if they won a big prize in the lottery. Read their comments and match the names with the drawings.

Ana, 18 años

Si me ganara la lotería, lo primero que haría sería pagar todas mis deudas y las de mis padres con quienes vivo actualmente. También me compraría una gran casa en la playa y la amueblaría lujosamente y, además, compraría un yate, en el que mi novio y yo daríamos la vuelta al mundo. Al regresar nos casaríamos. Si todavía me quedara dinero, lo invertiría muy bien y viviríamos holgadamente. Pero no dejaría mi trabajo, ya que me gusta lo que hago ...

Luis, 48 años

Si a mí me tocara la lotería, mi vida cambiaría completamente. No sé si sería más feliz o no, pero sí sé que resolvería mis actuales problemas económicos. Para empezar, renunciaría a mi puesto de administrativo en la empresa donde trabajo e instalaría mi propia empresa, y la administraría personalmente. Ya no tendría un jefe, ni tendría que trabajar ocho horas diarias para ganar un sueldo miserable.

En lo personal, me mudaría con mi familia al mejor barrio de la ciudad. Mi mujer y yo tendríamos cada uno su propio coche, y enviaríamos a nuestro hijo al mejor de los colegios. En verano tomaríamos unas largas vacaciones en la playa y en invierno nos iríamos a esquiar a la montaña. Y todavía nos quedaría suficiente dinero para invertir en la bolsa y vivir bien el resto de nuestras vidas ...

Raquel, 32 años

Soy profesora y, si tuviera la suerte de ganar la lotería, haría una gran fiesta para celebrar. No dudaría en dejar mi actividad actual y dedicarme totalmente a escribir novelas, que es lo que siempre he soñado. Ayudaría también a mi familia y a la gente más necesitada de mi pueblo, especialmente a los niños y a los ancianos. Donaría una gran cantidad de dinero al colegio donde trabajo y donde yo misma hice mis estudios. No malgastaría el dinero, pero sí lo disfrutaría mucho ...

Who said the following? Read the comments again and match the sentences below with the appropriate names.

i Dejaría mi trabajo.
 ii No renunciaría a mi puesto.
iii Yo mismo estaría a cargo de ella.
 iv Es lo que he querido hacer toda mi vida.
  v Antes que nada, pagaría todo lo que debo.

Y tú, ¿qué harías si te tocara la lotería?

6 ¡A escuchar!

◀) **CD2, TR 15**

¿Dónde compra Vd.? Where do people in your country normally buy their food: in traditional corner shops, or in small or large supermarkets? Compare their habits with those of Spanish people in the table below, then listen to or read some interviews conducted by a journalist on the subject of shopping.

TIENDAS DONDE LOS ESPAÑOLES SUELEN COMPRAR SUS ALIMENTOS (%)	
Hipermercados	37
Pequeños supermercados	32
Grandes supermercados	14
Tiendas tradicionales	9
Pequeños autoservicios	8

a The first interview is with Rosario Santos, a housewife. As you listen to or read the transcript, answer the questions which follow. Here are some key words.

grandes almacenes *(m pl) department stores*
comestibles *(m pl) foodstuff*
vecino/a *(m f) neighbour*
cotillear *to gossip*

   i ¿En qué ocasiones compra en la tienda de su barrio?
   ii ¿Cuándo compra en grandes almacenes? ¿Por qué?
  iii Y los comestibles, ¿dónde los suele comprar?

b The second interview is with Ana Belmar, a student. Listen to what she has to say, or alternatively, read the transcript, and as you do so, say whether the following statements are **verdaderos o falsos**. Learn first some of the key words.

rebajas *(f pl) sale*
aprovechar *to take advantage*
tratándose de ... *if it is to do with ...*
a la moda *fashionably*

   i Ana prefiere comprar en pequeñas tiendas porque es más barato.
   ii Hoy ha comprado en unos grandes almacenes porque hay ofertas especiales.
  iii Ana trabaja para comprar su ropa.

c The third interview is with Andrés Calle, an office clerk from South America. Listen to the complete conversation, or read the transcript. This key vocabulary will help you to understand it:

lo cierto es ... *the truth is ...*
encargarse de *to be responsible for*
acompañar *to accompany*

i Listen again, if you have the recording, and as you do so, complete the passage below with the missing words. Alternatively, read the interview once more and then, without looking at the text, try completing the passage below with the words which are missing.

Pues, lo cierto es ____ prefiero ir a una ____ más pequeña donde el ____ sea más directo, más ____. Pero eso sólo lo ____ hacer el fin de ____. Yo soy administrativo y ____ por la mañana y ____ la tarde y cuando ____ las tiendas ya están _____. Por eso vengo a ____ aquí, pues está abierto ____ mediodía. Aprovecho la ____ de la comida para ____ lo que necesito.

ii Listen again to (or read) the answer given by Andrés Calle to the second question: **¿Y la compra de comestibles, la hace Vd. también?** Summarize his answer in English.

7 A friend of yours who doesn't know any Spanish is thinking of renting an apartment in Spain for the summer. Your friend has been sent the information on consumer protection (in the box overleaf) by a Spanish acquaintance and he/she has asked you to translate it for him/her. Familiarize yourself with the new vocabulary before you do the translation in writing.

combustible (m) fuel (gas)
recogida de basuras (f) rubbish collection
señal (f) deposit
importe (m) cost, value
antelación (f) time in advance
aviso (m) notice

QUICK VOCAB

APARTAMENTOS TURÍSTICOS

En el precio del alojamiento van incluidos los siguientes servicios: agua, luz y combustible; recogida de basuras y servicios comunes.

En el momento de realizar la reserva se puede exigir, en concepto de señal, una cantidad que va del 15 al 40% del importe total que corresponda al precio contratado.

Si el usuario decide anular la reserva tiene derecho a una devolución de la señal con unas penalizaciones que van del 5 al 50%, según la antelación del aviso. Si la anulación se efectúa con menos de 7 días de antelación no tendrá derecho a devolución alguna.

ESTE VERANO VIAJA INFORMADO

(Oficina Municipal de Información al Consumidor, Ayuntamiento de Toledo)

8 Here is some advice given by a consumer magazine to its readers, in which some key words are missing. Fill in the gaps with an appropriate word from the following list:

precio	pena	bolsillo	lista	vergüenza	compra	tentación
		estantes	vacío	gastos		

Cómo mantener el consumo bajo control

a Antes de salir a comprar, lo mejor es hacer una ____ de lo que necesitas y un presupuesto aproximado.

b No compres alimentos con el estómago ____. Caerías fácilmente en la tentación de adquirir más de lo necesario.

c Si en un gran almacén ves un artículo que no tenías previsto comprar y parece interesarte, trata de no ceder a la primera ____ y déjalo para la próxima vez. Sólo así sabrás si merece la pena comprarlo.

d Muchas veces compramos cosas que no nos sirven para nada, sólo porque están en oferta. Piensa que una oportunidad sólo es real si se trata de un artículo que realmente necesitas y cuyo ____ es inferior al que suele tener habitualmente.

e Antes de pasar por el cajero de la tienda, compara el dinero que has gastado con el que habías previsto. Si excede, devuelve a los ____ los artículos menos necesarios.

f No sientas ningún tipo de ____ por salir de un establecimiento sin haber realizado compra alguna.

g Algunos expertos recomiendan, para luchar contra la adicción al crédito, romper la tarjeta o envolverla con el tícket de la última compra en la que se gastase mucho. Otro remedio es visualizar el dinero saliendo de tu ____ y llegando a las manos del dependiente cuando pagues con la tarjeta.

h Si tienes problema con el control de ____, divide con tu pareja el dinero disponible. De este modo evitarás llegar a un conflicto familiar.

(Revista Quo)

Read the text again and find the words and phrases which mean the following.
  i Cantidad de dinero calculado para hacer frente a ciertos gastos.
  ii Comidas o bebidas necesarias para subsistir.
  iii Establecimiento comercial dividido en departamentos.
  iv A precio rebajado.
  v La persona que recibe el dinero en una tienda.
  vi Persona encargada de atender a los clientes en una tienda.
  vii El marido o la mujer, o la persona con la que tienes una relación sentimental.

presupuesto *(m) budget*
ceder *to give in, yield*
cajero/a *(m/f) cashier*
estante *(m) shelf*
romper *to tear up, break*
pareja *(f) partner*

TEST YOURSELF

1 Complete the sentences on the left with an appropriate phrase on the right.

a	Si me invitaran	**1**	escogería este
b	Si supiera dónde está	**2**	puede cambiarlo
c	Si mereciera la pena	**3**	te lo diría
d	Si tuviera que elegir	**4**	te acompañaría
e	Si no le queda bien	**5**	lo haría reparar
f	Si tuviese tiempo	**6**	claro que aceptaría

2 Match each sentence on the left with a suitable phrase on the right.

a	La chaqueta te ha quedado grande.	**1**	Tengo que pagar con tarjeta (de crédito).
b	El lector de DVD no funciona.	**2**	Esto hay que celebrarlo con unas copas.
c	A mi hija no le ha gustado el regalo.	**3**	Tendrás que cambiarla por otra talla.
d	No tengo efectivo.	**4**	Habrá que mudarse.
e	¡Qué sorpresa y qué alegría que hayáis venido!	**5**	Tenemos que llevarlo al taller (de reparaciones).
f	El alquiler es demasiado alto para nosotros.	**6**	Tendremos que comprarle otra cosa.

Test 1 focuses on conditional sentences, while Test 2 assesses vocabulary and some key expressions. Check your answers in the Key to Test yourself before you go on to the next unit, or go back to the Key sentences or the Grammar section if you feel you need to revise some of the new language. Having reached so far in the course is a sign of good progress, but it is a good idea to go back to those bits that give you more trouble.

10

Estar en forma
Keeping fit and well

In this unit you will learn how to:
- *Describe minor ailments*
- *Refer to an action in progress*
- *Express indirect suggestions and commands*

1 En el consultorio *In the surgery*

A causa de un pequeño accidente, Carlos, un jugador de tenis,
consulta a un médico.

CD2, TR 16

Paciente	Buenas tardes. Tengo hora con la doctora Martínez.
Recepcionista	¿Su nombre, por favor?
Paciente	Carlos González.
Recepcionista	Bien …, tendrá que esperar un momento. La doctora está atendiendo a un paciente.
(Después de algunos minutos.)	Pase, por favor.
Paciente	Buenas tardes.
Doctora	Buenas tardes, señor. Siéntese, por favor. Dígame qué le pasa.
Paciente	Ayer, mientras estaba jugando al tenis me caí y me torcí un tobillo, el de la pierna derecha. Me duele mucho y lo tengo hinchado.

Doctora	A ver …, ¿Le duele aquí?
Paciente	Ay, sí, me duele mucho.
Doctora	Bueno, por suerte no es más que un esguince, pero suelen ser bastante dolorosos y tardará unos días en sanar. Le pondré una venda para proteger el tobillo. Y trate de no mover mucho el pie. Si de aquí a quince días no se le ha pasado el dolor y la hinchazón, vuelva a verme, pero no creo que sea necesario.
Paciente	Gracias, doctora.

caerse *to fall*
tobillo *(m) ankle*
torcerse *to sprain*
doler, duele *to hurt, it hurts*
hinchado *swollen*
esguince *(m) sprain, twist*
doloroso *painful*
venda *(f) bandage*
sanar *to recover*
hinchazón *(f) swelling*

Insight

One of the main revision points in this unit is the expression of actions in progress with **estar** followed by the gerund, the **-ando** or **-iendo** form of the verb: **Está atendiendo …** *She's looking after …* , **Estaba jugando** *I was playing*. See paragraph 1 of the Grammar section.

Language and comprehension check 1

What phrases are used in the dialogue to say the following?

a I have an appointment.
b I fell and twisted my ankle.
c Does it hurt here?
d The right leg.
e It hurts very much.

f It's swollen.

g Come and see me again.

h I don't think it'll be necessary.

> ## Insight
>
> The word **hora** is used for appointments with a fixed time such as those with doctors, dentists, and hairdressers: **Quería pedir/Tengo hora con el doctor Santana** *I'd like to ask for/ I have an appointment with Doctor Santana*. For other kind of appointments use the word **cita**: **Tengo una cita con el/la gerente** *I have an appointment with the manager*.

2 ¿Qué te dijo el doctor? *What did the doctor say?*

María Luisa, una amiga de Carlos, le pregunta sobre la visita al doctor.

CD2, TR 17

María Luisa	Hola, ¿cómo te has sentido?
Carlos	Pues, no muy bien, aún no se me pasa el dolor. Ayer por la tarde fui al médico.
María Luisa	Ah sí, ¿y qué te dijo?
Carlos	Bueno …, que no está roto el tobillo, es sólo un esguince. Me puso una venda y me dijo que tratara de no mover mucho el pie, y que volviera si de aquí a unos días no estoy bien. Ya ves, no podremos jugar al tenis juntos.
María Luisa	¡Hombre! Lo siento.

QUICK VOCAB

sentirse *to feel*

aún no se me pasa el dolor *the pain is still there*

roto (from **romper**) *broken (to break)*

puso (from **poner**) *she put, applied*

juntos *together*

168

Language and comprehension check 2

Match the words from the dialogue in the first column with their equivalents in the second column:

sentirse	intentar
sentir	dentro de
pasarse	encontrarse
romper	lamentar
tratar	acabarse
volver	quebrar
de aquí a	regresar

Key sentences

Describing minor ailments

Me torcí un tobillo.	*I sprained an ankle.*
Me duele mucho.	*It hurts very much.*
Lo tengo hinchado.	*It is swollen.*

Describing other minor ailments	
Me duele la cabeza/el estómago/el oído/la espalda/la garganta.	*I have a headache/ stomachache/earache/ backache/sore throat.*
Tengo fiebre.	*I'm running a temperature.*
Tengo indigestión.	*I have indigestion.*
Tengo estreñimiento/diarrea.	*I have constipation/diarrhoea.*
Estoy enfermo/a.	*I'm ill.*
Estoy malo/a.	*I'm unwell.*
	(Contd)

¿Cómo se/te encuentra(s)/ siente(s)?	How are you feeling? (formal/inf)
Me siento/encuentro mal/No me siento/encuentro bien.	I'm feeling unwell/not feeling well.
Estoy constipado/a.	I have a cold.
He cogido un catarro/la gripe.	I've caught a cold/the flu.
Me he roto la pierna/el brazo.	I've broken my leg/arm.

Insight

Doler *to hurt* is used in a construction with **me, te, le**, etc., just like **gustar** *to like*, so a sentence like **me duele la cabeza** translates literally as *to me hurts the head*.

The expression **tengo dolor de ...**, literally *I have pain of ...* has exactly the same meaning but is more restricted in use: **Tengo dolor de estómago** or **Me duele el estómago** *I have a stomach ache*.

Referring to an action in progress

Está atendiendo a un paciente.	She is looking after a patient.
Estaba jugando al tenis.	I was playing tennis.

Expressing indirect suggestions or commands

Me dijo que tratara de no mover mucho el pie y que volviera ...	She told me to try not to move my foot too much and to come back ...

Grammar

1 Estar with the gerund: *For actions in progress*

Estar with gerund, as in **Está atendiendo a un paciente**, refers to an action in progress at the time of speaking. To refer to an action which was in progress when something else happened, as in **Mientras estaba jugando al tenis me caí** *While I was playing tennis I fell*, you need to use the imperfect tense of **estar** (see Unit 5) followed by a gerund.

The gerund is formed by adding -ando, to the stem of -ar verbs, e.g. **jugar** *to play*, **jugando** *playing*, and -iendo to the stem of -er and -ir verbs, e.g. **correr** *to run*, **corriendo** *running*, **subir** *to go up*, **subiendo** *going up*.

A few verbs undergo a change in their spelling when forming the gerund: **dormir – durmiendo, morir – muriendo, poder – pudiendo, pedir – pidiendo, decir – diciendo, venir – viniendo, ir – yendo, leer – leyendo.**

Note that the second action will normally be expressed in the preterite tense: **Cuando me caí** *When I fell*. Here are some further examples:

Estoy esperando al médico.	*I'm waiting for the doctor.*
Estábamos trabajando cuando sucedió.	*We were working when it happened.*

The continuous form (e.g. **estoy trabajando**), present or past, can often be replaced by a non-continuous verb form (e.g. **trabajo**) without altering its meaning, for example:

¿Qué estás haciendo?	*What are you doing?*
¿Qué haces?	*What are you doing?*
Estaba jugando al tenis.	*I was playing tennis.*
Jugaba al tenis.	*I was playing tennis.*

The continuous forms, however, are more specific, with the emphasis more on the action in progress rather than on the action alone.

2 Expressing indirect suggestions and commands

Look at the way this suggestion has been reported.

Vuelva si de aquí a unos días no está bien.	*Come back if within a few days you are not well.*

Me dijo que volviera si de aquí a unos días no estoy bien.   *She told me to come back if within a few days I'm not well.*

If the verb in the first clause is in the past (e.g. **me dijo** ... *she told me* ...) the verb form of the direct suggestion or command (e.g. **vuelva** ... *come back* ...) changes into the imperfect subjunctive tense (e.g. ... **que volviera** ... *to come back*) in the indirect sentence.

Consider now this example:

Vuelva dentro de dos semanas.   *Come back within two weeks.*
Quiere que vuelva dentro de dos semanas.   *She wants me to come back within two weeks.*

If the verb in the main clause is in the present tense (e.g. **quiere** ..., *he/she wants* ...) the verb form in the second clause will be in the present subjunctive tense, which is the same as that for the polite imperative, therefore there is no change. Notice however that the verb changes if the direct command is a familiar imperative, e.g. **Vuelve** dentro de dos semanas, Quiere que **vuelva** dentro de dos semanas.

For the forms of the present subjunctive see Unit 1 and for the imperfect subjunctive see Unit 9.

Practice

1 Use the verbs in brackets to say what you or others were doing. Follow the example.

Example: Pareces cansado. (trabajar)

Estaba trabajando.

  a Pareces medio dormido. (dormir)
  b Te veo muy relajada. (hacer yoga)

c Antonio se ve muy sereno. (meditar)

d Elvira tenía la luz encendida. (leer)

e ¿Qué hacíais en la cocina tú y Esteban? (preparar la cena)

f ¿Qué hacías en tu habitación a esta hora, Pepe? (ver el fútbol en la tele)

2 Express indirect suggestions and commands.

Ejemplo: No mueva el pie. (Me dijo …)

Me dijo que no moviera el pie.

    a Vuelva Vd. mañana. (Me dijo que …)

    b Descanse Vd. un poco. (Me aconsejó que …)

    c No fumen mucho. (Nos recomendó que …)

    d Haz más ejercicio. (El doctor quiere que …)

    e Por favor, llegad a la hora. (Rosa nos pidió que …)

    f No trabajes tanto. (Mi mujer no quiere que …)

3 While on holiday in Spain you have problems with your stomach and you go to the chemist's to buy something. Play the part of the customer.

Farmacéutico	¿Dígame?
Cliente(a)	*(Say you would like something for a stomach ache).*
Farmacéutico	¿Tiene Vd. diarrea también?
Cliente(a)	*(Yes, you've also got diarrhoea. You had some fish the night before and later you began to feel unwell.)*
Farmacéutico	Mire, le voy a dar estas pastillas que son muy buenas. Tome dos tres veces al día hasta que se sienta mejor. Y tenga cuidado con la alimentación. No coma nada frito.
Cliente(a)	*(Thank you. How much is it?)*
Farmacéutico	Son seis euros.

Insight

In the case of a medical emergency during a visit to Spain you can dial 112 from wherever you are and get assistance in Spanish or in English. Calls to 112 are free of charge. If you are a member of the European Union, your European Health Card will give you free access to a GP at a local public health centre or at the place where you are staying. With a few exceptions, people from countries outside the European Union have to pay for medical attention.

4 Your Spanish friend wants to know what the chemist told you. Refer to the dialogue above and answer his/her question. Notice the construction **hasta que se sienta mejor**, which carries a verb in the subjunctive.

> **Amigo(a)** ¿Cómo te fue en la farmacia?
> **Tú** *(Tell your friend what the chemist gave you and what he suggested.)*

5 How would you express the following in Spanish?
  a He broke his leg while playing football, so he won't be able to play for some time.
  b I'm not feeling well. I have a headache and I'm feverish.
  c She said she wouln't be able to see me this afternoon. She has an appointment with the doctor at four o'clock.
  d The doctor told me to rest and to come back in a fortnight if I'm still not feeling well.
  e She phoned the office to say she's not coming to work because she's caught flu.
  f He fell and twisted his ankle. It is swollen and he says it hurts him very much.

6 To be healthy and in good shape we must eat a balanced diet. The following passage gives some information about the kind of food we ought to eat. There are some missing words in it. Fill them in with words from the list. New vocabulary will be found at the end of the book.

| huevos | músculos | alimenticia | comer | mantenimiento |
| leguminosas | alimentos | proteínas | productos |

El hecho de ____ en exceso no quiere decir que se estén consumiendos los ____ más ricos en nutrientes. Entre los ____ que contienen mayor calidad y cantidad ____ se encuentran las carnes, pescados, aves y ____. De igual manera las ____, nueces y alegrías, que son productos sumamente ricos en ____, necesarias para la producción, ____ y reparación de los tejidos, ____, órganos, sangre, piel, cabello, etcétera.

(*Diario Excélsior, México D.F.*)

7 ¡A escuchar!

🔊 **CD2, TR 18**

··

Insight
In Spain, as elsewhere in Europe, the pace of modern life is bringing changes to the traditional Mediterranean diet that is still popular among most people. Experts are afraid that the adoption of a less balanced diet may have a detrimental effect on people's health.

··

La dieta mediterránea
In a radio talk, a specialist on food and diet refers to Spanish people's eating habits and to the changes that are taking place. Listen to the talk, if you have the recording. Otherwise, use the transcript for reading comprehension. Look at the following key words and questions before you listen to the recording.

tierra adentro *inland*
alimentación *diet*
grasa *(f) fat*
fibra *(f) fibre*
meseta central *(f) central plateau*
riesgo sanitario *(m) health risk*
equilibrada *balanced*

a Which are the Spanish regions where the Mediterranean diet is most popular?

b Why is the health risk higher in the central plateau, and in the north and north west?

c How does the Madrid diet compare with that of other Spanish regions?

d What sort of breakfast do people in Madrid tend to have?

e Why are more and more people eating outside their homes?

f What sort of diet do people in Catalonia tend to have?

8 Four readers of a health magazine wrote to the editor seeking help with their problems. What are their problems? Read the letters and find out.

El sol y la piel blanca

Mi piel es sumamente blanca y cada vez que llega el verano me veo imposibilitada de tomar el sol con normalidad porque me pongo colorada y se me produce un ardor muy intenso. Además de eso, nunca consigo broncearme. ¿Qué puedo hacer? Rosa Saavedra

Problemas estomacales

Tengo 18 años y soy un gran aficionado al turismo aventura. Mi problema es que casi siempre me veo afectado por problemas estomacales que más de una vez han arruinado mis vacaciones. Esto suele ocurrir especialmente cuando viajo a zonas donde las condiciones higiénicas son precarias, y donde no siempre es posible encontrar asistencia médica. ¿Qué podría hacer para prevenir estos problemas? Ignacio Carrera

Problemas cardíacos

Desde hace unos meses siento palpitaciones muy fuertes en el pecho que, por lo general, se producen de día y sin una razón

---

aparente. Estoy muy preocupada porque nunca me había pasado y además sólo tengo 32 años. ¿Qué me aconseja? Claudia Parra

Desmayo por exceso de trabajo
Desde hace un año tengo un trabajo que me exige mucho esfuerzo físico y psicológico. Llego a casa muy cansado y por la mañana me cuesta mucho levantarme. Hace unos días estaba trabajando en el jardín y me desmayé. Fui al médico y me dijo que no me preocupara, que simplemente tenía que aprender a relajarme. ¿Qué me sugieren ustedes? Alejandro García

(Adapted from Revista Buena Salud)

Which of the following suggestions would be appropriate for each person?

a Haz ejercicios de respiración para evitar el estrés.
b Puedes tener algún problema al corazón. Será mejor que pidas consejo a un especialista.
c Utiliza un buen bronceador que te proteja.
d No consumas alimentos crudos.
e Evita la exposición a los rayos ultravioletas, especialmente al mediodía.
f Hierve siempre el agua que vas a beber.
g Tómate unos días de vacaciones e intenta descansar los fines de semana.
h No te alarmes, pero si el problema continúa pide hora con un cardiólogo.

verse imposibilitado *to be unable*
ponerse colorado *to turn red*
ardor *(m) burning*
verse afectado por *to suffer from*
pecho *(m) chest*
desmayarse *to faint*

TEST YOURSELF

1 Rephrase the following sentences using other constructions or verbs with the same meaning.
  a Tengo dolor de cabeza.
  b El niño tiene dolor de estómago.
  c No me siento bien.
  d ¿Qué decías?
  e Ángel dormía plácidamente.

2 Answer the following questions using indirect speech. The direct suggestions or commands are given in brackets.
  a ¿Qué le dijo (a Vd.) el especialista? (*Deje de fumar.*)
  b ¿Qué te aconsejó tu novio? (*No se lo digas a nadie.*)
  c ¿Qué os sugirieron? (*Aprended español.*)
  d ¿Qué te pidió tu madre? (*No sigas con la dieta.*)
  e ¿Qué le recomendó (a Vd.) la doctora? (*Haga algún deporte.*)

Test 1 assesses your ability to express certain key ideas in a different way, while Test 2 focuses on your ability to make the changes that are necessary when changing from direct into indirect speech. Check the Key to Test yourself to see how well you performed. If you are still uncertain about the construction in Test 2, go back to section 2 of the Grammar section before you go on to the next unit.

11

El mundo que nos rodea
The world around us

In this unit you will learn how to:
- *Ask and give opinions*
- *Agree and disagree*
- *Express relationships of cause and effect*
- *Offer solutions*
- *Express unfulfilled conditions*

1 ¿A qué se debe? *What is it due to?*

En una entrevista con una periodista española, el director gerente de una cadena de hoteles menciona el deterioro del medio ambiente como una de las causas de la disminución del turismo en España.

Periodista	Señor Riveros, desde hace un par de años se viene dando en España un cierto descenso del número de turistas que nos visitan. ¿A qué se debe, cree Vd., esta disminución?
Sr. Riveros	Pues, creo que este descenso obedece a varios factores. Por un lado está el deseo natural de la gente de conocer otros lugares. Países como Grecia, México y algunas naciones de Asia, para nombrar sólo algunos, están gastando una buena cantidad de recursos en promover sus atracciones turísticas,

(Contd)

🔊 **CD2, TR 19**

con resultados bastante positivos. Por otro lado, la mayor conciencia ecológica de la población europea está haciendo que esta mire hacia lugares más naturales, con menos contaminación, y sin las grandes aglomeraciones y el deterioro que se observa en nuestras costas.

Otra causa no menos importante es la económica. La crisis por la que han atravesado algunos países ha hecho que la gente limite más sus gastos de esparcimiento y vaya en busca de lugares que les resulten más favorables económicamente. España es hoy un país caro y al turista que proviene de otros continentes no le favorece pasar sus vacaciones en nuestro país.

Periodista Parece que se trata de una situación irreversible, ¿no cree Vd.?

Sr. Riveros No, en eso no estoy de acuerdo. Pienso que se trata de una situación pasajera. Podría durar todavía uno o dos años más, pero creo que al final se estabilizará. Pero no nos podemos quedar de brazos cruzados. Habría que tomar medidas para mejorar algunos de los aspectos que he mencionado. Tendríamos que descontaminar nuestras playas y nuestro mar, habría que ajustar los precios de manera que España resulte más atractiva económicamente y, naturalmente, sería necesario mejorar la calidad de nuestros servicios. Si no hacemos nada, la situación difícilmente mejorará.

Periodista Da la impresión de que las autoridades no han tomado muy en serio el problema. ¿No cree Vd.?

Sr. Riveros Sí, en eso estoy absolutamente de acuerdo con Vd. A mi juicio, lo que está sucediendo en el sector turismo es también responsabilidad de las autoridades de gobierno, no sólo de los que trabajamos directamente en él.

Insight

This dialogue is longer than most you have encountered so far and the language reflects its formal tone. It will help you to listen to it or read it several times, each time focusing attention on a different point. You could start by making a note of all the expressions used for asking and expressing opinions, then focus on phrases used for expressing agreement and disagreement, then on the way relationships of cause and effect are conveyed, and on phrases used for offering solutions. (See also Key sentences.)

medio ambiente *(m) environment*
cadena *(f) chain*
se viene dando un descenso *there has been a decrease*
obedecer a ... *to be due to ...*
atravesar *to go through*
esparcimiento *(m) entertainment*
con los brazos cruzados *twiddling one's thumbs*
tomar medidas *to adopt measures*
a mi juicio ... *in my opinion ...*

Insight

The number of foreign tourists visiting Spain each year exceeds the total number of Spain's population (46 million). Around 60 million people choose Spain as a holiday destination. The most popular places are Catalonia, the Canary Islands and Andalusia. Most people come from other countries in the European Union, with the United Kingdom in first place, followed by Germany, France and Italy.

Language and comprehension check 1
  i ¿Verdadero o falso?
   a En España ha disminuido el número de visitantes.
   b La gente prefiere pasar sus vacaciones en casa.
   c Otros países están promoviendo fuertemente el turismo.
   d La gente tiene más dinero para viajar.
   e España resulta económico para los visitantes extranjeros.
   f Las costas españolas están contaminadas y deterioradas.

ii How is the following expressed in the interview?

    a dos años

    b ¿Cuál es la razón/causa?

    c por una parte

    d Están invirtiendo mucho dinero.

    e por otra parte

    f una situación que no es permanente

2 ¿Cuál es su opinión? *What's your opinion?*

Uno de los problemas que preocupa a los españoles, como a otros europeos, es el excesivo aumento del tráfico en las grandes ciudades. Esta es la opinión de una madrileña sobre este tema.

Entrevistador	Señora, buenos días. Estamos haciendo un estudio sobre los problemas del tráfico en las grandes ciudades españolas. ¿Cuál es su opinión al respecto?
Señora	¿Cómo dice? Con el ruido del tráfico no le oigo nada.
Entrevistador	He dicho que estamos realizando un estudio sobre los problemas del tráfico en las grandes ciudades y me gustaría conocer su opinión.
Señora	Pues, ¡qué quiere que le diga! Que el tráfico en Madrid es insoportable. Aquí ya no se puede vivir. Hay cada vez más coches y más ruido.
Entrevistador	¿Estaría de acuerdo Vd. en que se limitara de alguna manera el acceso de vehículos privados al centro de la ciudad?
Señora	Desde luego. Creo que se debería favorecer más al transporte público. Si se hubiera hecho antes hoy no tendríamos este problema. Madrid sería una ciudad más limpia y con menos ruido.

QUICK VOCAB

preocupar *to worry*

¡qué quiere que le diga! *what can I say!*

cada vez más *more and more*

desde luego *certainly*

si se hubiera hecho *if it had been done*

Insight

Noise pollution is a major problem in large Spanish cities. In many areas, excessive noise from traffic, bars, discotheques, etc., is clearly affecting people's physical and mental health, increasing the levels of stress among those who have to put up with it. But things are beginning to change, and residents in the worst affected areas are pressing the government to take measures and are taking their cases to court. There have been favourable rulings in more than one case.

Language and comprehension check 2
Answer the following questions in Spanish.
 a ¿Qué opina la señora sobre el tráfico en Madrid?
 b Según ella, ¿cuál sería la solución para resolver el problema del tráfico?
 c ¿Cómo favorecería a Madrid esta solución?

Key sentences

Asking and giving opinions

¿Cuál es su opinión?	*What is your opinion?*
Me gustaría conocer su opinión.	*I'd like to know your opinion.*
¿No cree Vd.?	*Don't you think so?*
Creo que ...	*I think (that) ...*
Pienso que se trata de ...	*I think it is ...*
A mi juicio ...	*In my opinion ...*

Other ways of asking and giving opinions	
¿Qué opina Vd.?	*What do you think?*
¿Qué le parece esto?	*What do you think of this?*
Opino que ...	*I think that ...*
Me parece que ...	*It seems to me that ...*
Considero que ...	*I consider that ...*
A mi parecer ...	*In my opinion ...*

Agreeing and disagreeing

¿Estaría Vd. de acuerdo?	*Would you agree?*
Estoy de acuerdo.	*I agree.*
No estoy de acuerdo.	*I don't agree.*

Other ways of expressing agreement and disagreement

¡De acuerdo!	*Right, O.K., all right!*
¿Vale? (familiar)	*Is that all right?, O.K.?*
¡Vale! (familiar)	*All right, O.K.!*

Expressing relationships of cause and effect

¿A qué se debe ...?	*What is it due to?*
Se debe a ...	*It is due to ...*
Obedece a ...	*It is due to ...*

Other ways of expressing relationships of cause and effect

¿Cuál es la causa/la razón/ el motivo (de) ...?	*What is the reason for ...?*
La causa/razón/el motivo es ...	*The reason is ...*

Offering solutions

Habría que (plus the infinitive) ...	*One would have to ...*
Tendríamos que (plus the infinitive) ...	*We would have to ...*
Sería necesario (plus the infinitive) ...	*It would be necessary to ...*

Other ways of offering solutions

La solución sería (plus the infinitive)	*The solution would be to ...*
Podríamos (plus the infinitive) ...	*We could ...*
Se podría (plus the infinitive) ...	*One could ...*

Expressing unfulfilled conditions

Si se hubiera hecho antes, hoy no tendríamos este problema.	*If it had been done before, today we wouldn't have this problem.*

Grammar

1 Expressing unfulfilled conditions

The sentence **Si se hubiera hecho antes, hoy no tendríamos este problema** *If it had been done before, today we wouldn't have this problem* expresses an unfulfilled condition (*it was not done before*). The verb in the if-clause is in the pluperfect subjunctive (**hubiera hecho**) while the verb in the second clause is in the conditional (**tendríamos**). More often, however, in unfulfilled conditions, the pluperfect subjunctive in the if-clause is followed by a clause with a verb in the conditional perfect:

Si yo hubiera/hubiese sabido, no habría venido.	*If I had known, I wouldn't have come.*
Si nos lo hubieras/hubieses dicho, te habríamos ayudado.	*If you had told us, we would have helped you.*
Le habríais visto, si hubierais/hubieseis llegado a la hora.	*You would have seen him, if you had arrived on time.*

2 The pluperfect subjunctive

The pluperfect subjunctive is formed with the imperfect subjunctive of **haber** (for the formation of the imperfect subjunctive see Unit 9) followed by a past participle (for past participles see Unit 8). Remember that the imperfect subjunctive has two alternative endings, -ra or -se.

Si (yo) hubiera/hubiese llamado ...	*If I had called ...*
Si (tú) hubieras/hubieses sabido ...	*If you had known ...*
Si (él/ella/Vd.) hubiera/hubiese estado allí ...	*If (he/she/you) had been there ...*
Si (nosotros) hubiéramos/hubiésemos viajado ...	*If we had travelled ...*
Si (vosotros) hubierais/hubieseis bebido ...	*If you had drunk ...*
Si (ellos/ellas/Vds.) hubierais/hubieseis hablado español ...	*If they/you had spoken Spanish ...*

Consider now the use of the imperfect subjunctive in non-conditional sentences such as the following ones:

Ojalá hubiesen llegado.   *I wish they had arrived.*
¡Cómo desearía que me hubiese   *How I wish he/she had*
llamado!   *called me.*
Habría sido mejor que les   *It would have been better if you*
hubieras dicho la verdad.   *had told them the truth.*

In all three examples the action expressed by the pluperfect subjunctive is one that did not take place.

3 The conditional perfect

The *conditional perfect* is formed with the conditional of **haber** (see Unit 8) followed by a past participle (see also Unit 8).

.... (yo) habría aceptado.   *... I would have accepted.*
... (tú) habrías regresado.   *... you would have come back.*
... (él/ella/Vd.) habría comido.   *... he/she/you would have eaten.*
... (nosotros) habríamos salido.   *... we would have gone out.*
... (vosotros) habríais ganado.   *... you would have won.*
... (ellos/ellas/Vds.) habrían perdido.   *... they/you would have lost.*

In a sentence like **Si la casa no hubiera/hubiese sido tan cara, la habríamos comprado** *If the house hadn't been so expensive, we would have bought it*, the conditional perfect in the second clause may be replaced by the -**ra** form of the pluperfect subjunctive: ... **la hubiéramos comprado,** with exactly the same meaning.

Practice

1 Express unfulfilled conditions

Ejemplo:

Subieron los precios. Disminuyó el turismo.

Si no hubieran subido los precios, no habría disminuido
el turismo.

To get the right form of the past participle, look up the verbs in
your dictionary to see whether they belong to the 1st (**-ar**), 2nd (**-er**)
or 3rd (**-ir**) conjugation.

    a Perdí mi trabajo. No fui a España.

    b No teníamos dinero. No pudimos viajar.

    c Aumentaron los precios. Descendió el turismo.

    d No encontraron plaza en el avión. Tuvieron que esperar
       otro vuelo.

    e Carlos tuvo un accidente. Cancelamos el viaje.

    f No nos invitaron a la fiesta. No fuimos.

2 Rephrase the following sentences using a construction
   with the words in brackets.

    a ¿Qué le parece a Vd. el tráfico en Madrid? *(opinar)*

    b Creo que es demasiado caótico. *(parecer)*

    c ¿Qué le parece la prohibición de fumar en lugares
       públicos? *(opinión)*

    d Pienso que es una muy buena idea. *(creer)*

    e La menor llegada de turistas obedece a la crisis
       económica. *(deberse)*

    f También tendrían que descontaminar las playas. *(haber)*

    g ¿Cuál es la causa de tanta contaminación acústica?
       (deberse)

    h En mi opinión este es un problema cultural. *(mi parecer)*
       ¿No te parece? *(creer)*

3 More and more people are concerned about issues to
   do with the environment and their health these days.
   Take for example, smoking or the destruction of the ozone
   layer, to mention just two. Imagine you are being interviewed
   on the subject of smoking. Write the answers to these
   questions.

Pregunta	¿Qué le parece el hecho de que en España se haya prohibido fumar en lugares públicos? ¿Está usted de acuerdo con esa medida?
Tú	*(Yes, you agree with that completely. You think people should not be allowed to smoke in public places. People who disagree with this think only of themselves. It is a well-known fact that many deaths are due to cigarette smoking.)*
Pregunta	¿Está usted también de acuerdo con la prohibición de la publicidad al tabaco?
Tú	*(Certainly. Cigarette advertising should have been banned long ago. If it had been done earlier, many deaths would have been avoided. It would also be necessary to educate people, especially the young, so that they don't take up smoking.)*

Insight

A law banning smoking in public places, including public transport, came into effect in Spain on 1 January 2006. Although more than 30 per cent of Spaniards smoke, around 70 per cent were actually in favour of the ban. The number of deaths related to tobacco in Spain is higher than in many other European countries. The signs **No está permitido fumar** or **Se prohibe fumar** are now common in many bars and restaurants, but others have special designated areas for smokers. Smaller premises have the option of either allowing smoking or being smoke-free. If you are a smoker look for the sign **se puede fumar** or **está permitido fumar**.

QUICK VOCAB

permitir *to allow*
un hecho muy conocido *a well-known fact*
muerte *(f) death*
tabaquismo *(m) cigarette smoking*
prohibir *to ban*
evitar *to avoid*
empezar a *to take up*

4 The following passage considers the greenhouse effect caused partly by the destruction of the ozone layer. Read the passage and then answer the questions which follow.

EL AGUJERO DE OZONO, MÁS GRANDE

La falta de ozono es también una de las causas del llamado 'efecto invernadero', que está provocando el calentamiento de la Tierra.

'No creo que los seres humanos puedan sobrevivir sin una capa de ozono, y sin ella la cantidad de radiaciones ultravioleta que llegaría del espacio a la Tierra destruiría la mayor parte de las formas de vida tal como las conocemos', explicó el director de la división de ciencias aplicadas para la Tierra de la NASA, Shelby Tilford.

El ozono también influye sobre la temperatura de las capas superiores de la atmósfera. Sin el ozono, los patrones de lluvia cambiarían drásticamente junto a otros aspectos esenciales del clima terrestre, lo que afectaría a las cosechas agrícolas y a la vida acuática.

Los científicos informaron por primera vez acerca de la formación del agujero en la capa de ozono sobre la Antártida en 1985. El hueco ha ido agrandándose paulatinamente. Los científicos opinan que el agujero en el ozono sobre la Antártida, que aparece por esta época del año, es una clara evidencia de que la contaminación causada por el hombre está dañando la atmósfera. Si esta tendencia continúa, se puede prever una alta incidencia de los casos de cáncer en la piel, daños en las cosechas y en las aguas.

(*Diario Ya*, España)

a What expressions are used in the text to say:
  i the greenhouse effect?
  ii the earth's warming?
  iii ultraviolet radiation?
  iv the higher layers of the atmosphere?
  v rain patterns would change drastically?
  vi the hole in the ozone layer?

b What do the following mean?

    i No creo que los seres humanos puedan sobrevivir.

    ii Destruiría la mayor parte de las formas de vida.

    iii ... lo que afectaría a las cosechas agrícolas y a la vida acuática.

    iv El hueco ha ido agrandándose paulatinamente.

    v El agujero en el ozono sobre la Antártida está dañando la atmósfera.

Insight

In the Key to the exercises you will find the answers to exercises a and b. There is no correct way in which to translate the sentences in the second exercise and your own translations may well differ from the ones given. Once you have checked the answers go through the text again a few times and make a note of or look up other expressions or vocabulary that you think relevant.

QUICK VOCAB

calentamiento *(m) warming*
patrón *(m) pattern*
cosecha *(f) crop, harvest*
agujero *(m) hole*
hueco *(m) hole*
agrandarse *to enlarge*

5 ¡A escuchar!

◀) **CD2, TR 21**

Antonio García, leader of an action group which is fighting to reduce noise pollution in Madrid, is interviewed by a journalist. Listen to the conversation and the recorded exercises or, alternatively, study the transcript. Once you feel confident with the new material, answer the following questions:

    a What is the main purpose of the organization?

    b What examples of noise pollution does Antonio give?

    c What comparison does he make between Madrid and other European capitals?

d How does he propose to achieve his objectives?

e Can you complete the following phrases with the missing verbs? Listen to the interview again if necessary.

   i hacer que la gente _____ conciencia

   ii que las autoridades _____ normas legales

  iii que nos _____ una mejor calidad de vida

  iv no nos _____ dormir por la noche

   v la vida _____ insoportable

  vi seguiremos _____ hasta _____ oír

conseguir to get, achieve
vecinos (m pl) neighbours, residents
terraza (f) area outside a bar or café
desconsideración (f) lack of consideration
insoportable unbearable
bastar to be enough
hacer cumplir to uphold, enforce
mientras tanto in the meantime

6 The following passage looks at air pollution in Mexico City and other places. Look at these key words and phrases and consider the questions which come before the text, then read it through and answer them.

a su vez in turn
superan con creces they far exceed
fallecido/a dead
padecer una afección to suffer from an illness
adoptar medidas to adopt measures
rechazo (m) rejection
mejora (f) improvement
placa de matrícula (f) number/licence plate

a ¿Cuáles son las tres causas principales de la contaminación en la Ciudad de México?

b ¿Cuál es el nivel máximo de partículas contaminantes recomendado por la OMS (Organización Mundial de la Salud)? ¿En qué situación se encuentra la capital mexicana?

c ¿Cuántas personas mueren anualmente a causa de la contaminación atmosférica?

d El texto menciona tres razones que impiden que se tomen medidas más estrictas para combatir la contaminación. ¿Cuáles son?

e El texto menciona tres medidas que podrían adoptar las autoridades de gobierno para combatir la contaminación atmosférica. ¿Cuáles son?

La Ciudad de México, con aproximadamente 20 millones de habitantes, es la más grande de las capitales de Hispanoamérica y una de las más grandes del mundo. Pero, es a su vez una de las que presenta el mayor grado de contaminación atmosférica en todo el planeta. Otras ciudades hispanoamericanas, entre ellas Santiago de Chile, Lima y Bogotá, sufren también un problema similar.

Las causas se encuentran en la gran concentración humana y en la excesiva centralización, que lleva a que la mayor parte de las industrias se establezcan en la capital, y también al aumento constante en el número de automóviles, todo lo cual hace que los esfuerzos que se realizan por mitigar esta situación sean prácticamente estériles. La capital mexicana tiene una de las mayores concentraciones de vehículos del mundo y las emisiones de partículas contaminantes superan con creces las recomendaciones de la Organización Mundial de la Salud (OMS), cuyo índice máximo de tolerancia es de 90 milígramos por metro cuadrado. En el Distrito Federal mexicano, el IMECA (índice metropolitano de calidad del aire) supera a veces los 300 milígramos. Las cifras para Santiago de Chile, cuya población es de seis millones de habitantes, tres veces menos que la de la capital mexicana, son muy similares, y las causas que motivan la contaminación no son muy diferentes a las de otras ciudades con similar problema. Europa y Norteamérica tampoco escapan a esta grave situación. En España, Barcelona presenta unos de los mayores índices de contaminación. En los Estados Unidos, Los Ángeles es una de las más afectadas. Según estadísticas de la OMS, el número de personas fallecidas por causa de la contaminación atmosférica llega a los dos millones de personas cada año, mientras millones de otras padecen de afecciones respiratorias y cardíacas y otras enfermedades asociadas a la toxicidad del aire.

Las medidas adoptadas por las autoridades políticas y sanitarias no han sido lo suficientemente eficaces para mejorar la calidad del aire. Las restricciones impuestas a los agentes causantes de los gases tóxicos, principalmente a las industrias, son débiles y sólo se hacen evidentes durante episodios de alerta ambiental. Intereses económicos, presiones políticas, y el propio rechazo de muchos de los afectados, dificultan la aplicación de medidas más drásticas y permanentes en el tiempo. Las mejoras en el transporte público, la restricción vehícular y el cierre definitivo o temporal de las industrias más contaminantes, son algunas de las medidas que contempla la acción gubernamental.

En la Ciudad de México y Santiago de Chile, por ejemplo, se limita la utilización de vehículos particulares un día a la semana. En la capital chilena, el control de la llamada restricción vehicular se realiza a través del último dígito de la placa de matrícula del coche, cuatro dígitos en períodos de menos contaminación, más dígitos en días de alerta ambiental. En la Ciudad de México la restricción, conocida con el nombre de *hoy no circula*, también se realiza a través del último dígito de la placa de matrícula, afectando regularmente a dos terminaciones y en días de mayor contaminación a cuatro. Los conductores se informan sobre el programa de restricción y cómo les afectará a través de los medios de comunicación y de Internet.

Insight

This is the kind of text that you might find in any newspaper. The language has not been simplified, as the idea is that you should develop your reading skills through authentic material. Don't be satisfied with only answering the questions correctly. Go back to the text a few times, consider some of the constructions used and list some of the new words, both general and specific to the topic.

TEST YOURSELF

1 Link the following sentences using the Spanish equivalent of the construction *If (I) had (not) ..., (I) would have (not) ...*

 a (Yo) no tenía dinero. No salí de vacaciones.
 b No llegaron a la hora al aeropuerto. Perdieron el vuelo.
 c Bebió en exceso. Tuvo un accidente.
 d No tenían visado. No pudieron viajar.
 e Se acostó tarde. No despertó a tiempo.

2 How would you express the following in Spanish? Use the formal form.

 a What's your opinion? (Give three alternatives.)
 b In my opinion ... (Give three alternatives.)
 c Don't you think that ...?
 d Do you agree with me?
 e I agree with you. This is due to ...

As explained in the Grammar section, the constructions in Test 1 have alternative verb forms. Generally, in everyday speech, people tend to be consistent with the form they use. Do likewise and try to learn one of them, for example **Si hubiera ..., habría ...** *If I had ..., I would have ...*, but it is important that you are aware of and can understand the others. For further practice, think of situations in which you might have wanted to express unfulfilled conditions and express them in Spanish. Check your answers for both tests and if you are satisfied with your performance go on to the next unit.

12

Ellos y ellas

A question of gender

In this unit you will learn how to:

* *Express comparisons*
* *Express probability*
* *Express contrast or opposition*

1 Tan modernos como los demás *As modern as the rest*

Una periodista entrevista a un hombre español sobre el tema del machismo.

CD2, TR 22

Periodista	Pepe, a menudo se oye decir que el hombre español es más machista que los europeos del norte. ¿Estás de acuerdo con esta apreciación?
Pepe	Bueno, del tema del machismo se ha hablado mucho y se han escrito muchas cosas, pero fundamentalmente, creo yo, este es un concepto que en las generaciones jóvenes tiene cada vez menos importancia. Con esto no quiero decir que el problema esté superado. Aún quedan muchas situaciones de desigualdad hombre-mujer que sería necesario resolver. Pero eso también es cierto de otras sociedades europeas.

(Contd)

| **Periodista** | ¿Qué pasa dentro del hogar, por ejemplo? ¿Comparte el hombre español las labores domésticas? |
| **Pepe** | Hoy en día, creo que sí, aunque no mayoritariamente. Depende mucho de la edad de las personas y del medio social. Pero entre la gente joven no cabe duda de que ha habido un cambio de actitud. El hombre ayuda a fregar los cacharros, a hacer la compra, a cuidar de los hijos. Es lo que yo he podido observar. En eso creo que somos tan modernos como los demás. |

Insight

Traditional male attitudes towards women in Spain have changed a great deal in the last few years, especially among the young. Most Spanish men, however, especially the older generation, still regard housework as being the domain of women, who receive little, if any, help from their male partners. A new equality law (**Ley de Igualdad**), enforcing women's rights and equality with men, which includes housework, was passed in March 2007.

QUICK VOCAB

estar superado to be over
hogar (m) home
machismo (m) social attitudes which discriminate against women in favour of men
labores domésticas (f) housework

Language and comprehension check 1

i Here are three domestic activities mentioned in the text: **fregar los cacharros; hacer la compra; cuidar de los hijos.** Can you guess their meanings?

ii Can you think of other domestic chores people normally do? Fill in the blanks below with a suitable word from the list.

| la limpieza | al bebé | la aspiradora | el suelo | los cristales | la ropa |

- **a** lavar _____
- **b** pasar _____
- **c** limpiar _____
- **d** hacer _____
- **e** barrer _____
- **f** bañar _____

2 La mujer en la sociedad española *Women in Spanish society*

◆) **CD2, TR 23**

Un periodista entrevista a una dirigente feminista española.

Insight

This is a formal interview and it contains a number of useful words and phrases used in the development of an argument: **yo diría que ...** *I would say that ...*, **Creo que ...** *I think that ...*, **Sin embargo ...** However, **Bueno ...** *Well ...*, **A mí me parece que ...** *I think that... .* Listen to the conversation several times, first for general understanding, trying to make a note of the main points, then look at the questions in Language and comprehension check 2 and listen again, focusing attention on specific points.

Periodista	En su opinión, ¿cuáles han sido los cambios más importantes en lo que respecta a la situación de la mujer en la sociedad española?
Dirigente	A nivel general, yo diría que el cambio fundamental ha sido el abandono, por parte de la mujer, del papel netamente pasivo que la sociedad le había asignado, y su incorporación activa a la vida económica y social del país. A nivel más específico, creo que la principal transformación se ha dado dentro del área de la educación. La mujer española
	(Contd)

se ha incorporado masivamente al sistema educativo. Más de la mitad de los estudiantes de bachillerato son de sexo femenino, y en educación superior el porcentaje de participación femenina llega casi al 50 por ciento. Sin embargo, todavía persisten diferencias en lo que respecta a la elección del tipo de estudios a seguir. La mujer aún se inclina por las profesiones consideradas tradicionalmente femeninas, mientras que en las carreras de carácter técnico se nota un claro predominio del hombre.

Periodista   ¿Qué posibilidades hay de que este desequilibrio cambie en el futuro?

Dirigente   Bueno, de hecho ya está cambiando, pero es necesario que se dé una orientación profesional más adecuada y que las universidades y otras instituciones de educación superior entreguen más información sobre las carreras técnicas que actualmente ofrecen. De esta manera, es probable que se llegue a un mayor equilibrio, puesto que la mujer es tan capaz como el hombre de desempeñarse en cualquier área de la ciencia o la tecnología. En el campo de la informática, por ejemplo, se viene apreciando un notable aumento del elemento femenino.

Periodista   ¿Comó ve Vd. la situación de la mujer en el campo laboral?

Dirigente   A mí me parece que aquí aún existen fuertes desajustes que es necesario rectificar. Por un lado, ha habido un crecimiento de la población activa femenina, frente a una reducción de la masculina. No obstante, el paro ha afectado más a la mujer que al hombre, con las consiguientes frustraciones para aquellas mujeres que desean trabajar, muchas de ellas jóvenes, pues no hay que olvidar que la población activa femenina es más joven que la masculina.

Periodista	¿Qué repercusiones ha tenido en el ámbito familiar este nuevo papel que ha asumido la mujer?
Dirigente	Bueno, el cambio más importante ha sido, sin duda, el descenso de la tasa de natalidad. El número medio de hijos por mujer ha bajado ostensiblemente y probablemente seguirá descendiendo.
Periodista	Se dice que uno de los campos donde la mujer española ha tenido más dificultades para integrarse ha sido el de la política. ¿A qué se debe, cree Vd., esta situación?
Dirigente	A mi juicio, los partidos políticos, especialmente los más tradicionales, no se han preocupado lo suficiente de los problemas que afectan a la población femenina. Además, las dificultades con que la mujer se enfrenta para iniciar una carrera política son tales, que muchas desisten de hacerlo. Pero aquí también ha habido cambios trascendentales, y en los últimos años, frente a las presiones del elemento femenino dentro de los partidos, hemos visto cómo la mujer se ha venido abriendo camino y ocupando cargos de gran responsabilidad política. Probablemente, esta situación seguirá mejorando.

papel *(m) role*
bachillerato *(m) secondary school*
desequilibrio *(m) imbalance*
desempeñarse *to perform*
de hecho *in fact*
consiguiente *resulting*
en el ámbito familiar *within the family*
tasa de natalidad *(f) birth rate*
número medio *(m) average number*
abrirse camino *to force one's way*

QUICK VOCAB

Language and comprehension 2

Answer the following questions in English.

  a What percentage of secondary school students are women?
  b Which studies do women tend to choose?
  c What has happened in computing with regard to the recruitment of new students?
  d What contradiction does the feminist leader see when it comes to comparing the female and male working populations?
  e How does the female working population compare with the male one in terms of age?
  f What effect has the increase in the female workforce had on the family?

Key sentences

Expressing comparisons

La población activa femenina es más joven que la masculina. *The female working population is younger than the male one.*

La mujer es tan capaz como el hombre. *Women are as capable as men.*

Further comparisons	
menos que	*less than*
en comparación con	*in comparison with, compared with*
frente a	*in comparison with, compared with*
mientras que	*whilst*

Expressing probability

Es probable/posible que se llegue a un mayor equilibrio. *It is possible that a greater balance may be reached.*

Probablemente/posiblemente seguirá descendiendo. *It will probably continue to fall.*

More probability	
es improbable	*it is improbable, unlikely*
es poco probable	*it is not very likely*
quizá(s), tal vez, a lo mejor	*perhaps*

Expressing contrast or opposition

El porcentaje de participación femenina llega casi al 50%. Sin embargo, todavía persisten diferencias … *The percentage of women's participation has reached almost 50%. However, there are still differences …*

Ha habido un crecimiento de la población activa femenina, frente a una reducción de la masculina. No obstante, el paro ha afectado más a la mujer que al hombre. *There has been an increase in the female working population as opposed to a decrease in the male one. Nevertheless, unemployment has affected women more than men.*

Grammar

1 The pluperfect tense

The Spanish pluperfect tense (e.g. La sociedad le **había asignado** …) is equivalent to the English pluperfect (e.g. Society *had assigned* to her …). It is formed with the imperfect form of **haber** (**había, habías, había, habíamos, habíais, habían**) followed by a past participle which does not change (for the formation of past participles see Unit 8).

La sociedad le *había asignado* **un papel netamente pasivo.**

Society had assigned to her a purely passive role.

2 Comparisons

a Positive comparison
La población activa femenina es más joven que la masculina.

The female working population is younger than the male one.

b Negative comparison
La mujer hispanoamericana es menos liberal que la española.

Latin American women are less liberal than Spanish women.

c Comparison of equality
La mujer es tan capaz como el hombre.

Women are as capable as men.

d Irregular forms
bueno *good*	**mejor** *better*
malo *bad*	**peor** *worse*
grande *big*	**mayor** *bigger, greater, older* (also *más grande* for size)
pequeño *small*	**menor** *smaller, younger* (also **más pequeño**)

e Superlative forms

To say *the youngest*, *the most capable*, *the best*, use the construction **el/la/los/las** followed by **más** or **menos**:

el/la más joven or **el/la menor**	*the youngest*
los/las más capaces	*the most capable*
el/la mejor/peor	*the best/worst*

3 Expressing contrast or opposition

The word most commonly used for expressing contrast or opposition is pero *but*, but there are a number of others:

a Sino, sino que *but*. **Sino** is normally used instead of **pero** after a negative statement, while **sino que** is used before a verb phrase.

No hoy, sino mañana.	*Not today, but tomorrow.*
No le envié un email, sino que le llamé por teléfono.	*I didn't send him an email, but I phoned him.*

b Sin embargo *however*. This functions like **pero**, but its use is restricted to more formal spoken and written language.

No se llevan bien, sin embargo siguen juntos.	*They don't get on well, however they continue together.*

c Aunque *although, even though, even if*. If what follows is a fact, use an indicative verb, otherwise use the subjunctive verb, in which case **aunque** translates *even if*.

Aunque ella trabaja fuera de casa, él no ayuda con las tareas domésticas.	*Although/Even though she goes out to work, he doesn't help her with the domestic chores. (a fact)*
Aunque mañana llueva iremos a verte.	*Even if it rains tomorrow we'll come and see you. (not yet a fact)*

d **A pesar de** *in spite, despite.* You can use this with a noun, a pronoun or an infinitive.

A pesar de la lluvia/eso saldremos a cenar.	*In spite of/Despite the rain/that we'll go out for dinner.*
No nos ha olvidado a pesar de estar lejos.	*He/she hasn't forgotten us in spite of/despite being far away.*

e **A pesar de que** *in spite of/despite the fact that, even though, even if.* Use this with an indicative verb if what follows is a fact, otherwise use the subjunctive.

A pesar de que estoy ocupado, te ayudaré.	*In spite of/Despite the fact that I'm busy, I'll help you. (Even though I'm busy …)*
No volveré con él, a pesar de que me lo pida.	*I won't go back to him, despite the fact that he may ask me to. (…even if he asks me to.)*

f **No obstante** *nevertheless, despite, in spite of.* This is more formal than the other phrases and is restricted to writing or very formal speech.

El país ha progresado, no obstante todavía queda mucho por hacer.	*The country has progressed, nevertheless there is still a lot to do. (Despite the fact that the country has progressed, there is …)*

Practice

1 Translate the following sentences into Spanish.

   a She was better than him, and in spite of that she didn't get the job.

   b Although Carlos is older than Sofía, they get on very well together.

   c María had lived in the United States for several years, however her English wasn't as good as her brother's.

   d They hadn't lived in Madrid but in Barcelona, although they had been here more than once.

e Despite being younger, he is not as active as the others.
f We'll go on holiday, even if we have to borrow money.
(*pedir dinero prestado*)

2 Match each word or phrase with one of similar meaning from the list below. Words and phrases a–j are from Dialogues 1 and 2.

con frecuencia indudablemente en relación con por otra parte en realidad ya que a mi parecer por una parte así en la actualidad

   a por un lado
   b no cabe duda
   c de esta manera
   d a mi juicio
   e a menudo
   f además
   g puesto que
   h hoy en día
   i en lo que respecta a
   j de hecho

3 ¡A escuchar!

◀) **CD2, TR 24**

Entrevista con Teresa Morales, 27 años: Teresa Morales talks to a journalist of a Spanish magazine about her life with Paco, her husband. Listen to the interview, if you have the recording, or alternatively, read the transcript and then answer the questions which follow. First, study these key words and phrases.

¿cómo os arregláis? *how do you manage?*
tareas del hogar *(f/pl) housework*
eludir *to avoid*
asistenta *(f) charwoman*
planchar *to iron*
camino de casa *on the way home*

QUICK VOCAB

guisar *to cook*
labores compartidas *shared work*
ajuste(s) *(m) adjustment(s)*

¿Verdadero o falso?

a   Teresa y Paco llevan pocos años de casados.
b   La limpieza del piso la hace Teresa.
c   La comida la prepara Paco.
d   La asistenta friega los platos.
e   Teresa y Paco no funcionan bien como pareja.
f   Según Teresa, cuando vengan los hijos no habrá mayores cambios.

4   Carla wrote to a magazine seeking advice with a personal
    matter. What is Carla's problem? Read the letter and find out.

Mi marido no quiere que trabaje

Estimada Eli:

El problema por el que te escribo es que, en siete años de
matrimonio, aún no logro convencer a mi marido de que quiero
trabajar. Él dice que tenemos una situación económica muy
buena y que no es necesario que salga de la casa. Tenemos
una hija de seis años que ya va al colegio y creo que yo podría
conseguir una ocupación, al menos, de medio tiempo. Se trata de
sentirme útil, ya que terminé mi carrera de ingeniería comercial
y siempre soñé con realizarme en ella. Ahora no es eso lo que
persigo, pero al menos hacer algo relacionado con el tema que
estudié. Mi marido dice que podría hacer talleres, tomar cursos,
pero creo que el problema es que él teme que yo me desarrolle
profesionalmente, por miedo o celos. No sé qué hacer. ¿Cómo
hacerlo entender? Carla

(Revista de El Sábado de El Mercurio, Chile)

Why do you think Carla's husband is acting the way he is? And
what advice would you give her? Compare your ideas with those

of the newspaper editor below and, as you do, fill in the gaps in
the letter with an appropriate word from the list:

---

inseguridad   cambio   actividad   sensación   horizontes
razones   apoyo   estatus   necesidad   seria

Carla:

Da la _____ de que a tu marido le incomodaría que tú salieras a
trabajar por muchas _____: posiblemente por machismo, por _____
o por celos, pero también es probable que sea por _____ social o
porque piense que tu hija estará más protegida contigo en la casa.

Creo que debieras hablar en forma muy _____ con tu marido.
Dile que has decidido realizar una _____ de acuerdo a lo que
estudiaste y que le estás pidiendo su _____ porque es una _____
concreta que tienes. Explícale que este _____ te producirá
felicidad, satisfacción, que tus _____ van a cambiar, que van a
poder conversar de otros temas.

(Revista de El Sábado de El Mercurio, Santiago de Chile)

---

5 The article which follows looks at the birth rate in Spain and
explains why it has one of the lowest birth rates in Europe.

Which of the following reasons for the decrease in the birth rate
are mentioned in the text? Read the article and find out.

a El Estado sanciona a las familias que tienen numerosos hijos.
b La incorporación de la mujer al trabajo.
c Los españoles confían más en la ayuda estatal.
d Las viviendas son demasiado pequeñas como para una familia
   numerosa.

e La transformación de las costumbres que se produjo después de la desaparición de Franco.

f El tener hijos implica obligaciones que las parejas no quieren asumir.

g La adopción de medidas para el control de la natalidad.

Cuando los hijos son caros

A sus 34 años, Mariló Corral tiene un hijo de seis y duda al pensar en tener otro. Periodista de profesión, actualmente está desempleada, lo que condiciona su deseo de dar a luz de nuevo. Sin embargo, dice que la mayoría de sus amigas tienen sólo un hijo, 'pues tener un niño es muy caro'.

Este testimonio refleja algunos de los motivos del bajo índice de fecundidad que se registra en España, y que en 2007 sólo llegó a 1,39 hijos por mujer, según cifras del Instituto Nacional de Estadística Español, mientras que la media europea es de 1,5 hijos. Esta tasa no alcanza el 2,1 necesario para asegurar el relevo generacional, y es una de las más bajas de Europa.

Sin embargo, la caída de la natalidad en España preocupa, pero no alarma. De hecho constituye una tendencia desde 1984.

Según el sociólogo Salvador Giner, este fenómeno se debe al cambio cultural sufrido por España tras la muerte de Franco. Destaca la mayor confianza de los españoles en el Estado de bienestar, la revolución que significó el control de la natalidad y el ingreso de la mujer a la vida laboral.

Pensárselo dos veces

Inquieto y gracioso, Marc es el primer hijo de Rosalía Pallarés, una administrativa de 35 años. Casada hace cinco y medio, asegura que siempre quiso tener hijos, pero bajo una planificación familiar. 'Para traer niños al mundo es mejor pensárselo dos veces. No poder mantenerlos es una pena', dice.

Sin embargo, a juicio del investigador Diego Levis, detrás de las excusas económicas se esconde la incapacidad de las parejas para asumir la responsabilidad que representa criar y educar un hijo.

(El Mercurio, Santiago de Chile)

Read the text again and find another word or phrase meaning the following:

  i Está sin trabajo/en paro.
 ii Tener un hijo.
iii Otra vez.
 iv Las razones.
  v A juicio de …
 vi Oficinista.
vii Pensarlo muy bien.
viii Es una lástima.

Insight

According to official statistics, the current average age for marriage in Spain is 30 for women and 33 for men. Government statistics now include same-sex marriage, which became legal in Spain on 4 July 2005. Spain became the third country in the world, following the Netherlands and Belgium, to allow marriage between same-sex couples, giving them the right to adopt children.

cifra *(f)* figure
caída *(f)* fall
estado de bienestar *(m)* welfare state
esconderse *to hide*
criar *to bring up*
asignación familiar *(f)* child benefit
relevo *(m)* relay, replacement

Young Europeans as a whole base the decision of having children on a range of other reasons. Do you agree with them? Look at the chart below and compare these with the ones mentioned by the people in the article.

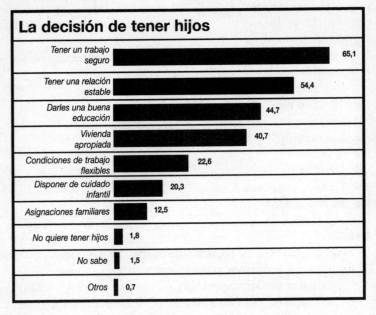

La decisión de tener hijos

Tener un trabajo seguro	65,1
Tener una relación estable	54,4
Darles una buena educación	44,7
Vivienda apropiada	40,7
Condiciones de trabajo flexibles	22,6
Disponer de cuidado infantil	20,3
Asignaciones familiares	12,5
No quiere tener hijos	1,8
No sabe	1,5
Otros	0,7

(*El Mercurio*, Santiago de Chile)

QUICK VOCAB

seguro *secure*
vivienda *(f) housing*
disponer de *to have*
cuidado infantil *(m) childcare*
asignación *(f) allowance*

TEST YOURSELF

1 Fill in the blanks with a suitable word.

  a Antes de casarse, Daniel y Marité ____ vivido en Santander.

  b Perdona, (yo) no te ____ visto. ¿Dónde estabas?

  c Ya (nosotros) ____ terminado de cenar cuando llegó Ricardo y su mujer.

  d El español no es tan difícil ____ el alemán.

  e Elena es ____ que su hermana. Elena tiene veintitrés años y su hermana dieciocho.

2 Fill in the blanks with a suitable word from the list.

> a pesar de   sino que   aunque   sin embargo   sino

  a No, no es ese el que quiero, ____ el otro.

  b ____ nos inviten, creo que no aceptaremos la invitación.

  c ____ las dificultades, logró terminar sus estudios universitarios.

  d Eran muy buenos amigos, ____ después de aquel incidente nunca más se vieron.

  e No fue en España donde se conocieron ____ coincidieron en unas vacaciones.

¡Enhorabuena! You have now reached the end of your Perfect your Spanish course but perhaps, in spite of your progress, you still feel uncertain about how to use certain forms or constructions. Once you have checked the answers to Tests 1 and 2 above, think of what areas of the language you might want to revise and establish your own plan for advancing your Spanish even further. The grammar notes in the units may serve as a guideline, but using a grammar book, preferably one containing exercises, is probably the best option. **¡Buena suerte!**

Key to the exercises

Unit 1

Language and comprehension check

1 a No tiene que perder el tiempo yendo de un punto a otro de la ciudad en el coche, y no tiene un horario fijo. **b** Se considera bastante disciplinado. **c** Se sienta frente al ordenador. **d** Su familia y sus amigos conocen sus hábitos y no lo llaman por la mañana, a no ser que sea para algo importante. **e** Recibe a sus amigos, escuchan música, toman unas copas y charlan. A veces van al cine o a cenar fuera.

2 a Difícilmente puedo hablar. **b** Ya que. **c** A eso de. **d** Tardaría mucho tiempo. **e** No está nada mal. **f** Lo que pasa es que. **g** Tomar una copa. **h** De vez en cuando.

3 See Dialogue 3 for answers.

Practice

1 me despierto / me levanto / me ducho / desayuno / salgo / voy / cojo / vuelvo / almuerzo / me marcho / voy / juego / doy / me acuesto

2 trabaja / se despierta / se levanta / se ducha / desayuna / sale / va / coge / vuelve / almuerza / se marcha / va / juega / da / se acuesta

3 a 6. **b** 3. **c** 5. **d** 1. **e** 4. **f** 2.

4 a ¿A qué hora sales de casa? Normalmente salgo a las ocho y media. **b** ¿Y cómo vas al trabajo? Voy en el metro. **c** ¿A qué hora llegas a la oficina? Generalmente llego entre las nueve menos diez y las nueve. **d** ¿Y qué haces por la mañana? Pues,

reviso el correo electrónico, abro la correspondencia, la leo
y la clasifico, escribo las cartas que me dicta mi jefe, recibo a
los clientes de la empresa y fijo citas con el gerente, contesto el
teléfono, asisto a reuniones … e ¿A qué hora y dónde almuerzas
normalmente? Normalmente almuerzo a la una y media con
algunos compañeros de trabajo en el bar de la esquina. f ¿A
qué hora sales de la oficina? Salgo a las siete de la tarde. g ¿Y
qué haces normalmente por la noche? Ceno, veo la televisión,
escucho música, doy un paseo con mi novio.

5 a V. b F. c F. d F. e V.

6 a sobre, hacia b nuevamente, otra vez, de nuevo, una vez más
c tal vez, quizá, a lo mejor d se ducha, toma una ducha e frugal,
ligero f se pone el bañador, para seguir entrenando, de vuelta en
casa g normalmente, casi siempre, nunca h consiga – conseguir,
sea – ser.

7 a lleguen b sale c regrese d llame e invite f se levantan g conozcas
h está i digas j trabaja.

Test yourself

1 a I don't usually eat much at night unless I have to go out.
b It bothers Julia to be interrupted but it doesn't happen very
often. c We are tied to a certain routine which, whether we like
it or not, we have to keep to. d We go to the supermarket once
or twice a week, depending on what is needed. e I don't want
you to call me unless it's absolutely necessary. f It would be
impossible to come back home for lunch, as I'd waste a lot of
time going in the car, the bus or whatever.

2 a estés. b sé. c recuerdo, envíes. d pueda, sea. e vienes, quieras.
f escribas, des.

Unit 2

Language and comprehension check

1 **a** No la ha visto, pero le gustaría verla. **b** Deciden ir al día siguiente. **c** Los fines de semana suele ir a la sierra. **d** Se va el viernes por la tarde y regresa el domingo por la noche.

2 **a** Porque no había piscina en su barrio. **b** Porque trabaja y está casada y tiene dos hijos pequeños. **c** Cogen el coche y se van con los chicos de paseo. **d** Le gusta pintar.

Practice

1 **a** Haces. **b** Me. **c** gustan. **d** prefiero – gusta – ti – te. **e** gustan – no. **f** prefieres. **g** más. **h** A – te. **i** me.

2 Follow Dialogue 1.

3 Tengo muy poco tiempo. Trabajo en una oficina de 9.00 a 5.00 y estoy casado(a) y tengo tres hijos. Pero cuando puedo, me gusta trabajar en el jardín y también me gusta leer. Ahora estoy leyendo una novela de García Márquez, que me gusta mucho. Ah, también estudio español, por supuesto. Me gusta mucho el español. / No siempre. Aunque me gusta mucho España, es un país caro ahora, así que prefiero ir a algún lugar más barato. / ¡Fantástico! Muchas gracias.

4 **a** One is a documentary and the other a comedy. **b** The documentary is about the Civil War and the events that took place in Catalonia during the Republic. The comedy is about a school teacher who uses his hypnotic powers to impose order in his classroom.

5 **a** He recibido tu email y me alegro mucho de que vengas a mi ciudad. **b** Estoy seguro(a) de que te gustará mucho. **c** ¿Por qué no te quedas en mi casa unos días? Me gustaría mucho. **d** Puedes llamarme por teléfono para confirmar tu llegada.

6 a i More than 80 works. **ii** At the Museo Español de Arte Contemporáneo. **iii** Mexico, Colombia, Argentina and Chile. **iv** se está realizando / podrán apreciar / fue inaugurada por. **b i** Festival de otoño de Madrid. **ii** It will include theatre, classical and contemporary dance, etc. **iii** Eastern European countries.

7 a F. **b** F. **c** V. **d** F. **e** V. **f** F.

Test yourself

1 a (A él) le gusta el teatro, pero a ella no. **b** Lo que más nos gusta de este lugar/sitio es la gente. **c** ¿Te gusta? Pues, a mí no. Prefiero a Pablo. **d** ¿Qué te parece si vamos a tomar una copa, Silvia? **e** Me parece bien. **f** Les encanta/fascina ver este programa. Pues, a mí no me gusta nada.

2 a de manera muy lenta. **b** con frecuencia. **c** de forma muy descortés. **d** con mucha amabilidad. **e** de manera muy clara. **f** con cuidado.

Unit 3

Language and comprehension check

1 i a de, por. **b** de, de. **c** de, por. **d** en, desde. **e** por, a or para. **f** de. **ii** c, e, f.

2 i a Está un poco aburrida de él. **b** No está nada mal. **c** Casi cinco años. **d** El contacto con el público. **e** Enseña español a extranjeros en un instituto de idiomas. **f** Le gusta su trabajo, pero no el sueldo. **ii a** I can't complain either. **b** The salary is not bad at all. **c** At the beginning I used to like it a lot. **d** The relationship is rather impersonal. **e** I do like teaching. **f** Come on, things are not so easy!

Practice

1 a ¿Cuánto tiempo llevas viviendo en Londres? Llevo tres años viviendo aquí. **b** ¿Cuánto tiempo llevas estudiando inglés? Llevo dos años y medio (estudiándolo). **c** ¿Cuánto tiempo llevas

jugando al fútbol? Llevo cinco años (jugando). **d** ¿Cuánto
tiempo llevas tocando el piano? Llevo cuatro años (tocando).
e ¿Cuánto tiempo llevas trabajando como camarero? Llevo seis
meses (trabajando como camarero). **f** ¿Cuánto tiempo llevas
haciendo yoga? Llevo tres semanas (haciendo yoga).

2 a Hace tres años que vive ... **b** Hace dos años y medio que estudia ...
c Hace cinco años que juega ... **d** Hace cuatro años que toca ...
e Hace seis meses que trabaja ... **f** Hace tres semanas que hace ...

3 desde / como / de / trabajo / él / posibilidad / diferente / busca /
lo; horario / empiezo / la / los / son; sueldo / gano / espero / viene;
gusta / trabajo / donde / irme.

4 Buenos días. Llamo por el anuncio en el periódico y quisiera
hablar con la señorita Toñi. / ¿Sí? / Está bien. Esperaré. / Buenos
días, soy (*name*), he visto el anuncio en el periódico y quisiera
más información acerca del puesto. / Sí, trabajé como vendedor(a)
durante algún tiempo, aunque nunca he vendido libros. Pero
estoy dispuesto(a) a aprender. Vivo en España ahora y necesito
ganar algo de dinero y este es el tipo de trabajo que busco. Me
interesa mucho. / Me llamo (*name*) y vivo en (*your address*).

5 Follow model letter and change relevant information.

6 Check transcript to complete the form. (**María del Carmen
Salas**) **a** ¿Podrías decirme a qué te dedicas? **b** Estoy a cargo
de ... **c** ¿Qué es lo que más te agrada de tu profesión? **d** El
trabajo en terreno. **e** Eso es lo que más me agrada. **f** ¿Hay algo
que no te guste de tu trabajo? **g** Son muy exigentes. **h** Hay que
renovarse constantemente. **Javier Molina a** Hace cinco años.
b Trabajaba en Madrid en una empresa privada. **c** Porque no
ganaba lo suficiente. **d** Es un puesto seguro y para toda la vida.
e Principalmente en dar información al público. **f** La mayoría pide
información sobre hoteles y sobre sitios de interés en la región.

7 a La que me lo dijo fue María/María fue la que me lo dijo. **b** A
Madrid llegó el viernes por la tarde/El viernes por la tarde llegó

a Madrid. **c** A las cinco de la mañana le llamó por teléfono su madre/Le llamó por teléfono su madre a las cinco de la mañana. **d** En el restaurante donde comimos dejé el teléfono móvil/Dejé el teléfono movil en el restaurante donde comimos. **e** Por Pepe, que nos llamó, supimos la noticia/Supimos la noticia por Pepe, que nos llamó. **f** El email de César lo recibió Antonia el sábado/El sábado recibió Antonia el email de César.

8 **a** Translation and interpreting. **b** She's selling books door-to-door. **c** She's living with her parents and two of her brothers (or brothers and sisters) because her income, which is low and fluctuating, doesn't allow her to rent a flat and live independently. **d** She looks up advertisements in the newspaper and sends her CV in the hope of being called for an interview. **e** Domina perfectamente el inglés y el francés. Trabaja vendiendo libros a domicilio. El haber hecho estudios universitarios. Con la esperanza de que la llamen al menos para una entrevista. **f** una universidad madrileña; puesto que; conseguir un empleo/encontrar trabajo; bien remunerado; el día que ello suceda. **g** pueda (poder), cambie (cambiar), deba (deber), consiga (conseguir), tenga (tener), llamen (llamar), suceda (suceder).

Test yourself

1 **a** Soy ingeniero. Construyo … **b** Soy enfermera. Cuido … **c** Soy bombero. Apago … **d** Soy carpintero. Fabrico … **e** Soy conductora. Conduzco … **f** Soy director. Dirijo … **g** Soy profesora/catedrática. Enseño … **h** Soy cartera. Reparto …

2 **a** Llevan cinco años viviendo en la Costa del Sol. **b** ¿Cuánto tiempo hace que trabajas en/para esta empresa? **c** Victoria va a Nueva York por negocios, pero yo voy de vacaciones. También voy de compras. **d** Lo que más le gusta de enseñar es el contacto con la gente. Lleva mucho tiempo enseñando español. **e** Normalmente las compras las hace mi jefe, pero hoy me toca a mí. Or Normalmente es mi jefe quien/el que hace las compras, pero hoy … **f** Lo que no me gusta de mi trabajo es el sueldo, aunque viajar sí me gusta/sí me gusta viajar.

Unit 4

Language and comprehension check

1 **a** F. **b** V. **c** F. **d** V. **e** F. **f** F.

2 **a** Porque para profesores extranjeros de español tienen cursos especiales. **b** Cuatro semanas y dos semanas respectivamente. **c** Porque no dispone de mucho tiempo. **d** Le da un folleto informativo.

Practice

1 Me alegré / fue / hiciste / estudié / conseguí / tuve / asistí / abrió / aprendí / Tuve que / mereció.

2 **a** Me / te / la **b** Lo **c** le **d** le / me / le / se / lo **e** me / se / la / le

3 Gracias. Es Vd. muy amable. / Lo aprendí en la escuela, pero también pasé seis meses en España. ¿Habla Vd. inglés? / ¿Dónde estudió francés? / Sí, hice varios años de francés en la escuela y tuve una excelente profesora. Y también voy a Francia todos los veranos. El año pasado estuve en Cannes. Me gustó mucho.

4 **a** ¿Podría decirme si tienen Vds. cursos de español de verano? **b** ¿Cuándo empiezan? **c** ¿Qué niveles ofrecen? **d** ¿Cuánto cuestan? **e** ¿Y cuál es el horario? **f** ¿Pueden ayudarme a encontrar alojamiento?

5 Dear Sir, This is to request information about the Spanish courses for foreigners which the University of Málaga is running this summer. Please send me detailed information about the dates on which they will take place, the levels which are offered, the timetable and the registration fees. I would be grateful too if you could tell me whether it would be possible to get accommodation through you with a Spanish family. I look forward to hearing from you. Yours sincerely,

6 **a** By sending the registration form, two photographs and a photocopy of the document showing that payment has been sent. **b** Certificate in Spanish Language, Diploma in Hispanic Studies. **c** With families or in apartments. **d** They are grouped according to their knowledge of the language: beginners, intermediate and advanced levels. **e** 20 hours. **f** Concerts, shows, films, visits to the main monuments in the city and excursions to other cities.

7 Muy señores míos: He visto el anuncio sobre los cursos que ofrece el Centro de Estudios Eva y estoy interesado/a en el curso de … Les ruego que me envíen toda la información referente al curso, incluyendo la fecha en que se realiza, el valor de la inscripción, el horario y la forma de inscripción. Les agradeceré que me hagan llegar la información lo antes posible. Les saluda muy atentamente.

8 **a** F. **b** V. **c** F. **d** F. **e** V. **f** F.

9 **a** She used to read and write a lot. When she returned to school she discovered that the rest of the girls did not play her games (reading and writing). **b** She felt ugly, although she was in fact pretty, and she was also lonely, quiet and shy. **c** She had an unhappy childhood, full of fears and questions without answers. She was extremely sensitive and proud, which derived from a low self-esteem and by feeling very threatened and vulnerable. **d** His father bought a chemist's and went bankrupt. **e** He describes the relationship with his father as dreadful, and that with his mother's family as the Golden Age.

Test yourself

1 **a** hizo – hicieron – hice. **b** estuvo – estuvimos. **c** dije – dijo. **d** pusiste – puse. **e** fue – fueron – fuimos. **f** vino – vinieron – vine.

2 **a** ¿Podría darme/Me podría dar información sobre los cursos de español de verano, por favor? **b** ¿Nos envía/Nos puede enviar información sobre alojamiento también? Le daremos nuestros emails. **c** Me da vergüenza decirlo, pero mi español no es tan bueno como mi francés, aunque lo estudié durante un año.

d Mi hijo domina perfectamente el francés y el español. Los aprendió en la escuela/el colegio y también pasó algún tiempo en Francia y en España.

3 a This is to request an information brochure ... **b** Please/Kindly let me know what the registration fees are ... **c** I'd be grateful if you would get me accommodation with a Spanish family ... **d** I look forward to hearing from you.

Unit 5

Language and comprehension check

1 a Las pasó en Cuba. **b** Estuvo allí diez días en total. **c** El hotel era excelente y estaba a cinco minutos de la playa. Tenía piscina, discoteca ... **d** No, fue a través de una agencia de viajes, porque de otra manera les habría resultado muy caro. **e** Era muy maja. **f** Los viajes organizados no le gustan nada. **g** a través de, de otra manera, mereció la pena.

2 a México. **b** un amigo mexicano. **c** en julio. **d** agosto. **e** su amigo. **f** al Oriente.

3 a ¿Sigue lloviendo? **b** No ha parado de llover. **c** Está lloviendo a cántaros. **d** ¡Qué lástima! **e** ¡Es una pena! **f** ¡Ojalá!

Practice

1 viajaremos / saldremos / llegaremos / nos quedaremos / Podrás / Estaremos / daré / harás

2 a fueron, estuvieron. **b** era, iban, estaban. **c** resultó, llegó, esperaba, vivía. **d** pasaron, conocía, llevó. **e** tomaron, pareció, era. **f** fueron, soñaban.

3 Las pasé en San Sebastián, en el norte de España. / Me gustó mucho San Sebastián. Es una ciudad muy bonita, y el hotel donde me quedé era excelente. Estaba enfrente de la playa, tenía piscina y un restaurante excelente. Y tuve mucha suerte con el tiempo. No hacía mucho calor. / Fui con unos amigos. Nos llevamos muy bien, eran gente muy maja. / No estuvimos mucho tiempo. Desgraciadamente, todos tuvimos que volver a trabajar. / Me encantaría volver, pero el próximo año espero ir a Sudamérica. Pienso viajar a Argentina y Chile. Si tengo dinero me quedaré allí un par de meses. Pienso tomar otro trabajo para pagar mis vacaciones. Y tú ¿fuiste de vacaciones a algún lugar? / ¡Qué lástima!

4 a We're flying with Spanair. b It's a direct flight. c On a private bus. d By airplane. e Six days. f No, from Cancún.

5 a Iré a Cancún y Ciudad de México. b Primero visitaré Cancún. c Me quedaré dos semanas. d No, me quedaré en hoteles.

6 a No. b It will be misty and later on it will be hazy. c It will be misty and in the afternoon it will be cloudy. d Pollution will be relatively low. e 8.36 p.m.

7 a Estará nublado y habrá lloviznas. b La mínima probable será de 11 grados y la máxima de 23. c La mínima fue de 13,1 a las 8.00 de la mañana y la máxima de 26,8 a las 15.30. d Habrá nubosidad parcial, variando a despejado. e 14,7 grados.

8 a La mayoría prefiere el viaje organizado, pero con cierto grado de flexibilidad. b Prefieren visitar monumentos, museos, parques naturales.

Test yourself

1 a pasará, pasarán, pasaré. b hará, haremos. c tendrá, tendré. d pondréis, pondremos. e dirás, diré, dirá. f vendrán, vendrá, vendrás.

2 a El hotel donde se quedaron era excelente. No estaba lejos de la playa y también tenía una piscina, pero lamentablemente llovió a cántaros la mayor parte del tiempo. b Pero mereció la pena ir. La ciudad era interesante, aunque era un poco ruidosa. c Pensamos

viajar a Brasil el año que viene/próximo. Patricia estuvo allí hace dos años y habló/me contó maravillas de Río. d No, no tomaremos/vamos a tomar un viaje organizado. Preferimos viajar por nuestra cuenta/de forma independiente/ independientemente, de otra manera resultará/será demasiado caro. Reservaremos nuestros billetes a través de una agencia de viajes. e Pues/Bien, espero ir de vacaciones a/hacia finales de agosto. Hay unas vacaciones en el Caribe que no son nada caras. Ya veremos. Aún/Todavía falta mucho tiempo. f – ¿Sigue lloviendo? – Lamentablemente sí, no ha parado de llover desde que nos levantamos. – ¡Qué lástima/pena! Pensaba jugar al tenis.

Unit 6

Language and comprehension check

1 i a Una habitación con una cama de matrimonio y dos camas individuales. b Para el 24 de agosto y para siete noches. c 80 euros. d Está incluido. ii a No se oye bien. b Tengo entendido que. c Se paga aparte. d En caso de que Vd. prefiera. e A partir del 24 de agosto. f ¿Me dice su nombre?

2 i a F. b F. c F. d V. e V. ii a Llamo por el anuncio. b ¿... está disponible ...?, ¿Estará disponible ...? c Ahora le pongo ... d Está muy bien de precio. f Es justamente lo que busco. g Lo acaban de pintar.

Practice

1 está, es, está, es, son, será, está

2 para, para, para, para, para, por, para, por, por, por

3 Follow model letter.

4 Llamo por el anuncio en el periódico. / Eso es. Busco algo para alquilar. ¿Podría darme más información sobre el apartamento? / Necesito algo que esté disponible inmediatamente. / Pues,

también busco algo que no sea demasiado caro. ¿Cuánto es el alquiler mensual? / Gracias. Eso es demasiado para mí.

5 **a** Vive con sus padres y sus dos hermanos menores. **b** Es grande y muy antiguo. **c** Es muy bonito, es de principios del siglo pasado y está muy bien conservado. **d** Tiene siete habitaciones en total. **e** No, tiene su propia habitación. **f** Es una calle muy ruidosa, pero con una arquitectura interesante. **g** En la esquina. **h** Porque alquilar un piso cuesta una fortuna.

6 **a** 'Pablo se va a mudar este fin de semana a un piso estupendo a sólo quince minutos de la Plaza Mayor. Es un piso de tres habitaciones y tiene vistas al río. Va a compartirlo con dos amigos y van a pagar setecientos ochenta euros mensuales en total.' **b i** V. **ii** F. **iii** F. **iv** V.

7 The economic situation and unemployment prevents them from leaving their homes. **i a** Vive con su madre. **b** Dejan el hogar cuando aún son muy jóvenes. **c** Nos llevamos perfectamente. **d** No tienes que hacer nada. **e** La casa donde nació. **f** Todavía viven con sus padres. **g** El deseo de independencia se ha obstaculizado. **ii a** No suelen quedarse. **b** Más allá de los 20 años. **c** Normalmente suele matricularse en una universidad. **d** Para siempre. **e** Si acaso regresan a su ciudad. **f** No se trata, por supuesto, ... sino.

Test yourself

1 **a** por – para – para – para **b** para – para **c** por **d** por – por **e** para – por **f** por – por – por.

2 **a** El apartamento que se alquila en la calle Pelayo, ¿está/estará disponible todavía? **b** Es un apartamento amueblado. **c** Está en muy buen estado y es muy bonito. Lo acaban de pintar. **d** Es exterior. **e** Es justamente lo que busco. **f** – ¿En qué piso está? – No estoy seguro, pero ahora le pongo con la persona encargada.

Unit 7

Language and comprehension

1 i a V. b F. c F. ii a Coja la línea uno. b Hasta … c Cambie a la
   línea …

2 i a 2.30 b 20 minutos c 2.50. ii a la hora de llegada. b ¿A qué
   andén llega? c el tablero de llegadas.

3 i … right and go as far as Plaza Antón Martín which is 100 metres
   from here. There we take calle de León on the left and continue as
   far as calle Lope de Vega. We have to go straight on along Lope de
   Vega until we reach Paseo del Prado. The museum is on the other
   side of the Paseo. ii a Dígame. b ¿Nos puede decir …? c Al salir …
   d Tuerzan a la derecha. e Sigan todo recto. f … hasta llegar …

4 i a en tren o en autocar. b la estación de Atocha. c la estación
   Sur. d cada hora, a la hora. e siete de la mañana. f 11.00 p.m.
   ii a ¿Podría decirnos …? b el horario de (los) trenes. c cada hora
   a la hora (exacta). d a partir de las siete de la mañana. e No nos
   queda ninguno.

Practice

1 coge / bájate / cruza / sube / sube / sigue

2 Bien, gracias, ¿y Vd.? / Coja la línea 2 en dirección a Ventas. /
   Sí, va directo, / Coja la línea 4 en dirección a Esperanza y bájese
   en América. Allí cambie a la línea 1 en dirección a Castilla. Esa
   línea le llevará a Colombia. / Voy a ir al Museo del Prado y
   después almorzaré con un amigo español. / ¡Por qué no! Volveré
   al hotel sobre las 7.00.

3 Model dialogues: a A: ¿Podría decirme por dónde se va al
   Banco Central? B: Sí, mire, siga Vd. todo recto por la calle Juan
   Bravo hasta General Pardiñas y allí doble a la derecha. El Banco
   Central está a una calle de allí, en la esquina de Ortega y Gasset,

al lado de la Oficina de Turismo. **b** A: Perdone, ¿puede decirme dónde está el Hotel Plaza? B: Sí, siga Vd. por la calle de Serrano hasta Ortega y Gasset y allí doble a la izquierda. Suba por Ortega y Gasset. El Hotel Plaza está en la Plaza del Marqués de Salamanca, entre Velázquez y Príncipe de Vergara.

4 salir / doble / vaya / más / tome / dirección / bájese / está / cuadras / dirección / doble / siga / hasta / esquina.

5 Le / decirle / tiene que buscar / coja / bájese / cruce / siga / verá / su derecha / siga / tuerza / se pierda.

6 **a** ¿De qué estación sale el Eurocity a París? **b** ¿A qué hora sale de Madrid? **c** ¿Cuántas paradas hace? **d** ¿Cuánto tarda (el viaje)? **e** ¿A qué hora llega a París? **f** ¿A qué estación llega? **g** ¿Se puede reservar/hacer una reserva por teléfono?

7 **a** To go to the airport, you must go straight on as far as the second traffic light, there you have to turn left and continue along that street till the end. There you'll find the main road. To go to the airport you have to turn right. **b** The tourist office is far from here, but you can go on the metro. Take line 1 to La Unión station. On leaving the station you'll see the Museum of Modern Art. The tourist office is behind the museum, on calle Libertad.

8 **a** viaja / viajar, elige / elegir, pide / pedir, no dudes / dudar, haz / hacer, contrata / contratar, aprovecha / aprovechar, ten / tener. **b** acceder, planear, listado, por separado, la tarifa global, con soltura. **c** alta temporada – un paquete turístico – Te puede salir mucho más económico – No dudes en ... – un seguro de cancelación – Aprovecha las ofertas de última hora – Pero ten en cuenta que ...

Test yourself

1 **a** coja. **b** mire. **c** gire. **d** siga. **e** bájese. **f** cruce. 2 **a** No se los des. **b** No se lo digas. **c** No la pongáis aquí. **d** Por favor, no lo hagas. **e** No se la envíes por email. **f** No te bajes aquí.

Unit 8

Language and comprehension check

1 a Aún/Todavía no ha llegado/No ha llegado todavía. **b** ¿Está seguro/a? **c** Estoy completamente seguro/a. **d** He revisado todas las transferencias. **e** mañana sobre el mediodía. **f** Es mejor que llame Vd. por teléfono o escriba a su banco.

2 i espere (esperar) / marque (marcar) / pase (pasar) **ii a** ¿Qué prefijo tengo que marcar? **b** el tono (de marcar). **c** el número del abonado. **d** la cabina (telefónica).

3 Correos / muestras / recomienda / postal / urgencia / ventaja / certificado / entrega / caro / conviene

4 a Lo alquilaron en Manchester. **b** La hicieron para el día catorce. **c** La hizo el Sr. Brown. **d** La tenía para el día quince. **e** Porque no tienen ningún coche disponible. **f** Les aconsejan que hablen con el encargado.

Practice

1 ha llamado / han llegado / han reservado / he ido / he dejado / ha invitado.

2 a la transferencia llegaría mañana. **b** tardaría una semana. **c** la carta estaría allí el lunes. **d** nos entregarían el coche esta tarde. **e** me repararía el coche ahora mismo. **f** me llamaría por teléfono esta noche.

3 a Yo mismo/a he hecho la reserva. **b** No me cabe duda de que era para hoy. **c** ¿Está seguro/a de que no hay ninguna reserva a mi nombre? **d** ¡Es el colmo de la incompetencia! **e** ¡Es increíble! **f** Exijo que nos den una habitación inmediatamente. **g** Pues, quisiera hacer una reclamación. **h** Es la primera vez que nos sucede algo así.

4 a 5. **b** 3. **c** 1. **d** 6. **e** 4. **f** 2.

5 Primero pon varias monedas de (una libra) en la ranura, enseguida levanta el auricular y espera el tono de marcar. Marca el 00 y después el 3493, seguido del número de tus padres. Las monedas caerán cuando se establezca la comunicación.

6 **a i** A service for you to express your opinions and complaints. **ii** You have to dial phone 31 45 45. It is an automatic answerphone which operates 24 hours a day. **b i** in a hotel. A guest complains about the delay in bringing clean towels to her room **ii** in a garage. A customer complains to the person in charge about the state of his car. **iii** in a restaurant. A customer complains about the delay in bringing their order.

7 **Model answers: 1** El primer lector se queja de las molestias que le causó una línea aérea por la sobreventa de billetes, la que le impidió a él y su mujer realizar el viaje que tenían planeado. **2** La segunda persona se queja sobre la utilización del inglés en lugar del español en las indicaciones en un hotel en Ibiza, donde pasó sus vacaciones. **a** ya que. **b** insólito. **c** nos quejamos. **d** iniciar. **e** indignación. **f** descortés. **g** nunca lo había experimentado. **h** una suerte de.

Test yourself

1 **a** ha vuelto/vuelve – vendría. **b** escrito – aconsejado – haga. **c** recomendado – contrate – hecho. **d** diga – dicho. **e** entreguen – harían. **f** marque /Vd. marca – entendido.

2 **a** prefijo. **b** tono. **c** seguro – entrega – ventaja. **d** cabina. **e** reclamación – encargado. **f** reserva.

Unit 9

Language and comprehension check

1 **a** Es para regalo. **b** Están de oferta. **c** Puede cambiarlo. **d** Deberá traer la factura. **e** Me lo quedo. **f** Pagar en efectivo. **g** Pagar con tarjeta de crédito. **h** ¿Me lo puede envolver?

2 ¿Verdadero o falso? a F. b F. c V. d F.

3 a The picture is not very clear. b He's going to check it and then he'll give the client an estimate. c The client must accept the estimate.

Practice

1 a Si tuviera vacaciones viajaría a España. b Si el coche no estuviera en mal estado lo compraría. c Si mereciera la pena lo haríamos reparar. d Si no tuvieran que volver al trabajo se quedarían. e Si no estuviera ocupado los recibiría. f Si él hablara bien español ella le entendería.

2 a Tuve que vender el piso. b Tenía que decirte algo importante. c No hay nada que hacer. d Debo llevar el pasaporte. e Necesitaba comprar una maleta. f Habrá que traer algo para beber.

3 a Quisiera comprar unos pantalones. ¿Tiene algunos de oferta? No quiero gastar demasiado. b Sí, son para mí. Busco algo (que sea) de buena calidad. c Sí, son muy bonitos. Me gustan mucho. ¿Los tiene en negro? d Tengo la talla 46. ¿Tiene algunos en esa talla? e Quisiera probármelos. ¿Dónde está el probador? f Me quedan muy bien. ¿Cuánto cuestan? g Son un poco caros, pero me gustan. Me los quedo. ¿Aceptan tarjetas de crédito? No llevo dinero.

4 Dear Pat, What a surprise to hear from you again! I'm glad you're well and I hope you do very well in your final exams. Thank you very much for your invitation for this summer, but unfortunately I don't have enough money to travel. If I could, I would certainly come and see you. You don't know how much I'd like it! Next year perhaps, but I'll have to work very hard to save money as the trip is very expensive. You will have to come to Venezuela too some day. I don't need to invite you formally. I'll be waiting for you. Love Raúl.

5 a Luis. b Raquel. c Ana. d Raquel. e Ana. f Luis. i Luis. ii Ana. iii Luis. iv Raquel. v Ana.

6 **a i** Cuando necesita algo con urgencia. **ii** Cuando necesita varias cosas, porque pierde menos tiempo, hay más variedad, y no resulta más caro. **iii** En el supermercado. **b i** F. **ii** V. **iii** F. **c i** Check words in script of ¡A escuchar! in the A escuchar section. **ii** No, that is done by his wife. Sometimes he accompanies her, but normally he hasn't got time. They have a small supermarket in the area where they buy almost everything. Except for fruit and vegetables, which are bought in the market. It is cheaper and fresher.

7 Tourist Apartments – The following services are included in the price of accommodation: water, electricity and gas, rubbish collection and service charges. / When making your reservation, you may be asked to pay a deposit of 15 to 40 per cent of the total price agreed. / If you decide to cancel your reservation, you are entitled to a refund of the deposit, minus a deduction of five to 50 per cent, depending on how much notice is given. If the cancellation is made less than seven days in advance, there is no refund.

8 **a** lista. **b** vacío. **c** tentación. **d** precio. **e** estantes. **f** vergüenza. **g** bolsillo. **h** gastos. **i** presupuesto. **ii** alimentos. **iii** gran almacén. **iv** de oferta. **v** cajero/a. **vi** dependiente/a. **vii** la pareja.

Test yourself

1 **a** 6. **b** 3. **c** 5. **d** 1. **e** 2. **f** 4.

2 **a** 3. **b** 5. **c** 6. **d** 1. **e** 2. **f** 4.

Unit 10

Language and comprehension check

1 **a** Tengo hora. **b** Me caí y me torcí un tobillo. **c** ¿Le duele aquí? **d** La pierna derecha. **e** Me duele mucho. **f** Lo tengo hinchado. **g** Vuelva a verme. **h** No creo que sea necesario.

2 sentirse / encontrarse; sentir / lamentar; pasarse / acabarse; romper / quebrar; tratar / intentar; volver / regresar; de aquí a / dentro de.

Practice

1 a Estaba durmiendo. b Estaba haciendo yoga. c Estaba meditando. d Estaba leyendo. e Estábamos preparando la cena. f Estaba viendo el fútbol en la tele.

2 a Me dijo que volviera mañana. b Me aconsejó que descansara un poco. c Nos recomendó que no fumáramos mucho. d El doctor quiere que haga más ejercicio. e Rosa nos pidió que llegáramos/llegásemos a la hora. f Mi mujer no quiere que trabaje tanto.

3 Quisiera algo para el dolor de estómago. / Sí, también tengo diarrea. Comí pescado anoche y después empecé a sentirme mal. / Gracias. ¿Cuánto es?

4 Me dio unas pastillas. Me dijo que tomara dos tres veces al día hasta que me sintiera mejor. También me aconsejó que tuviera cuidado con la alimentación y que no comiera nada frito.

5 a Se quebró la pierna mientras jugaba / estaba jugando al fútbol, así que / de manera que no podrá jugar durante algún tiempo. b No me siento / encuentro bien. Tengo dolor de cabeza / Me duele la cabeza y tengo fiebre. c Dijo que no podría verme esta tarde. Tiene hora con el doctor a las cuatro. d El doctor me dijo que descansara y que volviera de aquí a / dentro de quince días si aún / todavía no me siento bien. e Llamó por teléfono a la oficina para decir que no va a venir a trabajar porque ha cogido una / tiene (la) gripe. f Se cayó y se torció el tobillo. Está hinchado y dice que le duele mucho.

6 comer / alimentos / productos / alimenticia / huevos / leguminosas / proteínas / mantenimiento / músculos

7 a In Andalusia and Levante. b Because the diet in these regions includes an excessive amount of proteins, animal fats and sugar. c In Madrid, the diet is balanced and healthy, better than in the capitals of other Spanish communities. d Breakfasts are light.

e Because of their work. **f** The diet in Catalonia includes an excessive amount of proteins, fats and not many carbohydrates.

8 Rosa's skin is too white and she easily gets sunburnt. Ignacio suffers from stomach upsets when on holiday. Claudia suffers from palpitations. Alejandro is working too hard and he fainted while working in the garden. Rosa, c and e. Ignacio, d and f. Claudia, b and h. Alejandro, a and g.

Test yourself

1 a Me duele la cabeza. **b** Al niño le duele el estómago. **c** No me encuentro bien. **d** ¿Qué estabas diciendo? **e** Ángel estaba durmiendo plácidamente.

2 a Me dijo que dejara/dejase de fumar. **b** Me aconsejó que no se lo dijera/dijese a nadie. **c** Nos sugirieron que aprendiéramos/ aprendiésemos español. **d** Me pidió que no siguiera/siguiese con la dieta. **e** Me recomendó que hiciera/hiciese algún deporte.

Unit 11

Language and comprehension

1 i a V. **b** F. **c** V. **d** F. **e** F. **f** V. **ii a** un par de años **b** ¿A qué se debe? **c** por un lado. **d** Están gastando una buena cantidad de recursos. **e** por otro lado. **f** una situación pasajera.

2 a Piensa que el tráfico en Madrid es insoportable. **b** Ella cree que se debería favorecer más al transporte público. **c** Madrid sería una ciudad más limpia y con menos ruido.

Practice

1 a Si no hubiera perdido mi trabajo habría / hubiera ido a España. **b** Si hubiéramos tenido dinero habríamos / hubiéramos podido viajar. **c** Si no hubieran aumentado los precios no habría / hubiera descendido el turismo. **d** Si hubieran encontrado plaza en el avión no habrían / hubieran tenido que esperar otro vuelo. **e** Si Carlos no hubiera tenido un accidente, no habríamos/hubiéramos cancelado el viaje. **f** Si nos hubieran invitado a la fiesta, habríamos/hubiéramos ido.

2 **a** ¿Qué opina Vd. sobre/acerca de ...? **b** Me parece que es ... **c** ¿Cuál es su opinión sobre/acerca de ...? **d** Creo que es ... **e** La menor llegada de turistas se debe a ... **f** También habría que ... **g** ¿A qué se debe tanta ...? **h** A mi parecer este es ... ¿No crees tú?

3 Sí, estoy totalmente de acuerdo con eso. No debe permitirse que la gente fume en lugares públicos. Es un hecho muy conocido que muchas muertes se deben al tabaquismo. / Por supuesto. La publicidad al tabaco debería haberse prohibido hace mucho tiempo. Si se hubiera hecho antes se habrían evitado muchas muertes. También sería necesario educar a la gente, especialmente a los jóvenes para que no empiecen a fumar.

4 **a i** el efecto invernadero. **ii** el calentamiento de la Tierra. **iii** radiaciones ultravioleta. **iv** las capas superiores de la atmósfera. **v** los patrones de lluvia cambiarían drásticamente. **vi** el agujero en la capa de ozono. **b i** I do not believe that the human species can survive. **ii** It would destroy the majority of life forms. **iii** ... which would affect crops and sea life. **iv** The hole has been gradually growing. **v** The hole in the ozone layer over Antarctica is damaging the atmosphere.

5 **a** Its main purpose is to make people aware of the problems caused by noise pollution, and to get the authorities to establish legal rules which can give us a better quality of life. **b** Other than traffic noise, he mentions problems caused by neighbours who, with their radio and television too loud, bother other people. And bar and disco owners who, with their music at full volume, disturb people's sleep. **c** He says there is a lack of consideration which is not seen in other European capitals. **d** By establishing prohibitions and enforcing them by means of legislation. **e i** tome. **ii** establezcan. **iii** den. **iv** dejan. **v** se ha hecho. **vi** protestando / hacernos.

6 a La gran concentración humana; la excesiva centralización; el aumento constante en el número de automóviles. **b** OMS: 90 milígramos por metro cuadrado; Ciudad de México supera a veces los 300 milígramos. **c** 2 millones. **d** Intereses económicos; presiones políticas; el propio rechazo de muchos de los afectados. **e** Mejoras en el transporte público; restricción vehicular; cierre definitivo o temporal de las industrias más contaminantes.

Test yourself

1 a Si hubiera/hubiese tenido dinero, habría/hubiera salido ... **b** Si hubieran/hubiesen llegado a la hora al aeropuerto, no habrían/hubieran perdido ... **c** Si no hubiera/hubiese bebido en exceso, no habría/hubiera tenido ... **d** Si hubieran/hubiesen tenido visado, habrían/hubieran podido ... **e** Si no se hubiera/hubiese acostado tarde, habría/hubiera despertado a tiempo.

2 a ¿Cuál es su opinión?/¿Qué opina/piensa usted? **b** En mi opinión/A mi parecer/juicio ... **c** ¿No cree usted que ...? **d** ¿Está (usted) de acuerdo conmigo? **e** Estoy de acuerdo con usted. Esto se debe/obedece a ...

Unit 12

Language and comprehension check

1 i a to wash the dishes/do the washing up. **b** to do the shopping. **c** to look after the children. **ii a** la ropa. **b** la aspiradora. **c** los cristales. **d** la limpieza. **e** el suelo. **f** al bebé.

2 a More than half of secondary school pupils are women. **b** Women tend to choose studies which traditionally have been considered as appropriate for women. **c** There has been a notorious increase in the number of women. **d** On the one hand, there has been an increase in the female work force and a decrease in the male work force. However, unemployment has affected women more than men. **e** The female working population is younger than the male one. f The average number of children per woman has gone down.

Practice

1 a Ella era mejor que él, y a pesar de/pese a eso no consiguió/ obtuvo el trabajo. b Aunque Carlos es mayor que Sofía, se llevan muy bien juntos. c María había vivido en los Estados Unidos durante varios años, sin embargo su inglés no era tan bueno como el de su hermano. d No habían vivido en Madrid, sino en Barcelona, aunque habían estado aquí más de una vez. e A pesar de/Pese a ser más joven, no es tan activo como los demás/ otros. f Iremos de vacaciones, aunque tengamos que pedir dinero prestado.

2 a por una parte. b indudablemente. c así. d a mi parecer. e con frecuencia. f por otra parte. g ya que. h en la actualidad. i en relación con. j en realidad.

3 a F. b F. c V. d F. e F. f V.

4 Carla's husband does not want her to go out to work. / sensación, razones, inseguridad, estatus, seria, actividad, apoyo, necesidad, cambio, horizontes.

5 b, c, e, f, g. i Está desempleada. ii Dar a luz. iii De nuevo. iv Los motivos. v Según. vi Administrativa. vii Pensárselo dos veces. viii Es una pena.

Test yourself

1 a habían. b había. c habíamos. d como. e menor.

2 a sino. b aunque. c a pesar de. d sin embargo. e sino que.

¡A escuchar! Transcripts

Unit 1

Antonio	Hola, Pilar. ¿Cómo estás?
Pilar	Muy bien, ¿y tú?
Antonio	Bien, gracias. Ayer vi a María y me dijo que ya habías encontrado trabajo. Me alegro mucho. Estarás muy contenta, ¿no?
Pilar	Por supuesto. Estoy trabajando en un colegio cerca de casa. Es un colegio muy bueno, pero hay que trabajar muchísimo. Empiezo a las ocho de la mañana y no salgo hasta la una.
Antonio	Te levantas muy temprano, entonces.
Pilar	A las siete de la mañana. Por suerte está muy cerca de casa, y en quince minutos estoy allí.
Antonio	¿Y por la tarde no trabajas?
Pilar	Por ahora no, pero con lo del colegio tengo bastante que hacer. Por la tarde preparo las clases, a veces tengo reuniones con los padres o con otros profesores. ¡En fin! Me falta tiempo para hacer todo lo que quisiera. Pero tenemos que vernos uno de estos días.
Antonio	Sí, por supuesto. No trabajas los sábados, ¿verdad?
Pilar	No, los sábados estoy libre.
Antonio	Bueno, ¿por qué no me acompañas a comprar un regalo el sábado por la mañana? Mi hermana está de cumpleaños y no sé qué regalarle.
Pilar	De acuerdo. ¿A qué hora?
Antonio	¿A las once te parece bien?
Pilar	Sí, está bien.
Antonio	Bueno, pasaré a buscarte a esa hora. Hasta el sábado, entonces.
Pilar	¡Chao!

Unit 2

Gran asistencia de público ha tenido la exposición de arte latinoamericano que se está realizando en Madrid, en el Museo Español de Arte Contemporáneo. Los asistentes podrán apreciar más de ochenta obras de los más connotados pintores iberoamericanos, provenientes de los principales países de la región, entre ellos México, Colombia, Argentina y Chile. La exposición, que fue inaugurada por la Reina Sofía, ha contado también con la presencia de importantes personajes del mundo artístico, tanto español como iberoamericano.

El viernes 25 se dará comienzo a un nuevo ciclo del Festival de Otoño de Madrid, que incluirá teatro, danza clásica y contemporánea, música clásica, y otras actividades, tales como cine, conferencias, coloquios y exposiciones. El Festival de este año dedicará una especial atención a los países de Europa del Este, en cada uno de los campos artísticos, en especial la danza y la música.

Este acontecimiento cultural servirá para mostrar aquellos espectáculos y creaciones que no se pueden contemplar habitualmente en los escenarios madrileños.

Unit 3

María del Carmen Salas

Periodista	¿Cómo te llamas?
M. del Carmen	Me llamo María del Carmen Salas.
Periodista	¿Cuántos años tienes?
M. del Carmen	Tengo 38 años.
Periodista	¿Podrías decirme a qué te dedicas?
M. del Carmen	Soy periodista. Trabajo en la revista Claudia. Es una revista femenina que se publica en Madrid una vez por semana.
Periodista	¿Tienes alguna responsabilidad especial dentro de la revista?

M. del Carmen	Bueno, la revista tiene varias secciones especializadas y yo estoy a cargo de la sección Salud. Escribo artículos relacionados con el tema de la salud, que sean de especial interés para la mujer. Además, realizo entrevistas con médicos y otros profesionales que tengan que ver con el tema.
Periodista	¿Qué es lo que más te agrada de tu profesión?
M. del Carmen	Pues, principalmente el contacto con la gente, el trabajo en terreno, salir a hacer entrevistas, también el contacto con las lectoras a través de correspondencia. Creo que eso es lo que más me agrada. Además, esta es una actividad muy creativa, hay que saber usar la imaginación y hacer cosas diferentes para satisfacer a la mayoría de las lectoras.
Periodista	¿Hay algo que no te guste de tu trabajo?
M. del Carmen	Que no me guste, no, pero debo confesar que es una profesión que exige mucha dedicación, hay que estar dispuesta a aceptar críticas, ya que las lectoras son muy exigentes, y hay que renovarse constantemente. Y eso no es nada fácil.

Javier Molina

Periodista	¿Cómo te llamas?
J. Molina	Me llamo Javier Molina Sánchez.
Periodista	¿Qué edad tienes, Javier?
J. Molina	Tengo 29 años.
Periodista	¿En qué trabajas?
J. Molina	Soy funcionario de la Oficina de Turismo de Alicante.
Periodista	¿Llevas mucho tiempo trabajando allí?
J. Molina	Trabajo allí desde hace cinco años.
Periodista	¿Dónde trabajabas antes?

(Contd)

J. Molina	En Madrid. Trabajaba en una empresa privada, pero no ganaba lo suficiente y decidí cambiarme. Tuve suerte al encontrar un puesto aquí. Ahora tengo un trabajo seguro y para toda la vida. Al menos así lo espero. Y el sueldo no está nada mal. Por otra parte, Alicante es una ciudad muy agradable para vivir, es un lugar tranquilo. Y la propiedad aquí está más barata que en Madrid. Así he podido comprarme un pequeño piso. En Madrid ahora es imposible. ¡Con esos precios!
Periodista	¿En qué consiste tu trabajo específicamente?
J. Molina	Pues, principalmente en dar información al público. A Alicante vienen muchísimos turistas, muchos ingleses, alemanes … Muchos no hablan castellano y yo sé inglés y algo de alemán también. La mayoría viene a pedir información sobre hoteles y sobre sitios de interés en la región. Es una región muy bonita y el clima es estupendo.

Unit 4

Pregunta	Gloria, me gustaría que hablásemos un poco acerca del tema de la educación y de tu propia experiencia como estudiante. Seguramente tendrás muchos recuerdos de aquella época. Después de todo eres muy joven y no te habrás olvidado aún, ¿verdad? ¿Cuándo dejaste el colegio?
Respuesta	Hace casi dos años. Tengo muchos recuerdos agradables del colegio. Fue una época muy feliz de mi vida.
Pregunta	¿Dónde hiciste tus estudios?
Respuesta	En un colegio religioso de La Coruña. Era un colegio sólo para chicas. La verdad es que me habría gustado ir a un colegio donde hubiese habido chicos, pero vamos, mis padres quisieron que fuese allí y no estuvo nada mal. Por el contrario, disfruté muchísimo y me hice de excelentes amigas allí.
Pregunta	En pocas palabras, ¿cómo describirías el colegio donde fuiste?

Respuesta	Pues, era bastante bueno. Los profesores eran muy estrictos y nos hacían trabajar mucho. En general, guardo un buen recuerdo de ellos. Había excepciones, claro, como es normal. La profesora de matemáticas, por ejemplo, no me gustaba nada. No tenía sentido del humor y nos llevábamos muy mal. En cambio, con otros no. La profesora de historia era una persona simpatiquísima y mis relaciones con ella fueron siempre estupendas.
Pregunta	¿Fuiste una buena estudiante?
Respuesta	Ni buena ni mala. Dependía de la asignatura. Había asignaturas que me gustaban mucho y otras que simplemente no me gustaban. En historia y en inglés, por ejemplo, nunca tuve problemas. Eran mis asignaturas favoritas y estudiaba muchísimo. En cambio, en matemáticas y ciencias me iba bastante mal y más de una vez suspendí.
Pregunta	¿Y a qué te dedicas ahora?
Respuesta	Estudio en una escuela de traductores e intérpretes.

Unit 5

El tiempo

Nublado con lloviznas y temperaturas extremas probables de once la mínima y veintitrés grados la máxima anunció para hoy en Santiago la Dirección Meteorológica de Chile. Las temperaturas extremas de ayer en la capital fueron trece grados, una décima (13,1), la mínima, a las ocho de la mañana y veintiséis grados, ocho décimas (26,8), la máxima, a las quince horas y treinta minutos (15,30). Perspectivas para mañana viernes veintiuno de febrero en el área metropolitana, nubosidad parcial variando a despejado. Temperatura del momento, catorce grados, siete décimas (14,7) con una humedad relativa de un ochenta y siete por ciento (87 %).

Ocho de la mañana, dieciséis minutos (8,16). Hasta aquí las informaciones. Por su atención muchas gracias y buenos días.

(Radio El Conquistador, Santiago de Chile).

Unit 6

a Un nuevo piso

Soledad	Hola, ¿qué hay?
Pablo	Hola.
Soledad	¿Y cómo os ha ido con la búsqueda de piso? ¿Habéis encontrado algo?
Pablo	Pues, sí, por fin hemos encontrado lo que buscábamos. No sabes lo difícil que ha sido.
Soledad	¡Hombre!, me alegro. ¿Y qué tal es?
Pablo	Pues, no está nada mal. Está a unos quince minutos en autobús de la Plaza Mayor, en la calle Conde de Villaseca. ¿La conoces?
Soledad	Sí, sí, por allí vive mi hermana. Es un barrio bastante bueno y muy tranquilo.
Pablo	Y el piso es bastante grande. Tiene tres habitaciones, mucho sol y una vista estupenda. Desde allí se puede ver el río.
Soledad	¡Qué maravilla! Y de precio, ¿qué tal?
Pablo	Un poco caro, setecientos ochenta euros al mes, pero vamos …, somos tres, doscientos sesenta cada uno, que tampoco es demasiado. ¿No te parece?
Soledad	Está bien. Yo estoy pagando sobre quinientos. ¿Os habéis mudado ya?
Pablo	No, todavía no, pero lo haremos este fin de semana. Tendrás que venir a vernos.
Soledad	Por supuesto.

b Hotel O'Higgins

Hotel O'Higgins de Viña del Mar le ofrece un fin de semana grande con precios para chicos. Dos noches, tres días, para dos adultos y hasta dos niños menores de doce años sin costo en la misma habitación por sólo treinta y cinco mil pesos. Incluye desayuno e impuesto. Además, sus niños disfrutarán del plan familiar del Hotel O'Higgins donde personal especializado realiza actividades y entretenciones para que usted pueda tomar un merecido descanso. Reservas en Santiago, teléfonos 713165 y 696 6826.

(Radio Clásica, Santiago de Chile)

Unit 7

a En viaje al aeropuerto

Conductor	Perdone, ¿la carretera para el aeropuerto, por favor?
Guardia	Sí, mire, siga Vd. todo recto hasta el segundo semáforo y allí doble Vd. a la izquierda y continúe por esa calle hasta el final. Allí encontrará Vd. la carretera. Para ir al aeropuerto tiene que torcer a la derecha.
Conductor	Muchas gracias.
Guardia	De nada.

b Buscando la oficina de turismo

Turista	Por favor, ¿sabe Vd. dónde está la oficina de turismo
Transeúnte	Pues, está un poco lejos de aquí, pero puede ir en el metro. Coja Vd. la línea 1 hasta la estación de La Unión. Al salir de la estación verá Vd. el Museo de Arte Moderno. La oficina de turismo está detrás del museo, en la calle Libertad.
Turista	Gracias.

Unit 8

a ¡Dígalo por la PR!, un espacio que hemos dedicado para que usted exponga sus comentarios y sus quejas. ¡Dígalo por la PR: el sistema de contestación automático que opera durante las 24 horas para que Vd. pueda ser escuchado. Llame ahora mismo al 31 45 45 y ¡dígalo por la PR! La Romántica, XHPR 101.3 MHz, transmitiendo las 24 horas del día desde Veracruz.

(Radio La Romántica, Veracruz, México)

b ¡Quejas y más quejas!

i ¿Oiga? ¿Quiere Vd. enviar a la camarera a la habitación 320, por favor? Le he pedido que me traiga toallas limpias. Esto fue hace más de una hora y todavía estoy esperando. Las necesito ahora mismo.

ii Vd. es el jefe, ¿verdad? Mire, he traído el coche a reparar y vea Vd. el estado en que lo han dejado. Está peor que antes. El trabajo que han hecho no vale nada. Esta es la última vez que traigo el coche aquí.

iii Perdone Vd., pero ¿a qué hora nos trae lo nuestro? Hemos pedido hace casi media hora. Tráiganos al menos el vino.

Unit 9

a Rosario Santos

Periodista	¿Compra Vd. normalmente en grandes almacenes como estos o prefiere comprar en una tienda pequeña?
Rosario	Bueno …, la verdad es que eso depende … Hombre, si se trata de una cosa que necesito con urgencia, la compro en cualquier tienda de mi barrio, pero cuando tengo que comprar varias cosas prefiero venir aquí. Así no tengo que andar de un lado para otro. Vamos, que a veces se pierde mucho tiempo. Además, mire Vd., aquí hay más variedad y si va Vd. a una tienda pequeña del barrio muchas veces no encuentra lo que busca o es más caro.
Periodista	¿Y los comestibles dónde los suele comprar?
Rosario	Pues, normalmente voy al supermercado, hay uno cerca de casa y allí hago la compra para toda la semana. Así me resulta más barato y más cómodo. Vamos, yo sé que hay gente que va todos los días a comprar una o dos cosas, luego se ponen a charlar con las vecinas, a cotillear y qué sé yo. Yo no, señor, eso no, que en casa hay muchísimo que hacer.

b Ana Belmar

Periodista	Ana, ¿tú compras normalmente en grandes tiendas como esta o en tiendas más pequeñas?
Ana	Bueno, hoy he venido aquí porque están de rebajas y, claro, hay que aprovechar. Pero por lo general prefiero ir a alguna tienda pequeña donde haya más cosas exclusivas, sobre todo tratándose de ropa. A veces pagas un poco más, pero te llevas algo que realmente te gusta.
Periodista	¿Te gusta vestir a la moda?
Ana	Vaya, sí, aunque no siempre puedo comprar lo que quisiera. Si trabajara, quizá sí, podría hacerlo, pero soy estudiante y el dinero me lo da mi padre.

c Andrés Calle

Periodista	Vd., señor, ¿suele comprar aquí, en una gran tienda o prefiere hacerlo en una tienda pequeña?
Andrés	Pues, lo cierto es que prefiero ir a una tienda más pequeña donde el trato sea más directo, más personal. Pero eso sólo lo puedo hacer el fin de semana. Yo soy administrativo y trabajo por la mañana y por la tarde y cuando salgo las tiendas ya están cerradas. Por eso vengo a veces aquí, pues está abierto al mediodía. Aprovecho la hora de la comida para comprar lo que necesito.
Periodista	¿Y la compra de comestibles la hace Vd. también?
Andrés	Pues no, de eso se encarga mi mujer. A veces la acompaño, pero normalmente no tengo tiempo. Pero tenemos un pequeño supermercado en el barrio donde compramos casi todo. Excepto la fruta y las verduras, claro, eso se compra en el mercado. Es más barato, más fresco …

Unit 10

La dieta mediterránea

Presentador: Buenos días. Damos comienzo a un nuevo programa de la serie La buena mesa. En la primera parte del programa de hoy tenemos una invitada especial, la experta en nutrición Angélica Muñoz quien se referirá a los cambios que ha experimentado la dieta de los españoles.

Invitada: Buenos días. En primer lugar quisiera referirme a la llamada dieta mediterránea. Pues bien, la dieta mediterránea está de moda, aunque hasta hace poco no gozaba de muy buena reputación. Los médicos y nutriólogos han descubierto que en los países mediterráneos la incidencia de enfermedades cardiovasculares es mucho menor que en tierra adentro.

En España, las características de este tipo de alimentación se dan, sobre todo, en Andalucía y en el Levante. Allí, la base de la dieta es el pescado, las grasas vegetales y los vegetales que contienen gran cantidad de fibra.

Por el contrario, es en la meseta central, norte y noroeste, donde el riesgo sanitario es más alto, pues se consume un exceso de proteínas, grasas animales y azúcares. La preocupación de los científicos es que España se contamine de la dieta continental, en vez de que los demás se contagien de la dieta mediterránea.

Ahora, veamos lo que pasa en Madrid. La dieta de los madrileños es equilibrada y saludable, mejor que la del resto de capitales comunitarias. No obstante, los madrileños toman menos verduras de las necesarias y demasiadas proteínas y sal. Como complemento, hay que decir que en Madrid se come poco pan y patatas y mucha fruta, leche y pescado.

¿Y qué hay de los desayunos? Pues, los desayunos que se toman los madrileños son ligeros y se advierte una tendencia a no cocinar por la noche en casa. Uno de cada cinco escolares no desayuna y muchos de los que lo hacen consumen menos calorías de las aconsejables.

El comer cada vez con más frecuencia fuera de casa por razones laborales, sobre todo, es otra de las características de los cambios alimentarios de los madrileños. Madrid está siguiendo la tendencia de la Comunidad Europea, donde casi el 4 por ciento de la población activa realiza cinco almuerzos semanales fuera de casa.

Algo similar sucede en Cataluña. Los catalanes ingieren demasiadas proteínas y grasas y pocos hidratos de carbono ...

(Cambio 16, N° 886)

Unit 11

Periodista	¡Ya era hora! Este verano, un gran número de madrileños ha comenzado a protestar por el ruido que hacen otros españoles. En una entrevista, preguntamos la opinión de Antonio García, quien dirige el grupo 'Por una ciudad más tranquila'.
Antonio	Pues, el propósito principal es hacer que la gente tome conciencia sobre los problemas causados por la contaminación acústica, y conseguir que las autoridades establezcan normas legales que nos den una mejor calidad de vida. Y no me refiero sólo al ruido causado por el tráfico. También están los propios vecinos, que con su radio o televisión demasiado altos molestan a los demás, así como los propietarios de terrazas y discos, que con su música a todo volumen y a toda hora no nos dejan dormir por la noche. En fin, existe una desconsideración hacia el resto de las personas que no se observa en otras capitales europeas. En ciertos barrios de Madrid la vida se ha hecho insoportable y el nivel de estrés va en aumento.
Periodista	¿Crees tú que la acción de este grupo pueda conseguir su objetivo?
Antonio	Vamos ... sabemos que no será fácil y que no basta con hacer una campaña al respecto. Simplemente hay que establecer prohibiciones y hacerlas cumplir mediante una legislación. Mientras tanto seguiremos protestando hasta hacernos oír.

Unit 12

Entrevista con Teresa

Pregunta	Teresa, tú y Paco os habéis casado hace muy poco tiempo, ¿verdad?
Teresa	Sí, hace poco más de un año.
Pregunta	Y ambos sois profesionales, ¿no es así?
Teresa	Sí, Paco es arquitecto y yo soy psicóloga.
Pregunta	¿Y cómo os arregláis con las tareas del hogar? Con la limpieza, la cocina, la compra, y todas aquellas tareas que hay en toda casa y que no se pueden eludir. ¿Quién las hace? ¿Tenéis a alguien que os ayude?
Teresa	Pues, tenemos una asistenta que viene dos veces por semana a limpiar el piso y a planchar, pero todo lo demás lo hacemos Paco y yo. La compra la hago yo, pues salgo antes del trabajo y camino de casa paso por el supermercado. En cambio, Paco, que cocina mucho mejor que yo, se encarga de guisar. Los fines de semana lo hacemos juntos, pero vamos, a él le encanta la cocina y a mí no. Pero yo soy la que friega los platos.
Pregunta	¿Son labores compartidas, entonces?
Teresa	Totalmente. De otra manera, quizá no funcionaríamos bien como pareja. Me molestaría tener que encargarme yo de todo. En cambio así, las cosas marchan muy bien y no hay ningún tipo de resentimiento. Por el contrario, Paco y yo tenemos una excelente relación.
Pregunta	¿Y cuando vengan los hijos?
Teresa	Pues, probablemente tendremos que hacer ciertos ajustes, pero fundamentalmente, no creo que las cosas vayan a cambiar.
Pregunta	¿Sois una pareja feliz, entonces?
Teresa	Sin duda.

Taking it further

Sources of authentic Spanish

Spanish newspapers and magazines

El País (http://www.elpais.es)
El Mundo (http://www.el-mundo.es)
La Vanguardia (http://www.lavanguardia.es)
ABC (http://www.abc.es)
El Periódico (http://www.elperiodico.es)

For general information, including Spanish current affairs and world news, try the following magazines: *Cambio 16*, *Tiempo* and *Tribuna*.

For light reading and entertainment you might like to look at *Hola*, *Quo*, *Mía*, *Pronto*, *Lecturas* and *Semana*. These are by far the most popular magazines amongst Spaniards and, as a beginner, you may find some of the articles easier to follow.

Latin American newspapers and magazines

Latin American newspapers and magazines will be more difficult to find outside each country, but if you have internet facilities you will be able to access their websites, although they may be special net versions. The following is a list of some of the main Latin American newspapers:

Argentina: *La Nación* (http://www.lanacion.com.ar), *Clarín* (http://www.clarin.com)
Chile: *El Mercurio* (http://www.diario.elmercurio.com)
Colombia: *El Espectador* (http://www.elespectador.com)
Cuba: *Granma* (http://www.granma.cu)
Mexico: *El Universal* (http://www.el-universal.com.mx)
Peru: *El Comercio* (http://elcomercio.pe), *Correo* (http://www.correoperu.com.pe)

Radio, television and internet news

An excellent way to improve your understanding of spoken Spanish is to listen to radio and watch television. On medium wave after dark (in Europe) and via satellite you will be able to gain access to Radio Nacional de España, Televisión Española (TVE) and other stations. For Spanish language news on the internet you may like to go to BBC Mundo (http://www.bbc.co.uk/mundo), or to Podcast BBC Mundo Radio, which offers a 15-minute world news summary from Monday to Friday, with a special focus on Latin America.

Travelling in Spain and Latin America

Travelling in a Spanish-speaking country is probably the best way to practise what you have learnt and improve your command of the spoken language. If you are planning to do this, there are a number of good guidebooks which will help you to plan your journey. The well-known Lonely Planet series covers not just specific countries, but also main regions and cities, including Spain and Latin America. For the latter, the Mexico and Central American Handbook and the South American Handbook have a long tradition amongst travellers in the region. Time Out, Michelin and Fodor's, among others, have also become well established in the travel guide market.

For travellers in Spain, the following websites may prove useful, with information on tourist attractions, accommodation, travel and restaurants:

http://www.sispain.org/english/travelli
http://www.worldtravelguide.net/country/259/
country_guide/Europe/Spain.html
http://www.red2000.com
http://www.spaindata.com/data/1index.shtml

Spanish National Tourist Office: http://www.tourspain.co.uk
Rail travel in Spain:
http://www.renfe.es/horarios/english/index.html
Madrid metro: http://www.metromadrid.es

Travellers in Latin America will find useful information in:
http://www.travel.org/latin.html
http://www.travelnotes.org/LatinAmerica/index.htm

Culture and history

Internet users interested in Spain may like to try the following sites:
España en la Red (Spain on the net):
http://www.sispain.org/spanish/history
http://www.sispain.org/spanish/index.html
http://spanish.about.com

Spanish language courses

For the Spanish language, the Instituto Cervantes is a worldwide
organization offering courses in Spanish and generally promoting
Spanish culture. The Hispanic and Luso Brazilian Council in the
United Kingdom, based in London, may be able to help you with
enquiries about Spanish language courses and aspects of life in
Spain and Latin America. For information on Latin American
Spanish you can contact the Hispanic Council or the embassy of
the country you are interested in.

For the Instituto Cervantes go to: http://www.cervantes.es

For the Hispanic and Luso Brazilian Council go to
www.canninghouse.com

For other related information, including Latin America, go to:
http://spanish.about.com
http://www.spanish-language.org
http://www.spanishabroad.com
http://planeta.com/schoolist.html

For information on Spanish language courses in Latin America you
can also contact the embassy of the country you are interested in.

Irregular verbs

The following list includes only the most common irregular verbs. Only irregular forms are given (verbs marked with an asterisk are also stem- or radical-changing).

Pluperfect subjunctive forms, which are derived from the third person plural of the preterite tense, are not included.

abrir   *to open*
past participle: **abierto**

andar   *to walk*
preterite: **anduve, anduviste, anduvo, anduvimos, anduvisteis, anduvieron**

conducir   *to drive*
present indicative: **(yo) conduzco**
present subjunctive: **conduzca, conduzcas, conduzca, conduzcamos, conduzcáis, conduzcan**
preterite: **conduje, condujiste, condujo, condujimos, condujisteis, condujeron**

dar   *to give*
present indicative: **(yo) doy**
preterite: **di, diste, dio, dimos, disteis, dieron**
present subjunctive: **dé, des, dé, demos, deis, den**

decir*   *to say*
present indicative: **(yo) digo**
present subjunctive: **diga, digas, diga, digamos, digáis, digan**
preterite: **dije, dijiste, dijo, dijimos, dijisteis, dijeron**
future: **diré, dirás, dirá, diremos, diréis, dirán**
conditional: **diría, dirías, diría, diríamos, diríais, dirían**
imperative (familiar, singular): **di** (formal, singular): **diga**

gerund: **diciendo**
past participle: **dicho**

escribir *to write*
past participle: **escrito**

estar *to be*
present indicative: **estoy, estás, está, estamos, estáis, están**
present subjunctive: **esté, estés, esté, estemos, estéis, estén**
preterite: **estuve, estuviste, estuvo, estuvimos, estuvisteis, estuvieron**
imperative (familiar, singular): **está**

hacer *to do, make*
present indicative: **(yo) hago**
present subjunctive: **haga, hagas, haga, hagamos, hagáis, hagan**
preterite: **hice, hiciste, hizo, hicimos, hicisteis, hicieron**
future: **haré, harás, hará, haremos, haréis, harán**
conditional: **haría, harías, haría, haríamos, haríais, harían**
imperative: **(Vd.) haga, (tú) haz**
past participle: **hecho**

ir *to go*
present indicative: **voy, vas, va, vamos, vais, van**
present subjunctive: **vaya, vayas, vaya, vayamos, vayáis, vayan**
imperfect: **iba, ibas, iba, íbamos, ibais, iban**
preterite: **fui, fuiste, fue, fuimos, fuisteis, fueron**
imperative: **(Vd.) vaya, (tú) ve**
gerund: **yendo**

leer *to read*
preterite: **(él, ella, Vd.) leyó, (ellos, ellas, Vds.) leyeron**
gerund: **leyendo**

oír *to hear*
present indicative: **oigo, oyes, oye, oímos, oís, oyen**
present subjunctive: **oiga, oigas, oiga, oigamos, oigáis, oigan**
preterite: **(él, ella, Vd.) oyó, (ellos, ellas, Vds.) oyeron**
imperative: **(Vd.) oiga, (tú) oye**
gerund: **oyendo**

poder* *to be able to, can*
preterite: pude, pudiste, pudo, pudimos, pudisteis, pudieron
future: podré, podrás, podrá, podremos, podréis, podrán
conditional: podría, podrías, podría, podríamos, podríais, podrían

poner *to put*
present indicative: (yo) pongo
present subjunctive: ponga, pongas, ponga, pongamos, pongáis,
pongan
preterite: puse, pusiste, puso, pusimos, pusisteis, pusieron
future: pondré, pondrás, pondrá, pondremos, pondréis, pondrán
conditional: pondría, pondrías, pondría, pondríamos, pondríais,
pondrían
imperative: (Vd.) ponga, (tú) pon
past participle: puesto

querer* *to want, love*
preterite: quise, quisiste, quiso, quisimos, quisisteis, quisieron
future: querré, querrás, querrá, querremos, querréis, querrán
conditional: querría, querrías, querría, querríamos, querríais,
querrían

saber *to know*
present indicative: (yo) sé
present subjunctive: sepa, sepas, sepa, sepamos, sepáis, sepan
preterite: supe, supiste, supo, supimos, supisteis, supieron
future: sabré, sabrás, sabrá, sabremos, sabréis, sabrán
conditional: sabría, sabrías, sabría, sabríamos, sabríais, sabrían
imperative: (Vd.) sepa

salir *to go out*
present indicative: (yo) salgo
present subjunctive: salga, salgas, salga, salgamos, salgáis, salgan
future: saldré, saldrás, saldrá, saldremos, saldréis, saldrán
conditional: saldría, saldrías, saldría, saldríamos, saldríais, saldrían
imperative: (Vd.) salga, (tú) sal

ser   *to be*
present indicative: **soy, eres, es, somos, sois, son**
present subjunctive: **sea, seas, sea, seamos, seáis, sean**
preterite: **fui, fuiste, fue, fuimos, fuisteis, fueron**
imperfect indicative: **era, eras, era, éramos, erais, eran**
imperative: **(Vd.) sea, (tú) sé**

tener*   *to have*
present indicative: **(yo) tengo**
present subjunctive: **tenga, tengas, tenga, tengamos, tengáis, tengan**
preterite: **tuve, tuviste, tuvo, tuvimos, tuvisteis, tuvieron**
future: **tendré, tendrás, tendrá, tendremos, tendréis, tendrán**
conditional: **tendría, tendrías, tendría, tendríamos, tendríais, tendrían**
imperative: **(Vd.) tenga, (tú) ten**

traer   *to bring*
present indicative: **(yo) traigo**
present subjunctive: **traiga, traigas, traiga, traigamos, traigáis, traigan**
preterite: **traje, trajiste, trajo, trajimos, trajisteis, trajeron**
imperative: **(Vd.) traiga**
gerund: **trayendo**

venir*   *to come*
present indicative: **(yo) vengo**
present subjunctive: **venga, vengas, venga, vengamos, vengáis, vengan**
preterite: **vine, viniste, vino, vinimos, vinisteis, vinieron**
future: **vendré, vendrás, vendrá, vendremos, vendréis, vendrán**
conditional: **vendría, vendrías, vendría, vendríamos, vendríais, vendrían**
imperative: **(Vd.) venga, (tú) ven**
gerund: **viniendo**

ver   *to see*
present indicative: (yo) veo
present subjunctive: vea, veas, vea, veamos, veáis, vean
imperfect indicative: veía, veías, veía, veíamos, veíais, veían
imperative: (Vd.) vea
past participle: visto

volver*   *to come back*
past participle: vuelto

Spanish–English vocabulary

Words already listed in each unit have not been included in this
vocabulary. Basic vocabulary and grammatical words have also
been omitted

a lo mejor   *perhaps*
abierto/a   *open*
abogado/a   *lawyer*
abrirse   *to open up*
acceder   *to have access*
acerca de   *about*
además   *besides*
administrativo/a   *office worker*
adquirir   *to acquire, obtain*
afección (f)   *illness*
aficionado a   *fond of*
agencia de empleos
  (f)   *employment agency*
agenda (f)   *diary*
agradecer   *to be grateful*
ahorrar   *to save*
ajedrez (m)   *chess*
ajustar   *to adjust*
alcanzar   *to reach*
alegría (f)   *joy*
algodón (m)   *cotton*
alimentación (f)   *food*
alojamiento (m)
  accommodation
alumno/a   *student*
amenaza (f)   *threat*
amistades (f pl)   *friends*
ampliamente   *fully*
ampliar   *to expand*

amplio   *varied, wide*
antecedentes
  (m pl)   *background*
anuncio (m)   *advertisement,
  announcement*
aparcamiento (m)   *car park*
aplicar   *to apply*
aplicarse una ducha   *to take a
  shower*
aprender   *to learn*
aprovechar   *to take advantage of*
apuntar   *to point to*
arreglarse   *to get ready,
  dress up*
artículos electrodomésticos
  (m pl)   *electrical household
  appliances*
ascensor (m)   *lift*
asegurar   *to assure*
asépticamente   *aseptically*
así   *so, thus*
asignar   *to allocate (funds),
  assign*
asimismo   *likewise*
asistencia (f)   *attendance*
asombro (m)   *surprise*
asumir   *to assume, take on*
atajar   *to stop from spreading*
atender   *to look after*

atraer *to attract*
aumento (m) *increase*
aunque *although*
ausencia (f) *absence*
avance (m) *progress*
ayudar *to help*

bajarse *to get off*
barrio (m) *area, neighbourhood*
barroco/a *baroque*
boletín (m) *form*
bonificado *subsidized*
brevemente *briefly*
bruto *gross*
buscador (m) *hunter (treasure)*
buscar *to look for*
búsqueda (f) *search*

cabe: no – duda *there is no doubt*
cabello (m) *hair*
cabina (telefónica) (f) *telephone booth*
calidad (f) *quality*
camino (m) *road*
campo (m) *field*
campo de fútbol (m) *football pitch*
cansado *tired*
capa de ozono (f) *ozone layer*
capaz *capable*
cargamento (m) *cargo*
cargo (m) *post, charge*
carrera (f) *career*
carretera (f) *main road*
carta (f) *letter*
casamiento (m) *marriage*

caseta (f) *kiosk*
casi *almost*
cayo (m) *cay (geography)*
cercano *nearby*
certificado *registered*
charlar *to chat*
chófer (m) *driver*
ciencias aplicadas (f pl) *applied sciences*
cifra (f) *figure*
ciudadano/a *citizen*
clave *key*
cobrar *to charge*
cocina (f) *cuisine*
coger *to take (transport)*
colega (m/f) *colleague*
colocado *placed*
comienzo (m) *beginning*
compartir *to share*
concepto: en – de *by way of*
confección (f) *preparation*
conseguir *to get*
consignado *recorded*
consumidor (m) *consumer*
contabilidad (f) *accountancy*
contagiarse *to contaminate, infect*
contar *to tell*
contestación (f) *answer*
contratado *agreed*
contribuyente (m/f) *contributor*
convenir *to be convenient*
convivir *to live together*
corroborar *to corroborate*
cuidar *to look after*
culpable *guilty*

cumplir (años/meses) *to be (years/months) old*

cumplir un horario *to comply with a timetable*

dañar *to damage*

dañino *damaging*

dar un paseo *to go for a walk*

dato (m) *information*

de hecho *in fact*

de igual modo *likewise*

deberse *to be due to*

decir: es – *that is to say*

dedicarse a *to do*

dejar *to let*

dejar claro *to reveal*

deporte (m) *sport*

deportivo *sports (adjective)*

desafío (m) *challenge*

desajuste (m) *imbalance*

desarrollar *to develop*

descanso (m) *rest*

descrito *described*

descubrir *to discover*

desgraciadamente *unfortunately*

desigual *unequal*

desocupado *free, unoccupied*

despacho (m) *office, study, dispatch, sending*

despejado *clear, cloudless*

desplazarse *to travel*

destinatario (m) *addressee*

detallado *detailed*

devolución (f) *refund*

dibujos animados (m pl) *cartoons*

dictar *to dictate*

dirigirse *to go, address*

domiciliario *home (adjective)*

dotado/a *equipped*

duda (f) *doubt*

dudar *to doubt, hesitate*

duplicarse *to double*

edad (f) *age*

edad escolar (f) *school age*

edificio (m) *building*

efectivo (m) *cash;*
en – *in cash*

efecto invernadero (m) *greenhouse effect*

efectuar *to do, carry out*

elegir *to choose*

embarcarse *to board*

empresa *(f)* *company, firm*

encargarse de *to be responsible for*

encuesta (f) *survey*

enfrentar *to face*

enseñar *to show, teach*

entorno (m) *environment*

entregar *to give, hand in*

entrevistar *to interview*

envío (m) *correspondence, despatch*

envolver *to wrap up*

escoger *to choose*

escolares (m pl) *school children*

escritor/a *writer*

escritura (f) *writing*

espalda (f) *back*

espantoso/a *dreadful*

estar de moda *to be in fashion*

estudios superiores (m pl) *higher education*

etapa (f) *stage*
étnico *ethnic*
evitar *to avoid*
exigente *demanding*
expedito *quick, speedy*
exponer *to put forward*
extraño/a *stranger*

fabricante (m/f)
 manufacturer
facilitar *to provide*
factura (f) *receipt, invoice*
facultativo/a *optional*
falta (f) *lack*
faltar *to lack*
famoso/a *famous*
fatal *terrible*
favorecer *to favour*
ficha de inscripción (f)
 registration form
figurar *to appear*
fijar citas *fix appointments*
finalizar *to end*
folleto informativo (m)
 information brochure
formación (f) *training*
forzado *forced*
fregar los platos/los
 cacharros *to wash up,*
 do the washing up
frito/a *fried*
funcionar *to function, work*

gabinete (m) *section*
ganar *to earn, win*
gasto (m) *expense*
golpe (m) *coup*
graduado *graduate*

hacer falta *to be necessary*
hasta tal punto *to such a point*
hecho (m) *fact*
hora (f) *time, hour;*
 tener – *to have an*
 appointment (with doctor, etc.)
horario (m) *timetable, working*
 hours
hundido *sunk*

idioma (m) *language*
impartir *to teach*
impedir *to prevent*
imponerse *to prevail*
importe (m) *cost, value*
inclinarse *to be inclined*
incluso *even*
índice (m) *rate*
infeliz *unhappy*
informática (f) *computing,*
 computer science
ingeniero/a *engineer*
inquietante *disturbing*
insoportable *unbearable*
intimidad (f) *privacy*
investigación *(f)* *research*

jefe/a *boss*
jet (f) *jet set (Spain)*
joyería (f) *jewellery*
jugador/a *player*
juguete (m) *toy*
juventud (f) *youth*

lamentablemente *regrettably*
lástima: ¡qué – ! *what a pity!*
leguminosa (f) *pulse*
lento/a *slow*

líder *leading*
limpio/a *clean*
litoral (m) *coast*
llamada (f) *(telephone) call*
llevar a cabo *to carry out*
llevar *to bear, deliver*
llevarse bien/mal *to get on well/badly*
llover *to rain; – a*
cántaros *to rain cats and dogs, pour (down)*
locutorio (m) *telephone exchange*
lucha (f) *struggle*
lugar (m) *place*
lujo *luxury*

malestar (m) *illness*
maleta (f) *suitcase*
manera: de otra – *otherwise*
mano de obra (f) *labour*
maravilla (f) *wonder*
marcado *marked*
marchar *to go, leave*
marea (f) *tide*
mariachi (m) *band that plays popular Mexican music*
más bien *rather*
matricularse *to register, enrol*
mediante *through*
mejora (f) *improvement*
merecer la pena *to be worth it*
merecer *to deserve*
mesa (f) *table (food)*
método (m) *method*
microbús (m) *small bus*
miembro (m/f) *member*
mientras *whilst*

mismo: ahora – *right now*
modalidades (f pl) *facilities*
módico *moderate, reasonable*
modo: de igual – *likewise*
mundo (m) *world*
músculo (m) *muscle*
muy señor mío *dear sir*
muy señora mía *dear madam*

nacimiento (m) *birth*
nada mal *not bad at all*
nadar *to swim*
natación (f) *swimming*
netamente *purely*
nevera (f) *fridge*
nivel (m) *level*
novio/a *boy/girlfriend*
nuez (f) *nut*
nutriente (m) *nourishing food*
nutriólogo/a *dietitian*

obstante: no – *nevertheless*
obtención (f) *obtaining, securing*
ocio (m) *leisure*
oferta (f) *offer;*
de – *on offer*
ojalá *I hope so, let's hope so*
operador/a postal *postal worker*
ordenador (m) *computer*
orgullo (m) *pride*

padecer *to suffer*
papel (m) *role*
paradero (m) *stop*
paro (m) *unemployment*

particular *private*

partido político (m) *political party*

partir: a – de *from, starting*

pasajero/a *passing, temporary*

pasar a buscar *to pick up*

pasillo (m) *corridor*

paso subterráneo (m) *subway*

pastas (fpl) *small cakes*

pastilla (f) *pill*

paulatinamente *gradually*

peletería (f) *furs*

película (f) *film*

pena: es una – *it's a pity*

pensión (f) *board, boarding house;* **– completa** *full board;* **media –** *half board*

peor: en el – de los casos *at worst*

perder el tiempo *to waste time*

perderse *to get lost*

periodista (m/f) *journalist*

permanencia (f) *stay*

permitido *allowed*

peruano/a *Peruvian*

pesar: a – de *in spite of*

petición: a – de *at the request of*

piel (f) *skin, leather*

piscina (f) *swimming pool*

piso (m) *floor, flat*

planear *to plan*

plaza (f) *seat*

pleno *full*

pleno: en – centro *right in the centre*

población activa (f) *working population*

poner en conocimiento *to let know*

poner en marcha *to start up, move*

por el contrario *on the contrary*

por suerte *luckily*

por supuesto *of course*

potencia (f) *power*

precisar *to need*

predominio (m) *predominance*

prejuicio (m) *prejudice*

prever *to forsee*

probador (m) *fitting room*

promover *to promote*

propensión (f) *tendency*

propietario/a *owner*

proporcionar *to provide*

proteger *to protect*

proveniente *coming from*

puesto (m) *post*

puesto que *as*

quedar *to be left*

quedar: me lo/la quedo *I'll take it (m/f)*

queja (f) *complaint*

quejarse *to complain*

rastreado *tracked, traced*

recibir *to receive*

recibo (m) *receipt*

recogida (f) *from recoger (to pick up)*

rectificar *to rectify*

recursos (mpl) *resources*

regalar *to give a present*

reinstaurar *to restore, re-establish*

rellenar un impreso *to fill in a form*
remitente (m) *sender*
renovarse *to renew oneself*
reparto (m) *delivery*
resentimiento (m) *resentment*
respirar *to breathe*
restante *remaining*
resultar *to be*
revelar *to reveal*
revista (f) *magazine*
rivalizar *to rival*
rodeado/a *surrounded*
roto/a *broken*
ruego: le – *kindly, please*
ruido (m) *noise*
ruidoso/a *noisy*

salud (f) *health*
salvaje *wild*
seco/a *dry*
seguidamente *then*
seguro (m) *insurance*
semáforo (m) *traffic light*
sencillo/a *simple*
sentido del humor (m) *sense of humour*
sentimiento (m) *feeling*
ser *to be*; **a no –** *unless*; **o lo que sea** *or whatever*
siglo (m) *century*
sitio (m) *place*
sobre (m) *envelope*
sobrevivir *to survive*
solfeo (m) *music theory*
solicitar *to request*
solucionar *to solve*
sometido *subjected*

subir *to go up*
suceder *to happen*
sueldo (m) *salary*
suelo (m) *floor, ground*
suerte (f) *luck*
superar *to be over*

talla (f) *size (clothes)*
tardar *to take (time)*
tarea (f) *work, labour*
tarjeta (f) *card*
techo (m) *roof*
tejido (m) *tissue*
temporada (f) *season*; **– alta** *high season*
temprano *early*
tener en cuenta *to take into account*
teniente (m) *lieutenant*
tesoro (m) *treasure*
tienda (f) *shop*
Tierra (f) *Earth*
título (m) *degree, certificate*
título académico (m) *university degree*
título universitario (m) *university degree*
toalla (f) *towel*
tomar una copa *to have a drink*
tono (m) *dialling tone*
tono: a – *in harmony, in tune*
torcer *to turn*
traductor/a *translator*
tranquilo/a *quiet*
transbordar *to change (transport)*

trasladar   *to transfer*
traslado (m)   *transfer*
tratamiento (m)   *treatment*
través: a – de   *through*

usuario (m)   *user*
utilizar   *to use*

vale   *O.K.*
validez (f)   *validity*
valle (m)   *valley*
varón (m)   *man, male*
vecino/a   *neighbour, resident*
venda (f)   *bandage*
ventaja (f)   *advantage*
vergüenza (f)   *shame*
viaje (m)   *journey, trip*

viajero   *travelling; (m) traveller*
vías respiratorias (f pl)
  respiratory tract
vidrio (m)   *glass*
vista (f)   *view*
vivienda (f)   *house, housing*
vuelo (m)   *flight*
vuelta (f)   *return*

ya   *already*
ya no   *no longer*
ya que   *as, since, for*
yate (m)   *yacht*

zapatería (f)   *shoe shop*
zapato (m)   *shoe*

English–Spanish vocabulary

about   **acerca de; sobre, a eso de** *(time)*
accommodation   **alojamiento** *(m)*
accompany: to –   **acompañar**
account   **cuenta** *(f)*
accountancy   **contabilidad** *(f)*
address: to –   **dirigirse**
addressee   **destinatario/a**
advantage   **ventaja** *(f)*
advantage: to take –   **aprovechar**
advertisement   **anuncio** *(m)*
agree: to –   **estar de acuerdo, acordar; contratar**
agreement   **acuerdo** *(m)*
almost   **casi**
already   **ya**
although   **aunque**
ankle   **tobillo** *(m)*
answer   **respuesta, contestación** *(f)*
appear: to –   **aparecer, figurar**
apply: to –   **aplicar; solicitar** *(e.g. a job)*
appointment   **cita** *(f)*
arrival   **llegada** *(f)*
article   **artículo** *(m)*
as ... as   **tan/tanto como**
as   **como, puesto que, dado que**
ashamed: to be –   **tener vergüenza**
assign: to –   **asignar**

assume: to –   **asumir**
assure: to –   **asegurar**
attendance   **asistencia** *(f)*
attract: to –   **atraer**
available   **disponible**
avoid: to –   **evitar**

back   **espalda** *(f)*
background   **antecedentes** *(m pl)*
baker's   **panadería** *(f)*
bear: to –   **llevar, soportar**
bed   **cama** *(f)*
beginning   **comienzo, principio** *(m)*
besides   **además**
birth   **nacimiento** *(m)*
bored   **aburrido/a**
boss   **jefe/a**
boyfriend   **novio**
breathe   **respirar**
brief   **breve**
brochure   **folleto** *(m)*
broken   **roto/a**
building   **edificio** *(m)*
bus   **autobús, microbús** *(small bus)*, **camión** *(m) (Mexico)*
business   **negocio** *(m)*

cake   **pastel** *(m)*, **tarta** *(f)*, **pastas** *(f pl) (small cakes)*
car park (m)   **aparcamiento, estacionamiento** *(Latin Am.)*
card   **tarjeta** *(f)*

cargo **cargamento** (m)

carry out: to – **efectuar, realizar, llevar a cabo**

cartoons **dibujos animados** (m pl)

cash: to pay – **pagar en efectivo**

century **siglo** (m)

certain **seguro/a**

challenge **desafío** (m)

change: to – **cambiar; transbordar** (transport)

charge: to – **cobrar**

chat: to – **charlar, conversar, platicar**

check: to – **revisar, checar** (Mexico)

citizen **ciudadano/a**

clean **limpio/a**

clear **claro/a; despejado** (sky)

clerk **administrativo/a**

clothes **ropa** (f)

cloudless **despejado**

coach **autocar, autobús, camión** (m) (Mexico)

coast **costa** (f), **litoral** (m)

code (telephone) **prefijo, código** (m)

colleague **colega** (m/f)

comfort **comodidad** (f)

company (firm) **empresa, compañía, firma** (f)

complain: to – **quejarse**

complaint **queja** (f)

computer **ordenador, computador** (m), **computadora** (f)

consumer **consumidor** (m)

contaminate: to – **contaminar; contagiar, infectar**

contrary: on the – **por el contrario**

cook: to – **cocinar, guisar**

correspondence **correspondencia** (f), **envío** (m)

corridor **pasillo** (m)

cost **valor** (m), **coste** (m), **costo** (m) (Latin Am.), **importe** (m)

cotton **algodón** (m)

course **curso** (m)

course: of – **por supuesto, desde luego, claro**

cover: to – **cubrir**

credit card **tarjeta de crédito** (f)

cuisine **cocina** (f)

damage **daño** (m)

damage: to – **dañar**

damaging **dañino/a**

degree **título** (m) (university)

delay **retraso** (m)

delivery **reparto** (m), **despacho** (m)

demand: to – **exigir**

demanding **exigente**

describe: to – **describir**

deserve: to – **merecer**

despatch **envío** (m)

despatch: to – **enviar, despachar**

despite **pese a**

develop: to – **desarrollar**

development **desarrollo** (m)
devote: to – **dedicar**
diary **agenda** (f)
dictate: to – **dictar**
dietitian **nutriólogo/a**
discount **descuento** (m)
double room **habitación doble/con cama de matrimonio** (f)
doubt **duda** (f)
doubt: to – **dudar**
drink **copa** (f)
drink: to have a – **tomar una copa**
driver **conductor/a, chófer** (m/f)
dry **seco/a**
dry: to – **secar**

earn: to – **ganar**
electrical household appliances **electrodomésticos** (m, pl)
email **correo electrónico** (m)
employment **empleo** (m)
engineer **ingeniero/a**
enrol: to – **inscribirse, matricularse**
environment **medio ambiente** (m), **entorno** (m)
equipped **dotado/a**
even though **aunque, a pesar de que**
even **incluso**
executive **ejecutivo/a**
exhibition **exposición** (f)
expand: to – **ampliar**
expense **gasto** (m)

face: to – **enfrentar**
facilities **equipamiento** (m); **modalidades** (f pl)
fact **hecho** (m)
fact: in – **de hecho, efectivamente**
factory **fábrica** (f)
famous **famoso/a**
fashion **moda** (f)
favour: to – **favorecer**
field **campo** (m)
figure **cifra** (f), **número** (m)
film **película** (f), **film** (m)
fitting room **probador** (m)
flat **piso** (m), **apartamento, departamento** (m) (Latin Am.)
flight **vuelo** (m)
floor **planta** (f), **piso** (m); **suelo** (m)
fond of **aficionado/a a**
food **alimento** (m), **alimentación** (f)
foot **pie** (m)
football field **campo de fútbol** (m)
forced **forzado/a**
foreigner **extranjero/a**
foresee: to – **prever**
form **boletín** (m), **impreso** (m), **formulario** (m)
free **libre, desocupado/a**
fridge **nevera** (f), **frigorífico** (m)
fried **frito/a**
friends **amistades** (f pl)
full board **pensión completa** (f)

full **lleno/a, pleno/a**
fully **ampliamente,
totalmente, completamente**
function: to – **funcionar**
fur **piel** (f)

get off: to – **bajarse**
get: to – on well/badly **llevarse
bien/mal**
get: to – **conseguir,
obtener**
gift **regalo** (m)
girlfriend **novia**
give: to – **dar, entregar**
glass **vaso** (m); **vidrio** (m)
(material)
go: to – down **bajar**
go: to – up **subir**
graduate **graduado/a**
grateful: to be – **agradecer**
greenhouse effect **efecto
invernadero** (m)
gross **bruto**
ground **suelo** (m)
guest **invitado/a**
guilty **culpable**

habit: to be in the – of
acostumbrar, soler
hair **cabello, pelo** (m)
half board **media pensión** (f)
hand: to – in **entregar**
happen: to – **pasar, suceder,
ocurrir**
have: to – **tener, disponer de,
contar con**
heal: to – **sanar**
health **salud** (f)

help **ayuda** (f)
hesitate: to – **dudar**
higher education **estudios
superiores** (m pl)
higher **superior**
highway **carretera** (f)
housing **vivienda** (f)
however **sin embargo**
humour: sense of – **sentido del
humor** (m)
hurt: to – **doler**

ill: to be – **estar enfermo/a**
illness **enfermedad** (f),
afección (f), **malestar** (m)
impose: to – **imponer**
improvement **mejora** (f)
include: to – **incluir**
increase **aumento** (m)
increase: to – **aumentar**
information brochure **folleto
informativo** (m)
information **información** (f),
dato (m)
insurance **seguro** (m)
interpreter **intérprete** (m/f)
interview: to – **entrevistar**
invoice **factura** (f)
iron: to – **planchar**

jewellery **joyas** (f pl);
joyería
journey **viaje** (m)

keep: to – fit **mantenerse
en forma**
key **llave** (f); **clave** (f);
cayo (m) (geography)

kiosk   **cabina, caseta** *(f)*,
  quiosco *(m)*
kitchen: open plan –   **cocina
  americana** *(f)*

labour   **mano de obra** *(f)*
lack: to –   **faltar**
language   **idioma** *(m)*,
  lengua *(f)*
last   **último/a**
lawyer   **abogado/a**
learn: to –   **aprender**
leave: to –   **irse, dejar,
  abandonar**
leg   **pierna** *(f)*
leisure   **ocio** *(m)*
level   **nivel** *(m)*
lift   **ascensor** *(m)*, **elevador**
  (Mexico)
likewise   **asimismo, de igual/
  del mismo modo, de la misma
  manera**
longer: no –   **ya no**
look after: to –   **cuidar, atender**
look for: to –   **buscar**
luck   **suerte** *(f)*
luckily   **por suerte**
luxury   **lujo** *(m)*

magazine   **revista** *(f)*
main road   **carretera** *(f)*
male   **varón** *(m)*
manufacturer   **fabricante** *(m/f)*
marriage   **casamiento** *(m/f)*,
  matrimonio *(m)*
marry: to –   **casarse**
master: to –   **dominar**
member   **miembro** *(m/f)*

mobile phone   **teléfono
  móvil/portátil** *(m)*, **celular**
  (Latin Am.) *(m)*
mountain   **sierra** *(f)*, **montaña** *(f)*
muscle   **músculo** *(m)*

nearby   **cercano/a**
necessary: to be –   **ser
  necesario, hacer falta**
neighbour   **vecino/a**
neighbourhood   **barrio** *(m)*
nevertheless   **no obstante**
nut   **nuez** *(f)*

O.K.   **vale, de acuerdo**
often   **a menudo**
oil   **petróleo** *(m)*; **aceite** *(m)*
  (cooking and car oil)
optional   **facultativo/a**
owner   **propietario/a**
ozone layer   **capa de ozono** *(f)*

pain   **dolor** *(m)*
paint: to –   **pintar**
painting   **pintura** *(f)*
party   **fiesta** *(f)*; **partido** *(m)*
  (politics)
pay: to –   **pagar**
performance   **función** *(f)*
perhaps   **a lo mejor, tal vez,
  quizá(s)**
pick up: to –   **pasar a buscar,
  recoger**
pill   **pastilla** *(f)*, **tableta** *(f)*,
  píldora *(f)*
plan: to –   **planear, programar**
platform   **andén** *(m)*
player   **jugador/a** *(m/f)*

point to: to – **apuntar**

political party **partido político** (m)

post office **(oficina de) correos** (f)

post **puesto** (job) (m); **correo** (mail) (m)

power **potencia** (f)

prejudice **prejuicio** (m)

present: to give a – **regalar, hacer un regalo**

prevail: to – **imponerse**

private **privado/a**

progress **progreso** (m), **avance** (m)

promote: to – **promover**

protect: to – **proteger**

provide: to – **proporcionar, proveer**

pulse **leguminosa** (f)

purely **netamente, puramente**

quality **calidad** (f)

quick **rápido/a, expedito/a**

quiet **tranquilo/a**

rate **índice** (m)

rather **más bien**

reach: to – **alcanzar**

realize: to – **darse cuenta**

reasonable **razonable; módico/a** (e.g. price)

receipt **factura** (f), **recibo** (m)

refund **devolución** (f)

register: to – **inscribirse, matricularse**

registered **certificado/a**

regrettably **lamentablemente, desgraciadamente**

relax: to – **relajarse**

remain: to – **quedar**

rent: to – **alquilar, rentar** (Mexico)

representative **representante** (m/f)

request: to – **solicitar, pedir**

research **investigación** (f)

resident **vecino/a; residente** (m/f)

responsible: to be – for **encargarse de**

rest **descanso** (m)

return **regreso** (m), **vuelta** (f)

return: to – **volver, regresar; devolver** (to give back)

right now **ahora mismo, inmediatamente, enseguida**

road **camino** (m)

roof **techo** (m)

salary **sueldo, salario** (m)

save: to – **ahorrar**

school age **edad escolar** (f)

school children **escolares** (m pl)

school **colegio** (m), **escuela** (f)

science **ciencia** (f)

search **búsqueda** (f)

season **estación** (f); **temporada** (f) (period)

seat **asiento** (m); **plaza** (f) (e.g. on a plane)

send: to – **enviar, mandar**

sender **remitente** (m)

sew: to – **coser**

shame **vergüenza** (f)

share: to – **compartir**

shoe shop **zapatería** (f)

shoe **zapato** *(m)*

shop **tienda** *(f)*

shopping: to do the – **hacer la compra/las compras**

show **sesión** *(f) (cinema),* **función** *(f)*

show: to – **mostrar, enseñar;** *(film)* **poner, dar** *(Latin Am.)*

shower: to – **ducharse**

since **ya que, puesto que;** **desde** *(from)*

single room **habitación individual/sencilla** *(f)*

sink: to – **hundir**

size **tamaño** *(m);* **talla** *(f)* *(clothing)*

slow **lento/a**

so **entonces; tan**

solve: to – **solucionar**

speedy **expedito/a, rápido/a**

spite: in – of **a pesar de, pese a**

sport **deporte** *(m);* **deportivo/a** *(adjective)*

sports centre **polideportivo** *(m)*

stamp **sello** *(m),* **estampilla** *(f) (Latin Am.)*

start: to – **empezar, comenzar, poner en marcha**

stay: to – **quedarse**

stop **parada** *(f),* **paradero** *(m) (Latin Am.)*

stop: to – **parar, detener, atajar**

struggle **lucha** *(f)*

subway **paso subterráneo** *(m)*

suitcase **maleta, valija** *(Argentina) (f)*

survey **encuesta** *(f)*

survive: to – **sobrevivir**

swim: to – **nadar**

swimming pool **piscina** *(f),* **alberca** *(f) (Mexico);* **pileta** *(Argentina) (f)*

swimming **natación** *(f)*

swollen **hinchado/a**

table **mesa** *(f)*

take: to – time **tardar**

teach: to – **enseñar; impartir**

telephone booth **cabina telefónica** *(f)*

telephone exchange *(m)* **locutorio**

tell: to – **contar, decir**

tendency **tendencia, propensión** *(f)*

then **entonces, después, seguidamente**

though **aunque**

threat **amenaza** *(f)*

through **mediante;** **a través de, por**

thus **así, de esta manera/este modo**

tide **marea** *(f)*

timetable **horario** *(m)*

time: spare – **tiempo libre** *(m)*

tired **cansado/a**

tissue **tejido** *(m)*

toast **tostadas** *(f pl),* **pan tostado** *(m) (Mexico)*

towel **toalla** *(f)*

traffic light **semáforo** *(m)*

training **formación** *(f)*

transfer **traslado** *(m)*

translator **traductor/a**
traveller **viajero/a**
traveller's cheque
  cheque *(m)* **de viaje/de viajero**
treasure **tesoro** *(m)*
treatment **tratamiento** *(m)*
trip **viaje** *(m)*
turn: to – **torcer, girar, doblar**
turn: to be one's – **tocar**
  a uno/a

unequal **desigual**
unfortunately
  desgraciadamente,
  desafortunadamente
use: to – **usar, utilizar**
user **usuario/a**

validity **validez** *(f)*
valley **valle** *(m)*
varied **variado/a, amplio/a**
view **vista** *(f)*

walk: to go for a – **dar un**
  paseo

wash: to – **lavar, lavarse**
waste: to – **perder**
wear: to – **llevar, usar**
while **rato, momento** *(m)*
whilst **mientras**
wild **salvaje**
win: to – **ganar**
wonder **maravilla** *(f)*
wonder: to – **preguntarse**
wonderful **maravilloso/a**
work **trabajo** *(m)*, **tarea** *(f)*
work: to – **trabajar;**
  funcionar
worker **trabajador/a**
working hours **horario**
  de trabajo *(m)*
working population **población**
  activa *(f)*
world **mundo** *(m)*
worth: to be – it **merecer/**
  valer la pena
writer **escritor/a**

yacht **yate** *(m)*
young **joven**

Index

Key to 3-part references (e.g. 8:G:2): the first number refers to the unit (8); 'G' refers to the *Grammar* section within Unit 8; 2 refers to grammar point 2.

Abbreviations:

A   Activity
G   Grammar
D   Dialogue
KS Key Sentences
P   Practice
LE Listening exercise

Credits